THE GARDEN CONSERVANCY

Open Days Directory 2022

Open Days:
Celebrating and sharing America's gardens since 1995

www.gardenconservancy.org/opendays

Publisher's Cataloging-in-Publication
(provided by Quality Books, Inc.)
The Garden Conservancy Open Days Directory
2022 ed., 26th ed.
    p. cm.
    Includes index.
    ISSN: 1087-7738
    ISBN-13 978-0-578-35942-7
1. Gardens—United States—Directories.
2. Botanical gardens—United States—Directories.
3. Arboretums—United States—Directories.
    I. Garden Conservancy
    II. Title: Open Days Directory
    SB466.U65G37 2020 712'.07473
               QBI00-836

Published and distributed by
The Garden Conservancy
P.O. Box 608, Garrison, NY 10524

Covers: A view of the Mountsier Garden in Nutley, New Jersey
Photo by Land Morphology

Open Days Directory 2022

Hello garden enthusiast,

The printed Directory is back!

Go ahead: pick it up, turn it over, dog-ear your favorite pages—heck, tear them out to keep as a memento! Or preserve the book, add it to your shelf. Whatever your style, there's nothing quite like print, and we're happy this year, and in future years, to be offering both the printed and online versions of the *Open Days Directory* as complementing resources for the Open Days season. Each has something unique to offer, and we proudly present both to you.

The online Directory is where you'll find the most up-to-date listings and any last-minute changes—all important in the COVID-19 era. This Directory was compiled in December 2021, and we aim to add additional pop-up gardens to the Open Days season, so keep an eye on our social media channels for announcements. The online Directory will also connect you with our electronic ticketing, which was rolled out last year with overwhelming success. And for those who've forsaken print, the online Directory will be your reliable guide to the 2022 season, and yet I encourage you to enjoy the printed Directory.

A smartphone may be a brilliant tool for navigating a new city, and there's no doubt it can hold a whole lot of photos of our favorite plants, but a smartphone can also diminish our awareness of the places themselves as well as our connections to each other: two things that Open Days are all about. Then there's the almost magical qualities of a physical object designed for a *specific purpose*, like this Directory. When we interact with them, studies have shown, we end up getting so much more out of the experience and remember it for much longer.

This printed Directory is more editorially rich than prior years. In fact, it's a little unfair to call it a "directory." It's so much more! It's a yearbook for the Open Days family, a place to show off photographs and to share ideas. The Directory is also a window into the Garden Conservancy, containing news and updates from across the organization. Many of you are our biggest supporters and the reason behind our recent tremendous growth—including a *20 percent jump in membership in 2021*. So please consider this book a tool, a calling card for your work on our behalf, and a huge thank you for your continued support.

Have a wonderful 2022 season!

—*Horatio Joyce, PhD*
Director of Public Programs and Education

How to Use This Directory

The *Open Days Directory* features a comprehensive listing of participating gardens with garden descriptions and hours. The 2022 Directory is different from previous editions in that it does not include addresses or directions to gardens. Instead, please go online to register at **gardenconservancy.org/opendays**. Once registered, you will receive the garden's address and directions. Please also visit our website for the most current and up-to-date information.

Open Days by state
Garden descriptions and open hours can be found in the main listing by state, beginning on page 35.

Garden descriptions for each private garden are submitted by the individual garden owner. This year, we have added additional host insights and reflections on the horticultural world in a new section called "Trowel Talk." Look for the tan boxes with the 👍 icon.

States are sequenced alphabetically. Within each state, Open Days are listed chronologically by date. Gardens participating in each Open Day are organized alphabetically by county, then town, then garden name.

Indices
To find out which gardens are opening on specific dates, see the "By Date" index starting on page 248. For a comprehensive list of all Open Days gardens by state, see the next index, "Open Days by State" starting on page 260.

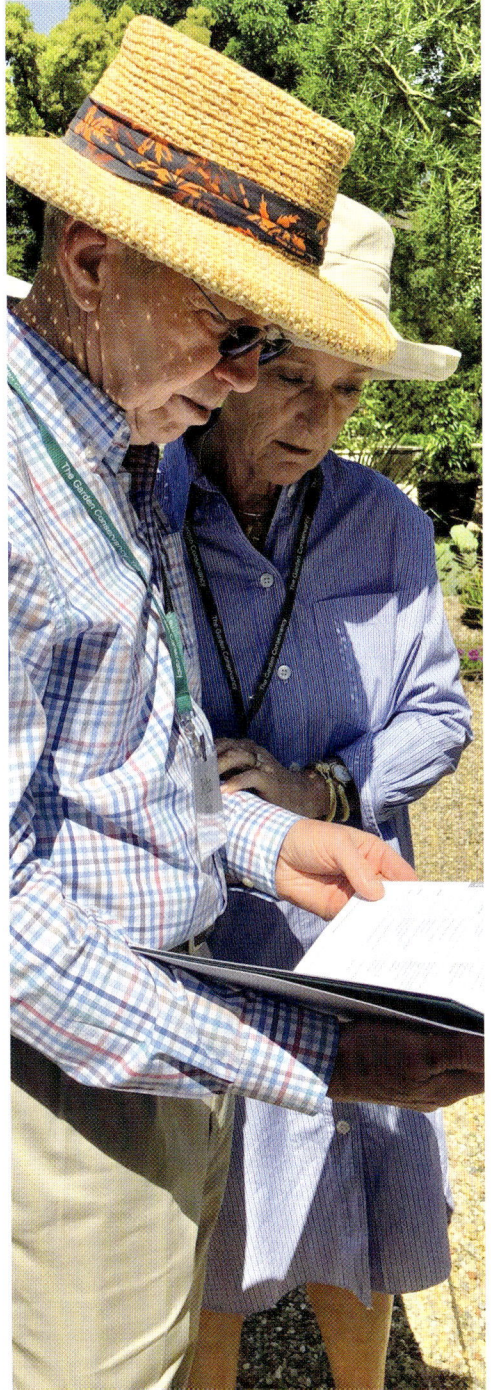

Plan Your Garden Visit

Open Days are self-guided tours that take place rain or shine.

Where possible, we have scheduled gardens to be within reasonable driving distance of one another. (Occasionally we find a garden that simply must be included, despite its being off the beaten path.)

We do our best to make sure the garden directions provided upon purchase are accurate. Always check directions before you leave home; bring a map or GPS system along with garden addresses provided on the electronic tickets.

Admission to Gardens
Admission to Open Days gardens is $5 per person for Garden Conservancy members and $10 per person for non-members, per garden. Children twelve and under are free.

Tickets for Open Days must be purchased on our website, gardenconservancy.org/opendays prior to entering the garden.

For assistance with registration, please call us at 1.888.842.2442, M–F, 9–5 Eastern.

Members' Discount
We save the best deals for Garden Conservancy members, who, in addition to getting 50 percent off Open Day tickets, also qualify for discounts on other Conservancy programs. To learn more about membership, see page 14.

Digging Deeper and Garden Master Series
Digging Deeper and Garden Masters Series programs offer special tours, demonstrations, and other in-depth experiences in the garden world. These special programs have very limited capacity and require additional fees.

To purchase a ticket, visit gardenconservancy.org/opendays or call 1.888.842.2442, M–F, 9–5 Eastern.

Cancellations and Changes
Occasionally, Open Days must be canceled or changed for unforeseen reasons. In the event of a cancellation, we will update our website and email those who have already purchased tickets. Please check our website for the latest news and information.

Children twelve and under are always FREE at Open Days!
We encourage you to bring your kids and grandkids, and share your love of nature and gardens with the next generation of gardeners!

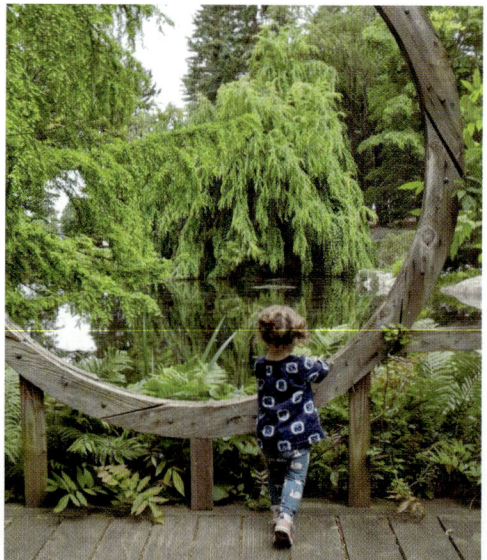

Guidelines for Visiting

Open Days are special invitations into private gardens. Please reward the generosity of our garden hosts by following these simple garden-visiting rules:

Sign In
Sign in at the admissions table. Hosts will have a list of everyone who purchased tickets. Please either check your name off the list or speak to the volunteer Garden Greeter and they will do so for you!

Hands Off
Plants and their parts must remain in the garden: no picking, pinching, or removing of plant pieces of any kind.

Greet the Hosts
Many Garden Hosts can be found in the gardens during their Open Day, identified by their "Garden Host" badge. Please say hello and let them know much you enjoyed their garden.

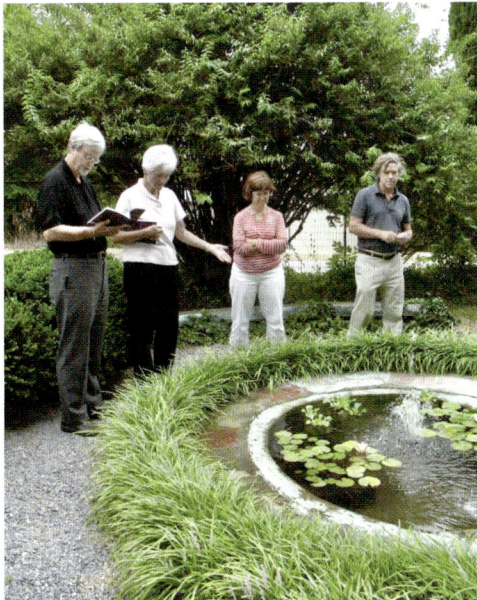

• Masks are required, at the discretion of the garden owners, and social distancing is encouraged at all in-person events.

• Take it with you! Do not litter in the garden, and please do not smoke!

•Stay on the designated paths (and out of people's houses)!

•Follow any posted signs and directions.

•Bring a friend, but not your furry friend. Sorry, no pets or therapy animals allowed.

•Children are very welcome at Open Days, but must be supervised at all times.

•Park your car so others can enter and leave the parking area easily.

•Respect the owner's preference for photographs! See garden listing or ask upon entry. Tripods are not permitted.

•Restrooms are not available, even if "it's an emergency!" Please go before you arrive, or ask at the admissions table for directions to the nearest public facility.

•Most gardens featured during Open Days are private and not normally open to the public. Please respect the privacy of these Garden Hosts and only view their gardens on the dates and times posted!

•Respect the privacy of our Garden Hosts by not contacting them directly outside of their Open Day.

Visitors at the Ann Spencer Garden, Lynchburg, Virginia

Nature Friendly Gardens

Starting this year, with the return of the beloved print version of the Directory, the Garden Conservancy will be recognizing the gardens that not only bring great pleasure to their owners and visitors, but also share their bounty with as many other life forms as possible.

Gardens that feed the caterpillars, which birds feed to their young. Gardens that are part of the web of life. Look for the nibbled leaf symbol as indicator of the properties that are managed without synthetic chemicals and with the environment in mind.

Gardens are never the same for any two consecutive moments. I used to think of this old truism strictly in terms of the effects of light, shadow, seasons, and years of growth on my plants, but now I look back on another growth cycle—my own. I started out obsessed with growing whatever was most difficult and exotic, but now I prefer plants that are perfectly fine

with the least amount from me, other than putting them where they will be happiest: close to where they evolved, and in touch with their ancestral community.

Is this new approach a function of my age, or the age I live in? Probably both, but it is not just me and my weary old body, it is the trend with gardeners of all ages: borne of the sadness of biodiversity losses and the joys of making gardens that provide homes for the species we can play a vital role in saving.

This is nature-based habitat gardening: choosing plants that aren't reliant on fertilizers, pesticides, or irrigation; plants that attract wildlife. It is using practices that respect the life cycles of insects and birds, and adding a clean water source to replace the puddles, ponds, and streams lost to development. It is leaving dead wood for insects and cavity-nesting birds. It is letting plants grow to their natural shapes. It is working with nature, not against it. It is learning to let go.

If you want to join the nibbled leaf team of Nature Friendly Gardens, just ask Amy Murray, Open Days Program Manager. There are no rules or requirements, but a commitment you make to yourself, your place, and the life it supports.

—Edwina von Gal
www.perfectearthproject.org

See Edwina's Garden, Marshouse, on September 17, followed by her Digging Deeper, "Designing for Nature—Keeping: A Garden's Commitment without Losing Its Looks". See page 192 for description and details.

Designer's Note

This year's Directory features a new icon for the category "Nature-friendly."

We had made the decision that a leaf with a bite taken out could symbolize the sharing by gardeners with nature. But my first attempt at a bite was too complex to be readable at the small size of an icon in the Directory:

So I simplified it:

Then we debated the look of the leaf—did it appear to be falling? Might that be depressing because it could signal autumn and, for many, the end of the gardening season? So I flipped the leaf:

We decided this was readable, recognizable, on-point, and reproducible at multiple sizes. Welcome to our new icon!

—Brian Jones
Graphic Designer

Glade Garden - East Hampton, NY
Photo by Abby Jane Brody

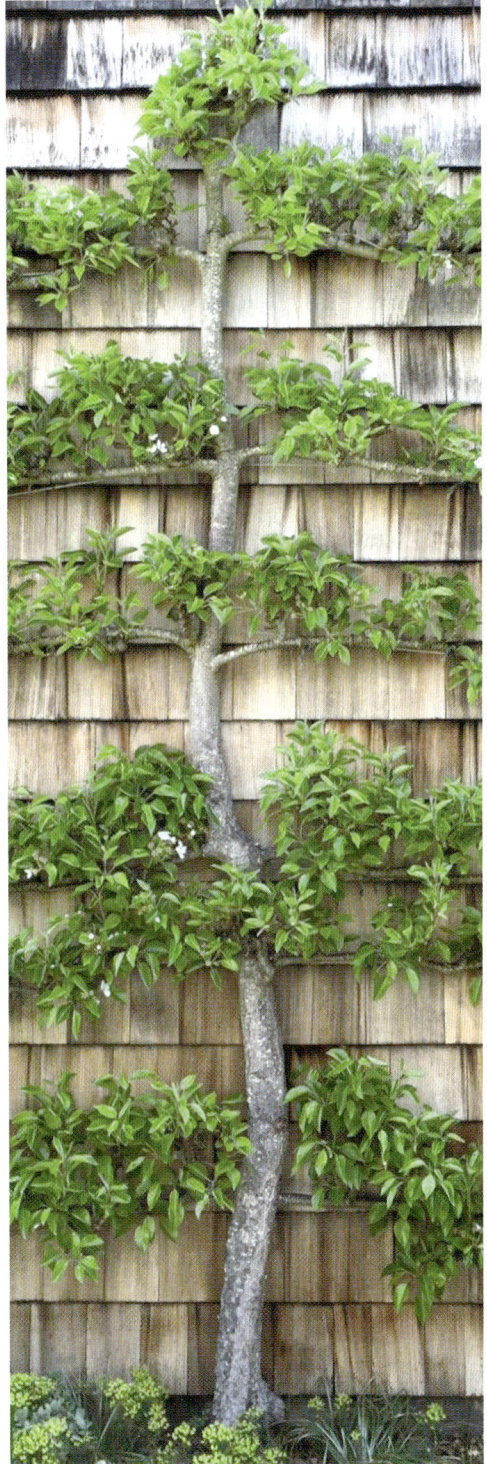

Glimpse Behind the Garden Gate:
The Mountsier Garden

The cover photo of the 2022 Open Days Directory shows the Mountsier Garden in Nutley, New Jersey. Like many Garden Hosts, owners Silas Mountsier and Graeme Hardie have long supported the Open Days program, graciously opening their garden since 2001. Horatio Joyce, Director of Public Programs and Education, and Amy Murray, Open Days Program Manager, conducted this interview to learn more about the Mountsier Garden's evolution, the owners' gardening philosophy, and their experience with the Open Days program. They were also fortunate to speak with landscape architect Richard Hartledge of Land Morphology, who has been involved not only with the Mountsier Garden since the early 1990s, but also with the Open Days program.

Tucked away in suburban New Jersey, only about eleven miles from Times Square, is a hidden oasis.

It was here that Silas Mountsier began his garden in 1945 on a half-acre plot. "It was used for town functions, weddings—all sorts of things," Graeme Hardie, his partner recalls. "It was always a beautiful garden."

By trade, Mr. Mountsier is a personal wealth manager, and Mr. Hardie an architect and anthropologist. Together, they've evolved the Mountsier Garden into the 2.5-acre strolling garden that exists today. Since 2001, the Mountsier Garden has been a part of Open Days, and the story of its making is one of continual growth and evolution, backed by a longstanding partnership between owners and garden designer.

While the garden had been in Mr. Mountsier's possession for many years, much of what is there today only began to take shape in the early 1990s. It was then that Richard Hartledge, of Land Morphology, became involved. "In many ways we feel like we tend his garden," Mr. Hardie said of Richard Hartledge. "We take care of his garden and make subtle changes, but it's his garden."

"The garden design is very important to me, and you augment design with sophisticated horticulture," Mr. Hartledge said of the garden. "This garden is very modern even though we've used older materials ... It's the closest thing I've done that acknowledges my love for the work of Roberto Burle Marx, who gardened as

if he was a cubist painter. [The Mountsier Garden] is planted in higher contrast."

This influence can be felt throughout the seasons in the garden. "Richard has designed a pretty amazing garden because it is multilayered. It's always a changing scene. It starts in spring with little scillas and small bulbs, and then the next layer comes. We have hills of daffodils—you don't often see that. We have 15,000 bulbs in May. Every year, Richard chooses the colors. We never know what we're planting until they emerge." Still, the longstanding relationship allows Mr. Hartledge to know what best suits the garden: "Pastels don't work well in the garden because of how [the bulbs] are used—they're a focal point, so either white or really saturated colors look best—[nothing] too dark." Such intimate knowledge of building an environment can only be built upon years of mutual trust.

Photo by Land Morphology

Photo by Land Morphology

As the season progresses, so too does the feeling evoked by the garden. Of the warmer seasons, Mr. Hardie says, "The heat here in July and August just kills all of our annuals. So we have a completely different attitude—we go tropical for July, August, and September. We have colored leaves throughout the garden—not flowers, but leaves. It is more of a green garden than a flower garden."

Underpinning the seasonally evolving landscape is an exceptional structure. "The garden is made up of many rooms," Mr. Hardie continues. "The whole garden is broken up—every time you move from one area to the next, it is a new experience. People that come here can't believe that it is two-and-a-half acres because there is so much to experience and to see ... I always say, look for the structure. Most gardens have little structure and lots of fluff. This garden has lots of structure and little fluff.

It's not focused on individual plants; it's massing of plants."

Punctuating the landscape are more than 80 sculptures and objects of different mediums—metalwork, stone, and wood. Placing them within the garden has been a delicate balancing act. "Richard had to wrap the garden around these pieces, and he has done an amazing job with that. They are in balance—they don't stick out." Whimsical structures, such as a cow, bull, cat, and lion are tucked throughout the property and surprise and delight visitors. "Even our cellar doors are sculptures. They take two people to open because they're heavy, but they're beautiful."

The house is a seamless part of the landscape, and the relationship between the building and garden is paramount. "The house is painted a patina copper color—a blue green—a very subdued color.

But there is no outlining of the windows—no distractions. I think that adds a lot to the presence of the garden because the buildings are integrated with the garden."

This interview was conducted via Zoom, as Mr. Hardie and Mr. Mountsier enjoyed their kitchen house on a cloudy December day and the warmth from the garden could still be felt despite the grey weather. Connected to the main house by a breezeway and heated by residual heat from the greenhouse, the kitchen house offers a 180-degree view of the gardens year round. "In the summer we eat outside in various places—except when it rains. We live in the garden as much as we can."

For the 2022 Season, the Mountsier Garden will be open as part of Open Days on four separate dates—April 16, May 15, June 4, and September 10—to allow visitors to experience the evolution of the seasons in the garden—"and it's always good because the structure is so good," Mr. Hardie adds.

We invite you to visit this exceptional garden and experience the oasis yourself.

> "There always has to be passion in the garden. It doesn't exist otherwise."
> —Graeme Hardie

Last year, the Mountsier Garden celebrated its twenty-year anniversary as an Open Days garden, opening for its first Open Day shortly after the attacks on the World Trade Center. "9/11 happened on a Tuesday, and we opened on a Saturday. It was very subdued, but people came. We had a fireman who was involved, and he was very grateful to be in the garden." Likewise, the garden provided solace in the early days of the COVID-19 pandemic. "When COVID started, we just put a sign on the street and people just came into the garden. It was like a public park. It's still like that—people still wander through the garden."

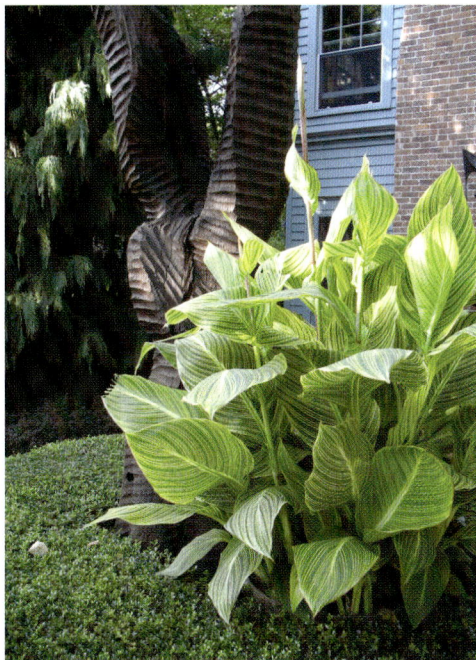

About the Garden Conservancy

A 501(c)(3) nonprofit organization incorporated in New York State, the Garden Conservancy was founded in 1989 by renowned plantsman Frank Cabot. The mission of the Garden Conservancy is to preserve, share, and celebrate America's gardens and diverse gardening traditions for the education and inspiration of the public.

PRESERVING

Since 1989, the Garden Conservancy has helped more than 100 of America's outstanding gardens survive and prosper. In partnership with garden owners, gardeners, communities, horticulturists, garden designers, and historians, we work to preserve outstanding gardens across America.

We help new and emerging public gardens become community-based public resources by drawing upon the expertise of our own dedicated staff as well as that of our network of experts in all aspects of garden design, management, and restoration. We also contribute to the welfare of existing public gardens, helping them manage both natural and man-made challenges to their survival. Many of the gardens we work with are National Historic Landmarks or on the National Register of Historic Places.

Read more about our garden preservation work on page 24.

SHARING

The best way to learn about gardening, garden design, and the transformative power of gardens is to experience gardens in person. Since 1995, more than 4,000 private gardens have participated in our signature **Open Days** program, welcoming more than 1.3 million visitors in states across the country. We also offer Digging Deeper educational programs in conjunction with garden visiting through Open Days.

Winter Hill, the Garden Conservancy headquarters

Frank Cabot planting at Stonecrop
Photo courtesy of Stonecrop Gardens

The Garden Conservancy also presents lectures, symposia, and other **public education programs** to foster the sharing of ideas and inspiration, as well as **garden-study tours**, which are open to members of our Society of Fellows.

C E L E B R A T I N G
Through all of our programs and outreach, we champion the vital role that gardens play in our history, our culture, and our quality of life.

The History of the Garden Conservancy

The Garden Conservancy was founded in 1989 by renowned plantsman **Frank Cabot** after his visit to Ruth Bancroft's dry garden in Walnut Creek, CA. He recognized an opportunity to create an organization to help preserve such exceptional gardens for future generations.

The Garden Conservancy's preservation and education programs have grown significantly over the years. Since 1989, the Conservancy has helped more than 100 outstanding American gardens survive and prosper. Every year since 1995, our signature garden-visiting program, Open Days, has been opening the gates to hundreds of private gardens across the country, allowing thousands of visitors to explore beautiful spaces not normally open to the public.

In 2020, in midst of the coronavirus pandemic, we launched our first virtual programs and celebrated the 25th anniversary of our Open Days program with the publication of a book, *OpenDays25: A Quarter Century of America's Gardeners and Their Gardens*.

In 2021, we published a companion piece to *OpenDays25*: a book about garden preservation, *GardenPreservation: Preserving, Sharing, and Celebrating America's Cultural Legacy,* and also introduced pre-registration and e-ticketing to enable a careful return to in-person programs.

Membership Matters

Thanks to the support and partnership of thousands of members across the country, we are able to pursue our mission to preserve, share, and celebrate America's gardens and diverse gardening traditions for the education and inspiration of the public

Members are not only our most committed supporters, they are also a national, diverse community of garden enthusiasts who value the boundless contributions gardens add to our lives.

Are you passionate about gardens and the vital role they play in our communities, quality of life, and culture?

Join us! We offer vast opportunities to learn and exchange information and ideas about gardening, sustainability, design, and preservation through our **educational events** and **publications**. Our **virtual programs** offer members a way to join the conversation regardless of location or season!

Together, we can preserve, share, and celebrate America's gardens and diverse gardening traditions so they may continue to nurture and inspire us for generations to come.

Thank you, members!

If You Dig Us, Then Join Us!

Membership opportunities start at just $50 and include exclusive benefits:

•Free copy of our *Open Days Directory*

•Complimentary member credits, redeemable for Open Days garden admissions or virtual program registrations

•Member-pricing on additional purchases of Open Days garden admissions or virtual program registrations—50% discount

•Subscription to the Garden Conservancy's print and electronic newsletter, containing articles about Conservancy projects, garden restoration, events, and tours

•Invitations to Conservancy-sponsored lectures, Digging Deeper, and Garden Masters Series events at member rates

•Invitations to special members-only events

•A 20% discount off your next order with White Flower Farm

•Subscription to *Better Homes & Gardens* or *Martha Stewart Living*

VISIT
gardenconservancy.org/membership

CALL
845.424.6500 M–F, 9–5 Eastern

EMAIL
membership@gardenconservancy.org

Celebrating and sharing America's gardens since 1995

Society of Fellows Programs

Members of the Garden Conservancy's Society of Fellows enjoy general membership benefits plus invitations to attend exclusive Garden-Study Tours, as well as salon sessions and other special events.

Each year, members of the Society of Fellows travel to domestic and international destinations to explore outstanding gardens and historic landscapes.

Everyone is welcome to become a member of the Society of Fellows. For more information about joining our Society of Fellows and becoming eligible for these Garden-Study Tours and other special events, please contact Bridget Connors at 845.424.6500, M–F, 9–5 Eastern.

Become Involved in Open Days

Visiting private gardens through Open Days is only one of the ways that you can support the Garden Conservancy's mission. As we look ahead to plan the future of Open Days, we want to capitalize on the passion and energy of our loyal supporters. There are lots of ways to become involved!

Become a Garden Host

Opening your garden through Open Days is a rewarding experience unlike any other. If you are proud of the work that you've done in your garden and wish to share it with others, you may be a perfect candidate to serve as an Open Days host. We are always on the lookout for gardens that showcase good design, creativity, and horticultural skill.

Contact our office to learn more about what it takes to become a garden host. We will do our best to connect you with a local Regional Ambassador in your area, or will discuss ways to expand Open Days to your region.

Become a Regional Ambassador

Are you passionate about the wonders of great gardens, and well-connected to your regional gardening community? Are you looking to become involved in a fun, rewarding, and worthy project? You might be a perfect fit to serve as a Regional Ambassador! The Garden Conservancy is dedicated to expanding the impact of our mission through Open Days, and we can do that only through the dedicated hard work of our Regional Ambassadors. Our Ambassadors make the program run— they identify Open Days host gardens, arrange logistics, help hosts to complete and submit the documentation needed to share their gardens through Open Days, organize volunteers to staff Open Days, and help to market Open Days through regional channels. We are truly grateful for our existing network of Regional Ambassadors, and we are enthusiastic to work with more people to join their ranks! Contact our office to learn more about the critically important work of Garden Conservancy Regional Ambassadors, and to see if it might work for you!

Volunteer at an Open Day

The Garden Conservancy works with a national network of volunteers who greet guests at Open Days, help orient guests at the Open Days gardens, and provide support in many other ways. It's also a fun and social experience! We so appreciate the work of each and every one of our volunteers. The commitment does not have to be major—volunteering at even one Open Day per year is tremendously valuable.

If you would like to become a part of our community of eager and enthusiastic garden-lovers and volunteers, then we would love to hear from you. Contact our office and we will put you in touch with a Regional Ambassador or Open Days host in your area. Thank you!

Call
845.424.6500, M–F, 9–5 ET

Email
opendays@gardenconservancy.org

Visit
Gardenconservancy.org/opendays

Introducing the Frank and Anne Cabot Society

The Garden Conservancy is delighted to announce the launch of the **Frank and Anne Cabot Society** for planned giving, established to recognize and thank our friends, members, and Fellows who have generously included the Conservancy in their estate plans.

The Cabots founded the Garden Conservancy in 1989 with the goal of guiding the transition of significant private gardens into vibrant public resources, a mission that continues to be central to all that we do.

With the creation of the Cabot Society, we celebrate those whose generosity supports the future of the Garden Conservancy, ensuring that the legacy of extraordinary gardens is available for generations to come.

There is no minimum dollar amount to become a member of the Frank and Anne Cabot Society. Benefits include complimentary admission to select programs and Open Days, recognition in the Conservancy's Annual Report, and a token of our appreciation created in partnership with Janet Mavec, celebrated jeweler and longtime friend of the Garden Conservancy.

For more information, please contact Director of Development Sarah Parker at sparker@gardenconservancy.org or 845.424.6500 ext. 214.

Photo courtesy of Caroline Burgess/ Stonecrop Gardens

The Garden Conservancy's Educational Programs

Since 1989, the Garden Conservancy has been sharing gardens and cross-pollinating ideas in many ways, including offering public educational programs in cities across the country, providing exclusive opportunities to tour private gardens through Garden-Study Tours for participants in our Society of Fellows, and through Open Days, our signature garden visiting program. We have expanded our educational offerings in recent years through Digging Deeper programs and the Garden Masters Series.

All of our efforts to share gardens and to facilitate a national dialogue around the most timely and important ideas in horticulture are designed to foster a community of people passionate and knowledgeable about the special importance of gardens. The more we celebrate great gardens, design, and horticulture, the more we can impact our world by supporting a community of garden stewards and by connecting people and nature.

Open Days

Fueling America's passion for gardens, Open Days is a nationwide community of gardeners and garden enthusiasts teaching and inspiring each other. We think there is no better way to improve as a gardener—from expert to novice—than by experiencing a diverse range of gardens firsthand.

Open Days provides opportunities to visit the county's most exciting, creative, and innovative private gardens. It has become our best-known and most beloved program.

Since 1995, Open Days has welcomed more than 1.3 million visitors into thousands of inspired private landscapes—from urban rooftops to organic farms, historic estates to innovative suburban lots—in 41 states.

Open Days is made possible thanks to the hard work and generous support of hundreds of volunteers who help us to showcase regional horticultural and stylistic expressions in a national context, celebrating the rich diversity of America's gardens. We are deeply grateful for the dedication of our regional ambassadors, without whom Open Days would not be possible. Special thanks also to our Garden Hosts for generously opening your gardens for public enjoyment, and to the hundreds of additional volunteers who provide other invaluable support on Open Days.

Our Open Days community is made up of a diverse and talented set of individuals. To provide a small introduction to a few of these impressive and accomplished individuals as well as a peek into the inner working of Open Days, please see "Glimpse Behind the Garden Gate: The Mountsier Garden" on page 8. This is just a sampling of the many special people who make Open Days a success.

Many Open Days hosts supplement the guest experience with guided tours and additional activities for visitors. These **Garden Extras** are free with garden admission. See the garden listings throughout this directory for more information.

Inspired by the rich informal conversations that typify Open Days, special site-specific programs were added to enhance the Open Days roster in 2015 and quickly became popular. In these **Digging Deeper** events, small groups of visitors come together for informative yet informal talks and demonstrations with experts from every facet of the garden world: landscape architects, garden writers, plant collectors, artists, and more.

Digging Deeper programs are a fantastic opportunity to explore the myriad connections between gardening and other creative pastimes. Advance registration and pre-purchase is required. Don't delay; space is limited and they fill up quickly! Visit gardenconservancy.org/opendays for more information and to register.

In 2019, we also introduced the **Garden Masters Series**—connoisseur-level educational and social opportunities at exclusive gardens not otherwise available through Open Days. A full list of Garden Master Series will be published in the spring. Please refer to our website often for the latest updates and more opportunities. Most of our 2021 Garden Masters Series programs sold out, so be sure to register early to avoid disappointment.

Other Educational Programs

The Garden Conservancy also presents and co-sponsors lectures, symposia, and many other educational programs across the country. Our Speaker Series presents some of the most important designers, authors, experts, theorists, practitioners, and other leaders in the gardening world who have influenced the public appreciation for gardens through their work. Gardens, after all, reflect cultural values and norms in the same way that other forms of art, architecture, and culinary practices do.

In 2020, in the midst of the coronavirus pandemic, we moved our Speaker Series to an online format, launching the first of our popular virtual program series that continue to today. We also began the *In My Garden: A Visual Diary* newsletter series, allowing members to explore and remain connected to gardens while at home. For the latest information on educational programs that we present or cosponsor, please **visit gardenconservancy.org**.

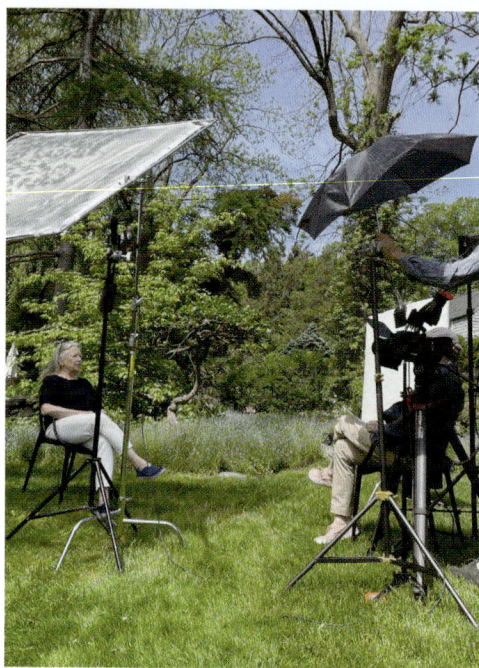

Speaking Out for Gardens

As an **advocate for garden preservation**, the Garden Conservancy takes a public stand to protect at-risk gardens. Recent examples include letters of support for the preservation of the Hirshhorn Museum Sculpture Garden in Washington, DC; the Los Angeles County Arboretum and Botanic Garden; and Marabar at the National Geographic Headquarters in Washington, DC.

Engaging with Small Public Gardens

In addition to working with individual gardens, the Conservancy provides educational and networking opportunities through the **Garden Conservancy Northwest Network**. Through this member-supported association of gardens, parks, and horticultural organizations, we support the "cross-pollination" of knowledge and resources and provide two annual workshops tailored to their specific interests and needs.

Gardens Tell Stories

Gardens are by nature ephemeral, and the Garden Conservancy's mission is to educate the public about these fragile cultural resources and help preserve the stories they tell. The Garden Conservancy's Documentation Program seeks to capture the essence of something intangible: the beauty of a garden and the many stories it embodies. Our Documentation Program uses film, photos, interviews, and archival material to bring gardens to life online and provide important insight for years to come.

Gardens for Good

In February 2021, the Garden Conservancy launched a new annual initiative, **Gardens for Good,** which allows us to award grants typically ranging from $5,000 to $13,000 to small public gardens and organizations that are making a significant impact in their communities through garden-based programming.

We are grateful for the generosity of donors and attendees of our 2020 Virtual Holiday Toast, who helped make possible the first round of grants. The Garden Conservancy is honored to support the work of the following organizations:

Gaiety Hollow
Salem, OR

The Elizabeth Lawrence House & Garden
Charlotte, NC

The Midland Gives campaign for the Pearl Fryar Topiary Garden
Bishopville, SC

Project EATS
New York, NY

Southside Community Land Trust
Providence, RI

The Anne Spencer House & Garden Museum
Lynchburg, VA

Sylvester Manor Educational Farm
Shelter Island, NY

Walnut Way Conservation Corp.
Milwaukee, WI

The John Fairey Garden
Hempstead, TX

The Gardens of Alcatraz
San Francisco, CA

The awardees represent a cross-section of gardens and organizations, all nonprofits, many of whom we have partnered with on preservation projects, as well as in Open Days and our other educational programs. We are delighted to support their work which makes a valuable impact in communities across the country.

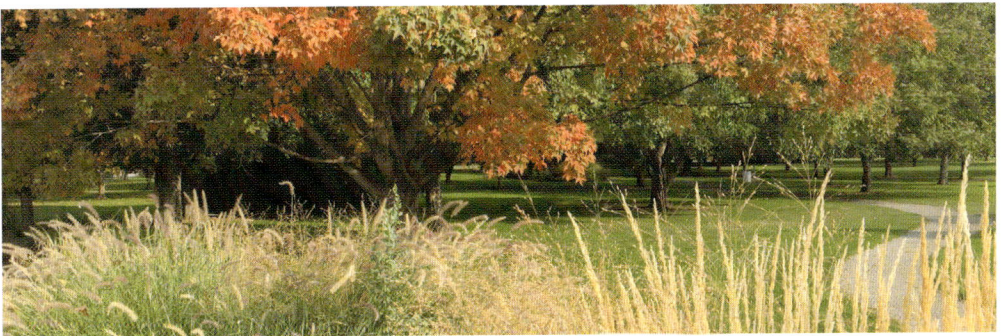

Preservation in Action

Since 1989, the Garden Conservancy has worked with more than 80 gardens in 26 states and two Canadian provinces to advance the Conservancy's mission to "preserve, share, and celebrate American gardens and diverse gardening traditions for the education and inspiration of the public."

The Garden Conservancy Preservation staff assists garden owners, managers, and community organizations from coast to coast to address the wide range of challenges they face, from historic rehabilitation and organizational development to collections management and documentation.

Reviving Gilded Age Beauty

Located on the Bard College campus in Annandale-on-Hudson, NY, Blithewood Garden is a nationally significant Beaux-Arts gem. We partnered with the college to rehabilitate this beautiful Italianate garden designed by Francis Hoppin circa 1903. Blithewood Garden's highly architectural elements have been hard-hit by the passage of time, leaving important design elements like the copper-roofed summer house, wisteria-covered pergolas, and terra-cotta balustrades in critical need of repairs.

With Bard College and the Friends of Blithewood, we are raising visibility for the project, conducting research, and establishing a rehabilitation plan, so that future generations can enjoy this nationally significant garden.

Celebrating the Legacy of American Designers

The Garden Conservancy helped to establish the Lord & Schryver Conservancy and to preserve Gaiety Hollow, the historic home and office of pioneering landscape architects Elizabeth Lord and Edith Schryver. The first all-female landscape architecture firm in the Pacific Northwest, Lord & Schryver designed more than 250 landscapes throughout the region in the first half of the twentieth century and was known for creating designs that adapted European and East Coast landscape styles to the climate of the Pacific Northwest.

The Garden Conservancy assisted the Lord & Schryver Conservancy with **organizational development**, advised on a multi-year restoration plan and a marketing plan, endorsed their capital campaign, and provided guidance on a Cultural Landscape Report. Now listed on the National Register of Historic Places, Gaiety Hollow is owned by the Lord & Schryver Conservancy and maintained as a resource and archive about women in landscape architecture.

Preserving Horticultural Collections

The John Fairey Garden (formerly Peckerwood Garden) in Hempstead, TX, has an important collection of more than 3,000 species of rare, drought-tolerant plants native to the southern United States and the remote mountains of Mexico and Asia. The Garden Conservancy helped form the Peckerwood Garden Conservation Foundation and guided strategic planning and collections management initiatives. We also hold a **conservation easement** on the property, preserving it in perpetuity.

As part of its goal to ensure the longevity of rare or threatened species, the John Fairey Garden participates in seed exchanges with numerous horticultural institutions such as the University of California at Berkeley, Harvard University, the Royal Botanic Gardens at Kew, and Chollipo Arboretum Foundation in Chingchongnam-do, South Korea.

Responding to Disasters

The historic Cummer Museum of Art & Gardens, in Jacksonville, FL, has undertaken **repairs to significant damage** from Hurricane Irma in 2017. The gardens are more than 100 years old and are listed in the National Register of Historic Places.

Some of the most important American landscape designers and horticulturists were involved with the gardens, including O. C. Simonds, Ellen Biddle Shipman, Thomas Meehan and Sons, and the legendary Olmsted firm. The Garden Conservancy donated $20,000 to help with the restoration.

Protecting Important Gardens for Future Generations

At the Elizabeth Lawrence House and Garden, in Charlotte, NC, the Garden Conservancy holds a **conservation easement** to protect the home and garden of one of the American South's most celebrated garden writers. Conservation easements set conditions for how a property is used and maintained and remain in effect in perpetuity.

Elizabeth Lawrence (1904–1985) considered her garden a "living laboratory," and preserving it is preserving her legacy. Lawrence wrote numerous books and was beloved for her regular articles on Southern gardens and gardening. Now a National Historic Landmark, her home and garden are part of the Wing Haven Foundation, open to the public as a horticultural learning center.

From the Open Days Program Manager

By training I am a historian, and I have worked in museum education for many years. Early on, it was impressed upon me that people learn best when there is a tangible connection between past and present: experiences that engage the senses are not only memorable, but also life changing.

As Coordinator of Horticulture at Old Sturbridge Village, I was tasked with building these connections in the museum's gardens. For five years, I had the privilege of delving into early nineteenth-century garden literature, diaries, and other ephemera not only to re-create period appropriate gardens, but also to maintain gardens using the same techniques written about 200 years ago.

Even though I am now firmly in the twenty-first century, I still return to this historic advice throughout the growing season: As I plant my hyacinths in the fall, I am reminded of Joseph Breck's 1851 advice that "an imperfect root is not worth planting." In the warmer months, Lydia Maria Child's 1829 receipt for "the best sort of catsup" is the only one I turn to when looking to use up an abundance of tomatoes.

Likewise, the jade plant from my great-grandmother has scions all over the country, residing in my family's homes and connecting us to each other and back to her. The rituals and traditions of gardening provide a tangible connection to gardens and gardeners past, with each season's experiences growing upon the last.

I was immediately captivated by the Open Days program because it not only connects us to a wider community of gardeners, but also connects us with the totality of experiences that leads to extraordinary gardens. More than simply peering over the garden gates, an Open Day allows us to learn from other gardeners and puts us in touch with generations of gardeners and their experiences before them.

A visit to an Open Day is a connection to every garden mentor, every visit to a breathtaking landscape, and every first horticultural love that sparked an all-consuming passion. It is no wonder that the program is so life-changing for so many visitors.

As we look toward the 27th season of Open Days, we too celebrate traditions: the return of the beloved Directory, the anticipation of visiting new gardens and seeing how returning gardens have grown each year. As you visit gardens this season, reflect not only on your garden mentors and experiences, but also on all those who have shaped you as a gardener.

—Amy Murray
Open Days Program Manager

Celebrating and sharing America's gardens since 1995

Celebrating and sharing America's gardens since 1995

Celebrating and sharing America's gardens since 1995

Women's Support Services proudly presents

TRADE SECRETS®

MAY 14 & 15, 2022

SATURDAY, MAY 14
Rare Plant & Garden Antiques Sale
Lime Rock Park, Lakeville, CT

SUNDAY, MAY 15
Tour an exquisite garden in
Falls Village, CT and explore
the Northwest Hills

A fundraiser for Women's Support Services:
Domestic Violence Intervention, Prevention, and Education
wssdv.org

TICKETS & INFORMATION:

TradeSecretsCT.com
or (860) 364-1080

Rain or shine
No pets

Proof of full COVID-19 vaccination
will be required for both events

Celebrating and sharing America's gardens since 1995

SEIBERT & RICE
FINE ITALIAN TERRA COTTA

www.seibert-rice.com
(973) 467.8266

Open Days 2022

Full Descriptions by State

Mountsier Garden - Nutley, NJ
Photo courtesy of Land Morphology

Dry Garden on Surrey - San Francisco, CA
Photo by John Priola

California

CALIFORNIA

Pasadena and Environs
Sunday, April 24

Los Angeles
Sunday, May 1

San Francisco East Bay
Saturday, May 7

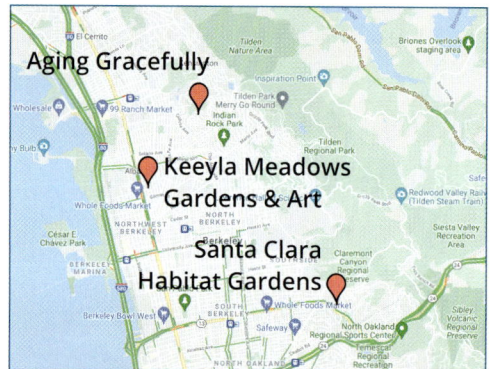

ALBANY
KEEYLA MEADOWS GARDENS & ART

📷 | ♿ partial | 🌿
Hours: 10 a.m. to 4 p.m.

Keeyla Meadows is a painter, sculptor, and garden designer who makes gardens that are full-scale works of art you can walk into and be a part of. Her own garden is a living painting of vibrant colors. Keeyla is known as a pioneer in making artistic gardens more adaptable to small-scale gardens, where color means filling the garden "frame" with attention to detail. Much of the color is provided by flowers.

The garden is an invitation to local pollinators: "hummers," bees, and butterflies. Many materials are incorporated into the garden work: painterly pavings, wavy walls, mosaic benches, bronze sculptures, and brilliantly colorful plantings. You will find images of Keeyla's garden in her book, *Fearless Color Gardens*.

BERKELEY
AGING GRACEFULLY

Hours: 10 a.m. to 4 p.m.

When we moved into our old, neglected carriage house and garden in 1987, I did not know a peony from a boxwood. I was busy working and raising children. We were so excited just to have fruit in the yard that we could actually eat and some flowers to put in a vase.

Over the years I have read, experimented, divided, planted, replanted, lost and gained. So much of my knowledge has come from sharing with others. I have learned much, especially the peace and joy a garden bestows. It is a place to contemplate, feel alive, and delight in the five senses.

I am most proud of the way our garden has given back over the years. What started as a clump of clivia is now hundreds, the hedgehog aloe that lived under the European oak has yielded 50+ babies, our agapanthus have graced the pathways of friends and neighbors from Berkeley to Napa, and our ancient acanthus is a spectacle in the spring, spreading its roots in nooks and crannies.

With California's water shortages and raging fires, the garden has evolved into a dryer version of itself. Succulents, grasses, and water wise plants have edged out hydrangeas and other thirsty perennials The true heroes of the garden have not only persevered but also flourished—regal beech and sculptural oak, the ancient

boxwoods and magnolias, the acanthus and elder hellebores—a true testament to the grandeur of nature.

> ## — TROWEL TALK—
>
> The garden and I have grown and aged together, nourishing one another and fulfilling each other's needs.
>
> This symbiotic relationship is one of the true gifts we give to one another.
>
> It is my happiness to be able to share this garden with others.
>
> — 👍 —

BERKELEY
SANTA CLARA HABITAT GARDENS

♿ partial | 🪶
Hours: 10 a.m. to 4 p.m.

Rich with color, texture, and plant-palette diversity, frequented by butterflies, bees, hummingbirds, songbirds, and more, Santa Clara Habitat Gardens enliven the senses and nourish the soul. They're artisanal and ecological by design, including many native plants, recycled redwood stairway treads and stepping "stones" of repurposed concrete.

Created as "Gardens of Delight for People & Pollinators" by Alisa Rose Seidlitz of Loving Gardens Designs, the three separate areas were planted over time, with gentle changes happening each year. The front garden, at about 14 years old, offers a variety of planting vignettes capturing one's attention on the way to the front door, and down the curving path to the back garden. The wide, tiered back garden, in its fourth season, with swaths of full sun and several seating areas, welcomes everyone to relax and breathe in the beauty. Sweet aroma abounds.

While the front and back gardens have some irrigation, there's an overall water-wise/low-water focus, with some parts needing no supplemental or only spot watering. The unfenced driveway side garden is the most recently planted, and has no irrigation at all. It requires only minimal, very occasional watering. With something in bloom year-round, it's untouched by deer, although they have been seen romping through without stopping!

Santa Clara Habitat Gardens sit on the territory of Huichin, the ancestral and unceded land of the Chochenyo Ohlone, the successors of the historic and sovereign Verona Band of Alameda County.

GARDEN EXTRAS

1:30 p.m. "Delightfully Delectable!"

Did you know that many familiar flowers can feed people as well as pollinators?

Expanding on last year's conversation, engaging speaker, Eco-Garden & Western Feng Shui Designer/Educator Alisa Rose Seidlitz will share ways to create spaces of beauty and delight for yourself, while staying in sync with nature.

Honoring Soil, Wind, and Water, she'll answer questions and discuss pollinator-habitat plants, edible flowers, water-wise design choices, surprising bee info, and some open secrets about California poppies, yarrow, and the plants we call "weeds." (A bit of rewilding can be key!)

Mendocino County

Saturday, May 21

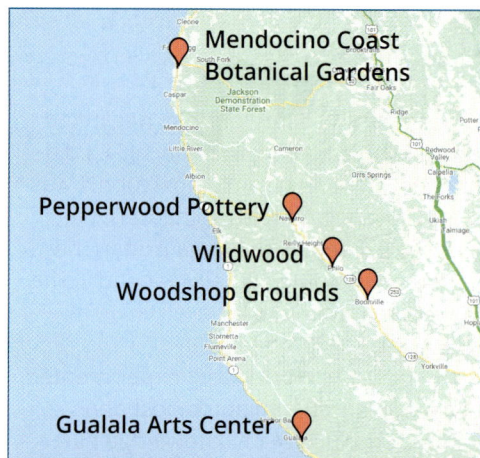

Mendocino Coast Botanical Gardens

Pepperwood Pottery

Wildwood

Woodshop Grounds

Gualala Arts Center

FORT BRAGG

PUBLIC GARDEN

MENDOCINO COAST BOTANICAL GARDENS

18220 N Hwy One
Fort Bragg, CA 95437

Mendocino Coast Botanical Gardens is a unique natural treasure located at 18220 North Highway 1, just two miles south of Fort Bragg and seven miles north of Mendocino. Our mission is to engage and enrich lives by displaying and conserving plants in harmony with our northern California coastal ecosystems and to preserve public access to the coast. This magnificent 47-acre site is one of few public gardens located directly on the ocean's shore. The unique environment on the Mendocino Coast makes the Gardens a wonder year-round, each changing season bringing new flora and fauna. We welcome visitors and our local community to experience the rugged beauty of the Mendocino Coast mixed with the peaceful tranquility of our garden by the sea.

For more information, visit www.gardenbythesea.org. Admission: $15 general (15 and older); $12 seniors (65 and older); $8 juniors (aged 6 to 14); children aged 5 and under are free; $10 Coast Resident (Gualala to Westport); $12/person for groups of 12 or more; members are free; $10 member's guests; free to American Horticulture Society Reciprocal Admissions Program members

GUALALA

PUBLIC GARDEN

GUALALA ARTS CENTER
46501 Old State Hwy
Gualala, CA 95445

Gualala Arts Center is a 15,000-square-foot visual and performing arts venue on eleven acres of redwood forest that sits one-quarter mile from the Pacific Ocean on the Mendocino Coast. This jewel of the Redwood Coast is tucked into the redwood forest next to the Gualala River and includes a Haiku Garden path, a Redwood Grove Events Area adorned with hand-built stone walls, multiple walkways, large bronze sculptures, large boulders, unique garden art, outdoor areas that invite you to pause and reflect, and a Meditation Grove of old-growth redwoods that stand tall among opulent ferns and lush greenery.

Patios and outdoor event areas are home to many annual and perennial plants and flowers native to the Mendocino-Sonoma

coastal area. Sculptures and outdoor artwork complement the forested grounds and gardens at every turn.

Indoor galleries change monthly, and Gualala Arts hosts many festivals and events throughout the year. Gualala Arts is thrilled to team up with the Stone Foundation and the Mendocino Stone Zone for Garden Conservancy Open Day garden tours. Many of the stone masons have created one-of-a-kind sculptures that remain on the grounds of Gualala Arts for all to admire. The newly remodeled Redwood Grove is a legacy build by the Stone Foundation and is a great place to stop for a picnic lunch among the towering redwoods, surrounded by the ancient art of stone masonry.

Gualala Arts is dedicating a new revolving outdoor sculpture garden in April 2022. Selected artists will display and sell their art for the year with a new map and catalogue each April.

Hours: The garden looks best March through November, although redwood forest and paths are lovely year-round. The Arts Center is open 7 days a week, 11 a.m. to 4 p.m. Grounds are always open to the public. Admission: Free. http://gualalaarts.org/

BOONVILLE
WOODSHOP GROUNDS
📷 | ♿ partial
Hours: 10 a.m. to 4 p.m.

My grandfather got me started in his vegetable garden when I was a boy, and, while continuing that, I also became interested in flowers. I discovered organic gardening when I was in junior high in Ohio and was considered somewhat weird then;

not so much today.

I have been a studio furniture maker all my working life, and the garden makes a wonderful setting for my shop and showroom. I have made garden furniture from reclaimed redwood as well as some concrete planters and border walls. I try to have something always blooming, and there will be a lot in May, including phlox, crocosmia, campanula, lychnis, heuchera, and more. My file folder of plants is more than 2½ inches thick and growing.

GARDEN EXTRAS

Easy Composting, 11 a.m. and 2 p.m.

— TROWEL TALK—

My grandfather got me started with this when I was a small boy. When it got to be time for Junior High and High School, I was raising roses, tomatoes, and gladiolas.

The thing that made me really stand out was my redworm farm. I went around town with my Radio Flyer wagon collecting throw-away produce to feed to the worms.

— 👍 —

NAVARRO
PEPPERWOOD POTTERY

📷 | ♿ partial | 🖋 | NEW
Hours: 10 a.m. to 4 p.m.

I moved onto my property 44 years ago with my ex-partner. She liked the garden at the Boonville Hotel so much, she had their gardener, Russell Link, wildlife biologist and landscape designer, put one in here. The perennial garden is well established with new plantings each year by my gardener, who maintains it now.

There are older fruit trees I planted 42 years ago and two grape arbors almost 100 years old. This was an old homestead, with the original house built in 1906. I did lots of gardening in my younger days and now just make my pottery and do some of the work on the six raised beds with vegetables that I grow year-round. I have been working on propagating an older peach tree that I believe to be close to 90 or 100 years old that is totally resistant to peach leaf curl.

The garden has a four-tier water fountain which makes beautiful sounds as people stroll through the walkways and visit my pottery showrooms.

— TROWEL TALK—

Most of my gardens now are taken care of by someone else while I do my pottery. I do work growing vegetables, with tomatoes being my favorite. I grew 32 this year and freeze large amounts to have them year round.

I do have a peach tree in my yard that is probably 90 to 100 years old and is totally resistant to the peach leaf curl which I have been working at propagating. I have started numbers of them from seed and have done a number of grafts of this tree onto some wild plum root stock.

— 👍 —

📷 Photos permitted   ♿ Partially accessible   NEW garden or section   🖋 Nature-friendly

PHILO
WILDWOOD

📷 | ♿ partial | 🌿
Hours: 10 a.m. to 4 p.m.

An idyllic 30-acre park of 150-foot-tall trees surrounds a conifer collection garden, a potager, and a small alpine garden. The garden contains a large collection of choice cornus, magnolia, perennials, and temperate region shrubs.

San Jose
Saturday, June 4

SAN JOSE
Garden of Cevan Forristt

Hours: 10 a.m. to 4 p.m.

Cevan's garden is an intensely private sanctuary. Here, water meets stone, the secular encounters the sacred, and nature adorns the man-made.

The understanding that this is not your typical suburban garden begins on the street; formidable walls and patinated iron gates announce his love of privacy, tell the tale of his travels throughout the Near and Far East, celebrate his fascination with use and reuse, and showcase his appreciation of the native and the exotic. His house and gardens not only reflect his sense of the mysterious and playful but also demonstrate his skill in combining diverse symbolic objects—stone urns and animal troughs, deities and chains, giant ceramic vessels and delicate woodcarvings.

Like an ambassador from some fantastic far-off land, Cevan has crafted a mazelike retreat that feels much larger than it actually is. Among ancient ruins of China and early California, stone paths, crenelated screens, and bamboo groves, he has magically formed from these material objects the sensation of venturing into space outside of time. Lush plantings and solid materials evoke his personal approach to the California outdoor lifestyle while reflecting his unique incantation of beauty.

GINKO FORRISTT TEA HOUSE

📷 | ♿ partial | NEW
Hours: 10 a.m. to 1 p.m.

Our garden is a pandemic collaboration (started in February 2020) with designer Cevan Forristt, who translated our love of east Asian gardens into an oasis that is both secluded and embraces our urban and dynamic downtown neighborhood.

The backyard of the historic 1914 Naglee Park craftsman home is characterized by pan-Asian detail, mature tree specimens curated for the site, a koi pond and redwood bridge, an open-sided tea house, and the kind of whimsical detail characteristic of a Cevan Forristt garden.

The front garden embraces a more formal

interpretation of classic Japanese and Korean gardens, utilizing large granite boulders, a sandstone path, mature maples, an imposing granite lantern, and an intricate stone and iron driveway inlay that invites neighborhood conversation.

San Francisco East Bay

Sunday, June 12

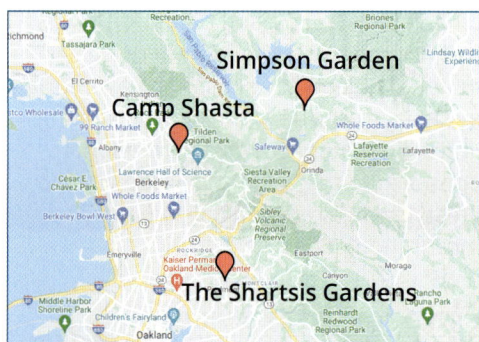

BERKELEY

CAMP SHASTA

📷

Hours: 10 a.m. to 4 p.m.

We call it "Camp Shasta" because we feel like we are at summer camp living here, in a park- like setting dominated by a house that looks like the National Park Service built it.

The garden is a deep canyon with Codornices Creek running through it year round. It is a mostly woodland setting, partly shaded, with sunnier areas near the house where the potager area, complete with fruit trees and chickens, is located.

Because of the size of the property, about three-quarters of an acre, I do not strive for a manicured look, but rather a look of tamed and enhanced nature. There are numerous sculptures, the best of which is a two-ton stone face in the creek, carved by Marcia Donahue.

ORINDA

SIMPSON GARDEN

📷 | ✐ |

Hours: 10 a.m. to 4 p.m.

The owners built the house and laid out the lower and upper gardens on the one-acre site in 1979 and over time have created a sculpture wonderland with their collection from around the world.

A playful abstract metal gate done by local artist Stan Dann sets the artistic tone for the guests when they arrive. The lower garden with its boxwood spheres and gently arching pergola was originally designed by Ron Lutsko. In setting a more formal mood, he created rooms of color to set off the sculpture. These seasonal changes make for something always in bloom.

By 2000, garden designer Suzanne Porter updated the plantings throughout and created a continuous garden up to and beyond the house. Subsequently, since 2005, Jane Sylvester has been involved in the next renovation. Through necessary editing, she has replanted various sections entirely as gardens change over time. The rear hillside is much cleaner now as the entire rear garden can once again be seen to the rear arbor. Shade-loving perennials hug the path toward the private terrace near the kitchen.

— TROWEL TALK—

📷 Photos permitted   ♿ Partially accessible   NEW garden or section   ✐ Nature-friendly

I used to do everything myself but now that the acre is developed, I have substantial help so can't take credit. I like the planning process and love working with Jane Sylvester. We bounce ideas off of one another until we come to some good solutions.

If a plant doesn't do well or turns out to be the wrong color, I have no trouble replacing it. I appreciate and love my garden every day, every season.

— 👍 —

PIEDMONT
THE SHARTSIS GARDENS

📷

Hours: 10 a.m. to 4 p.m.

The Shartsis Gardens surround the historic Sutro Mansion, built around 1910 on a five acre parcel that had been the site of writer Jack London's home. The Mansion, designed by architect Houghton Sawyer, now sits on a one-acre parcel secluded from the street below.

The house has five gardens that were completely redone in the 21st century. The front garden was reconstructed into two levels, the main brick staircase was enhanced, the lawns were added, and the garden enlarged. The lower level courtyard, paved with more than 4,000 hand-placed granite stones, features a medallion fashioned from more than 2,500 hand-cut bricks. Italian cypresses stand in front of a grand balustrade, frame the house, and also form a backdrop to a fountain with a whimsical bronze sculpture by American artist Larry Shank named *Colonel Mustard*, an homage to artist René Magritte. Extensive plantings of jasmine and laurels provide structure on both levels and

define annual planting beds. On the upper level, gravel pathways, a topiary, patterned flower parterres, and an elegant black iron fountain surrounded by 'Just Joey' rose trees are all bordered by miniature boxwoods. At the west end of the pathway is the bronze sculpture *Feeling* by French artist Jacques Le Bescond.

The morning garden on the east side of the house features an Italianate lion wall fountain surrounded by arborvitae, ground roses, and a border of boxwood globes. The patio is surrounded by camellias and boxwood hedges that form parterres for roses.

The third garden is a private walk on the west side of the house, with sculpted low hedges, arborvitae, camellias, and high pittosporum hedges. The private walk leads to the fourth garden and patio with breathtaking views of the San Francisco Bay.

On the upper lawn the monumental *Caballo Nileo* bronze sculpture by Spanish artist Carlos Mata stands on a two ton block of stone and looks out over the Bay. Custom brick designs tie together the walkways, the patio, the upper lawns, the citrus garden, the hydrangea garden, and the rose garden that surrounds part of the house. The back lawns are built on terraces constructed from 70 tons of rock. The cypress theme is repeated. The steep hillside below the main lawn features flowering plum trees and redwoods.

The fifth garden, the Italian vegetable garden, is sheltered below the main lawn, featuring stone terraces, a travertine Italian fountain, and a row of large Italian urns.

San Francisco
Saturday, June 18

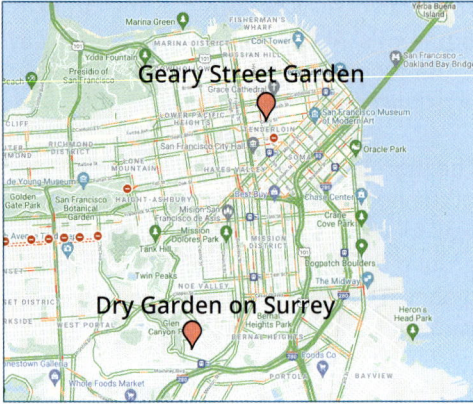

SAN FRANCISCO

DRY GARDEN ON SURREY

📷

Hours: 10 a.m. to 4 p.m.

This dry garden on Surrey is a bit of a succulent haven. Fifteen years of growing tree aloes, yuccas, agaves, and more. The yard features two very tall tree aloes that made it up here from Los Angeles in the back seat of a car in 2007.

This garden is self-made and designed as the plants come in. Ninety percent of the plants are traded, salvaged, or rescued. Many new homeowners may not want the scratchy, pokey plants, and they're out and rehomed right here. As you head to the Glen Park neighborhood, note the median on Bosworth, as this was planted almost ten years ago as a Street Park Steward.

— TROWEL TALK—

I was raised on a farm in Colorado and grew all kinds of flowers around the yard. It may have been a form of rebellion against how much work there was to growing food. My favorite plants are agaves and euphorbias.

— 👍

GEARY STREET GARDEN

📷 | 🖋

Hours: 10 a.m. to 4 p.m.

In the heart of downtown San Francisco lives a secret garden behind twin historic buildings. These structures were erected in the early 1900s in the theater district and are three blocks from Union Square, on the dividing line between upper-class Nob Hill and the notorious Tenderloin districts. It is extremely urban; however, from the treeless streets and filthy sidewalks you are just a garden gate away from an amazing urban oasis.

📷 Photos permitted   🏃 Partially accessible   **NEW** garden or section   🖋 Nature-friendly

Sean Stout and James Pettigrew of Organic Mechanics have designed a lush habitat garden for frogs, fish, bees, butterflies, songbirds, hummingbirds, mourning doves, nesting robins, and more. Even hawks regularly visit, bathing in the mosaic water feature after eating their pigeon in the trees.

The garden invites people with its soothing sound of water, many paths, and secret nooks. Recycled materials are used in fresh, creative ways in mosaic paths, unusual planters, and sculpture. Rare and unusual plants are featured in this can't-miss urban paradise.

Organic Mechanics has won numerous awards, including the American Horticultural Society Environment Award and the prestigious Best in Show at the San Francisco Flower and Garden Show. They have appeared in many television programs, newspapers, and magazines. Their design/build firm is founded on organic and sustainable principles.

Marin County
Saturday, June 25

A Panoramic Garden

Visions of Paradise

Garden of Sculpture

BOLINAS
GARDEN OF SCULPTURE
NEW
Hours: 10 a.m. to 4 p.m.

Landscape architect George Hargreaves is known for designing large urban master plans such as the Stanford's Engineering Quadrangle in Palo Alto, not for work on small, windswept, starkly beautiful sites atop cliffs that gradually step to the ocean as this property does.

"The sculpture collection drew me to work on this project," he says. Works by Henry Moore, Richard Long, and Barbara Hepworth are among those in the owner's collection. Hargreaves saw that the sculptures could be arranged in tiers to be viewed individually, as well as seen as a group from a distance. "We created a view corridor that steps down toward the ocean," he says. The flat-stepped terraces along this corridor provide a sculpted vista. Stacked stone fitted together forms retaining walls, and the stair treads and paths are covered in crushed granite.

At some points the property goes from natural to cultivated landscape. Hedges were used in windy areas where windbreaks were needed. Hedgerows separate the larger landscape from the garden landscape.

VISIONS OF PARADISE—
SALLY ROBERTSON GARDEN & STUDIO

📷

Hours: 10 a.m. to 4 p.m.

I like to think of walking through the garden gate as entering an enchanted and magical world. When asked to describe my garden, I refer to the title of one of my favorite garden books, *Visions of Paradise*. This expression has guided me for nearly four decades.

As a painter, I often choose plants as inspiration for a watercolor, but I give much thought to their placement, for the garden itself is a highly orchestrated color palette. As I mature as a gardener, shrubs and trees which give year-round structure become more and more important, and well-shaped shrubs mingle well with exuberant roses. Succulents have found their place, along with unusual specimens such as the exotic *Deppea splendens* from Mexico, or the lovely deciduous dawn redwood from China.

The koi pond and water garden offer an idyllic spot to linger and enjoy a reflective moment. The garden is an ever-changing project, evolving year after year, and I hope that even those who have visited in the past will find new inspiration here. Visitors are also invited to visit the studio, where art and garden meet.

— TROWEL TALK—

My coastal garden has evolved over more than four decades. Shaped shrubs, inspired in great part by gardens of Provence I visited over many years while teaching watercolor in the gardens of France, provide structure for the diverse flowering plants, including many unusual roses.

My large water garden and koi pond have become a major focus, and I can often be found tending it in my waders.

— 👍 —

STINSON BEACH
A PANORAMIC GARDEN

📷

Hours: 10 a.m. to 4 p.m.

Huge boulders on a steep hillside provide the framework for this unusual garden perched on the shoulders of Mt. Tamalpais. It was created twenty-plus years ago from a wilderness of brambles, poison oak, and native willows.

Now stone walks radiate from a centrally located house to a series of garden rooms defined by their plantings—various fuchsia species, tillandsia, and pendulous epiphyllums grow in the shade of ancient bay trees. On the hillside, protea and dozens of succulent species grow in the sparse soil among the rocks. In the sunny open areas, azara, pseudocydonia psoralea, and rare shrubs share space with perennials and self-seeding annuals. Water-loving plants such as papyrus and giant gunnera surround the seasonal stream and the koi pond.

The garden contains more than 200 species of plants, including unusual specimens from the Mediterranean, Australia, New Zealand, Chile, South Africa, and Mesoamerican cloud forests. Scattered among the plants are beautiful stone sculptures from Zimbabwe and comfortable weather-worn benches offering diverse views of the garden and the Pacific Ocean below.

— TROWEL TALK—

I am a retired Professor of Medicine. I have developed personal gardens in Southern California (Malibu), Cornwall, UK, and the San Francisco Bay area (city and coastal gardens).

My favorite plants are fuchsias, Mesoamerican cloud forest plants, and xerophytes.

— 👍 —

DIGGING DEEPER

**The Secret Lives of Plants:
Unusual Histories
and Unique Adaptations**
Martin Cline
Saturday, June 25, 4 p.m. to 6 p.m.

A Panoramic Garden
$30 Garden Conservancy members |
$40 General

Our garden has more than 200 species of plants from many parts of the world and many habitats. In their native environments, some of our plants grow under extremely moist conditions, whereas others survive under extremes of water deprivation.

Some have developed unique strategies for pollination; others have evolved mechanisms to survive the depredations of browsing animals. Several species have been rescued from the brink of extinction, and many have interesting histories of discovery or Indigenous uses.

For twenty years we have been adapting areas of this coastal garden to accommodate these diverse species. "Digging Deeper" will be the story of this journey.

Photo by Martin Cline

📷 Photos permitted   ♿ Partially accessible   **NEW** garden or section   🪶 Nature-friendly

Mendocino County
Saturday, October 22

Mendocino Coast Botanical Gardens

Frog Song Farm
Mendocino Stone Zone
Gualala Arts Center

FORT BRAGG

PUBLIC GARDEN

MENDOCINO COAST BOTANICAL GARDENS

18220 N Hwy One
Fort Bragg, CA   95437

Mendocino Coast Botanical Gardens is a unique natural treasure located at 18220 North Highway 1, just two miles south of Fort Bragg and seven miles north of Mendocino. Our mission is to engage and enrich lives by displaying and conserving plants in harmony with our northern California coastal ecosystems and to preserve public access to the coast. This magnificent 47-acre site is one of few public gardens located directly on the ocean's shore. The unique environment on the Mendocino Coast makes the Gardens a wonder year-round, each changing

season bringing new flora and fauna. We welcome visitors and our local community to experience the rugged beauty of the Mendocino Coast mixed with the peaceful tranquility of our garden by the sea.

For more information, visit www.gardenbythesea.org. Admission: $15 general (15 and older); $12 seniors (65 and older); $8 juniors (aged 6 to 14); children aged 5 and under are free; $10 Coast Resident (Gualala to Westport); $12/person for groups of 12 or more; members are free; $10 member's guests; free to American Horticulture Society Reciprocal Admissions Program members

GUALALA

PUBLIC GARDEN

GUALALA ARTS CENTER

46501 Old State Hwy
Gualala, CA   95445

Gualala Arts Center is a 15,000-square-foot visual and performing arts venue on eleven acres of redwood forest that sits one-quarter mile from the Pacific Ocean on the Mendocino Coast. This jewel of the Redwood Coast is tucked into the redwood forest next to the Gualala River and includes a Haiku Garden path, a Redwood Grove Events Area adorned with hand-built stone walls, multiple walkways, large bronze sculptures, large boulders, unique garden art, outdoor areas that invite you to pause and reflect, and a Meditation Grove of old-growth redwoods that stand tall among opulent ferns and lush greenery.

Patios and outdoor event areas are home to many annual and perennial plants and flowers native to the Mendocino-Sonoma coastal area. Sculptures and outdoor artwork complement the forested grounds and gardens at every turn.

Indoor galleries change monthly, and Gualala Arts hosts many festivals and events throughout the year. Gualala Arts is thrilled to team up with the Stone Foundation and the Mendocino Stone Zone for Garden Conservancy Open Day garden tours. Many of the stone masons have created one-of-a-kind sculptures that remain on the grounds of Gualala Arts for all to admire. The newly remodeled Redwood Grove is a legacy build by the Stone Foundation and is a great place to stop for a picnic lunch among the towering redwoods, surrounded by the ancient art of stone masonry.

Gualala Arts is dedicating a new revolving outdoor sculpture garden in April 2022. Selected artists will display and sell their art for the year with a new map and catalogue each April.

Hours: The garden looks best March through November, although redwood forest and paths are lovely year-round. The Arts Center is open 7 days a week, 11 a.m. to 4 p.m. Grounds are always open to the public. Admission: Free.
http://gualalaarts.org/

MENDOCINO STONE ZONE

Hours: 10 a.m. to 4 p.m.

For more than a decade, annually or biannually, for weeks at a time, Peter Mullins has hosted multiple masons from around the world to add to the splendor of his Gualala property.

With 50 acres of natural forested land, Peter has extensively worked on brush and tree thinning while lifting the canopy to add depth and create a more fire defensive environment. Adding hardscaping became a natural … clean the forest, add stone. Beautiful and functional, the hardscaping enhances the scenic environment and provides protection from erosion.

Guests are invited to explore the myriad of whimsical stone structures including garden follies, pebbled pathways, sculptural installations, stone patios, and walls, plus the completed Fish Rock Irish Watch Tower overlooking the forest and Pacific.

Come ready to walk, ask questions, discover traditional techniques, enjoy other newly completed installations—a Roman arch, pergola, and temple.

While in the area, other noteworthy outdoor installations in the Mendocino Stone Zone can be found at the Gualala Arts Center, constructed during the 2016 Stone Foundation Stone Symposium, as well as the stone "picket fence and labyrinth" installed recently at the Point Arena Lighthouse.

POINT ARENA
FROG SONG FARM

📷 | ♿ partial | 🖋

Hours: 10 a.m. to 4 p.m.

I am a naturalistic gardener, preferring to make a wide variety of plants happy together in my landscape. I'm never without my hori hori (soil knife) and my Felco pruners any time I step outside. I learned to garden at my father's side, begging him to let me help weed, and it still feels like a privilege to keep things tidy!

The climate here is Mediterranean, so I have collected plants from all over the world that like dry summers. Some are quite rare. I could never pick just one favorite!

Our ocean view is lovely, but it means that plants must withstand windy cool maritime conditions in the spring. Finding the right microclimate for each plant has taken repeated efforts on my part. I had to learn gardening all over again as we made this garden from scratch, starting 20 years ago with a clear-cut expanse of bare hillside, completely devoid of plants and not much soil either! Southern hemisphere plants have proved especially well adapted and I have tons of them. We even call one part of the garden "Australia." Our native plant palette provides a rich compliment to the rhododendrons and heathers that also grow well in this environment.

There is some formality in the garden design from the long axis, but my style is pretty relaxed. I call it a Tapestry Garden that concentrates on foliage texture and color as the backbone, and flowers as the bonus, adding seasonal interest. Particularly in the fall when the Hillside positively blazes with autumn colors. We feature a distinctly Japanese flavor in the grand stone staircase with its many dwarf conifers, as well as a stream that recirculates water from the 1/2-acre lily pond. The upper part of the garden is about growing food- orchard, perennial vegetables, berry cage, chickens, hoop house for heat-loving veggies and fruit, beehives, plus cut flowers for the soul and a large composting area for the planet. And we love to share the bounty.

There is always something going on throughout the year with my two greenhouses, wildflowers, unusual South African bulbs, a wall of daffodils in March, *Petanque* court, rock garden, and all of it surrounded by our native redwood, bishop pine, rhododendron, and Douglas fir forest. I look forward to welcoming you to Frog Song!

NOTES

Prospect Gardens Westport - Westport, CT
Photo by Melissa Ceriale

Connecticut

CONNECTICUT

Litchfield County

Saturday, April 30

FALLS VILLAGE

GARDEN OF BUNNY WILLIAMS

📷 | ♿ partial | 🖋

This garden is open twice this year: April 30 and July 23

Hours:
Morning session 10 a.m. to 1 p.m.
Afternoon session 1 p.m. to 4 p.m.

Interior designer and garden book author Bunny Williams's intensively planted fifteen-acre estate has a sunken garden with twin perennial borders surrounding a fishpond, a seasonally changing parterre garden, a year-round conservatory filled with tender plants, a large vegetable garden with flowers and herbs, a woodland garden with meandering paths, and a pond with a waterfall.
There is also a working greenhouse and an aviary with unusual chickens, an apple orchard with mature trees, a rustic

Greek Revival-style poolhouse folly, and a swimming pool with eighteenth-century French coping.

Fairfield County

Saturday, May 21

GREENWICH

SLEEPY CAT FARM

📷

This garden is open twice this year: May 21 and September 17

Hours:
Morning session 10 a.m. to 1 p.m.
Afternoon session 1 p.m. to 4 p.m.

The thirteen acres of Sleepy Cat Farm have evolved over the last 25 years in close collaboration between the present owner and Virginia-based landscape architect Charles J. Stick.

The landscape bordering Lake Avenue includes an extensive greenhouse and potager. The "Barn," distinguished by its half-timbered French Normandy vocabulary, is surrounded by thyme-covered terraces, providing an elegant

---

📷 Photos permitted   ♿ Partially accessible   NEW garden or section   🖋 Nature-friendly

stage set for a fine collection of garden ornament, sculpture, and boxwood topiary. The visitor's experience of the garden unfolds as pathways lead from garden room to garden room in a carefully orchestrated series of discoveries.

The central portion of the garden is distinguished by two parallel garden spaces; the first is dominated by a long reflecting pool, terminated on the north end by a wisteria-covered arbor, and on the south end by a pebble mosaic terrace and fountain basin. One of the great surprises of the tour is the adjacent garden space. Bordered by a precisely clipped hornbeam hedge, the green architecture of this room is meant to frame the view to the Chinese pavilion (or "ting"—a place to stop and take in the view) positioned on a small island in the middle of a pond teeming with koi. The north end of this garden is terminated by an impressively scaled statue of Atlas.

The heart of the original six acres is most joyfully experienced along the "Golden Path," a granite dust pathway that leads from the main house and formal terraces on top of the hill, out into the New England landscape. As it winds through the oak and beech woodland, one encounters fountains, statuary, an iris garden traversed by a Japanese spirit bridge and planted with 10,000 Japanese iris, and finally a rustic stone grotto. The woodland stream is bordered by native azaleas and a collection of spring flowering trees and bulbs, all planted for enjoyment throughout the year.

The most recent additions to the property include a limonaia used for the winter storage of citrus trees, a new fruit orchard, and a sacred woodland grove that is enjoyed from a series of pathways radiating from a newly planted meadow. The southern expansion of the property over the past three years has added a new dimension to the overall landscape experience of Sleepy Cat Farm.

A recent addition to the garden is an English-style perennial border directly across from the koi pond and, directly below, a viewing path framed by a wisteria arbor. This border is surrounded by decorative stone walls covered with hydrangea, climbing roses, clematis, and boxwood. It consists of four linear beds around a central axis of lawn pathway and features a mixed shrub and perennial border containing a succession of bloom through the seasons.

The iris garden was completed last year with many more Japanese iris cultivars added, as well as a winding bamboo railway path leading to it, featuring a fragrant Korean spice viburnum border interspersed with spring bulbs and fall blooming kirengeshoma. The garden is now bordered by a ring of bright red *Cornus* 'Arctic Fire' against a backdrop of topiaries *Ilex glabra*. In addition, seven new pieces of art have been installed in various spots along the paths.

New Haven County

Saturday, May 21

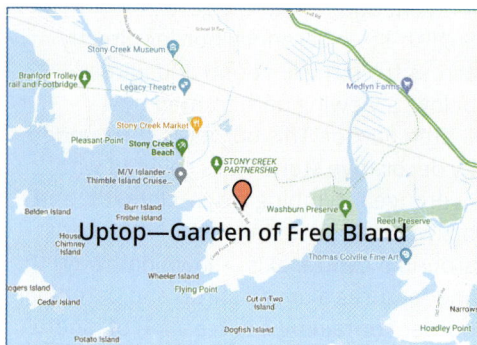

Uptop—Garden of Fred Bland

STONY CREEK

UPTOP—GARDEN OF FRED BLAND

📷 | ♿ partial

Hours: 10 a.m. to 4 p.m.

This is an intensively cultivated one-acre village weekend garden created by an architect/plant collector. The garden has more than 1,400 species of plants (mostly perennials, shrubs, and small trees) arranged in many gardens: a long double border, two woodland gardens, a pool garden hidden by a rollicking serpent-pruned tapestry hedge.

Many other hedges as well as rock walls (all quarried on site) add their charm. A main cottage and guest cottage with several other outbuildings are all purpose-designed to be subservient to the dominant garden. The owner is the chairman emeritus of the board of the Brooklyn Botanic Garden.

The garden was published in Jane Garmey's *Private Gardens of Connecticut* and other publications.

DIGGING DEEPER

Making a Garden, Leaving a Trace— An Afternoon Salon for Gardeners
Fred Bland
Saturday, May 21, 4 p.m. to 6 p.m.

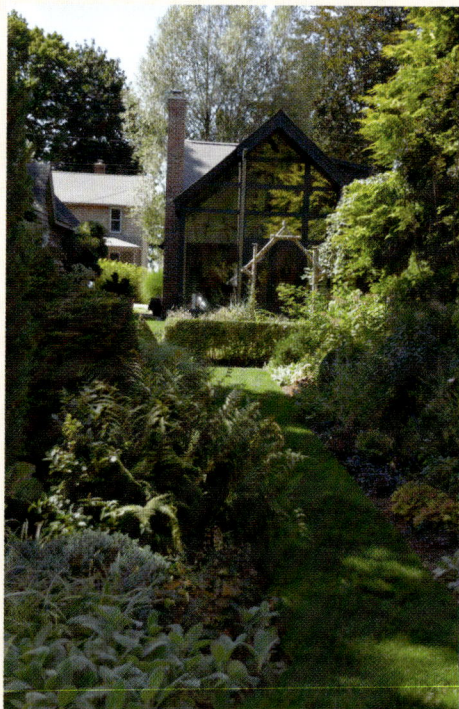

Uptop—Garden of Fred Bland
$30 Garden Conservancy members
$40 General

Join plant collector, gardener, and architect Fred Bland for a walk through

---

📷 Photos permitted   ♿ Partially accessible   **NEW** garden or section   🌿 Nature-friendly

his garden, where he works to weave his ever-growing collection of choice plants into a beautiful, engaging design.

In the spirit of a true salon, Fred will then gather guests with some refreshments for a leisurely and hopefully lively discussion of ideas about gardens and what drives us to make them. On that topic, Fred has written a short book, *The Making of a Garden(er): An Urbanist Architect in the Garden*. To fuel the afternoon's conversation, he hopes guests will read his booklet beforehand and come with ideas of their own. It is available on his firm's website, Beyer Blinder Belle, and a link is provided below.

Here are some of Fred's thoughts: "Many people view a garden as nature incarnate. It is the opposite: a garden is an artifact created by humans for human pleasure and edification. A garden is no more "natural" than a building is, even though it uses natural plant material to create its story just as a building uses bricks, steel, and glass to explain itself.

The creation of a garden, unlike some other so-called leisure pursuits, does not simply mark time but creates a product, a place, a physical record of accomplishment. This kind of hobby— so different from golf or bridge, for instance—is something that always appealed to me. It does not "fade into the void leaving no trace" (John Updike in *Toward the End of Time* describing the hours each day devoted to the practice and perfection of bridge).

I want to leave a trace. To make something always was important, perhaps as an architect is compelled

to make things. It is also an idea—this making of things—that grew in me over time, and became over time, the time of my life."

The Making of a Garden(er): An Urbanist Architect in the Garden, a link to the first part: http://www.beyerblinderbelle. com/stories/72_a_gardener_grows_the_ making_of_a_garden_er_installment_1 (Links to subsequent parts are at the end of each section.)

Fairfield County

Sunday, May 29

Blau House & Gardens

WESTPORT

BLAU HOUSE & GARDENS

📷 | ♿ partial | 🖋

This garden is open twice this year: May 29 and September 18

Hours: 10 a.m. to 4 p.m.

These two acres of formal and informal gardens were developed over 50 years by Barry Blau and include many mature specimens, especially rhododendron groves planted below towering oaks and surrounding a Mid-century Modern house.

An allée of pollarded crab apples leads to a Neptune fountain circle surrounded by columnar Norway spruce. Bamboo groves form a backdrop to the Asian garden with a large Buddha, waterfalls, and stream with water lilies and water iris, and a grass garden. A sunken rose garden is framed by stone retaining walls with boxwood parterre and fountain pools. A folly of astilbe-filled terraced beds is surrounded by stone retaining walls and steps. Lilacs, roses, and lilies are in other areas.

The house also includes front-entry sedum terraces, a roof deck with a commanding view of the gardens, and a skylit pool room and mezzanine filled with interior plants. Features incorporated throughout the garden include paths and walks, benches, ornamental gates, trellis, stone retaining walls, and sculptures.

Urns and planters filled with annuals punctuate the gardens and have been graciously funded by Bartlett Connecticut Arborists office in Monroe, CT

BARTLETT
BARTLETT
TREE EXPERTS
SCIENTIFIC TREE CARE SINCE 1907

DIGGING DEEPER

Thoroughly Modern Westport: From Stage to Garden
Matty Selman, Robert Cohen, & Emily Blau
Sunday, May 29, 5 p.m. to 6 p.m.

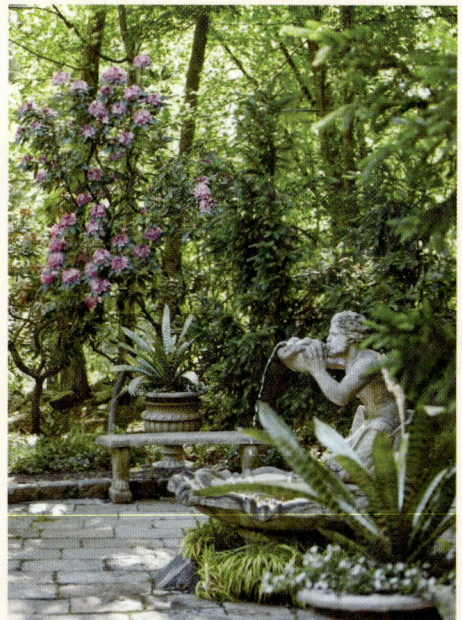

The Blau Garden in Westport, CT
$30 Garden Conservancy members
$40 General

Westport's arts community transformed from a small farming community into an "Avant Garde" cultural center made of institutions and stars in the performing, visual, and literary arts. Blau House & Gardens grew out of this engaging history—the house designed by stage set designer Ralph Alswang, and the garden created by Barry Blau, marketing executive.

Tour the grounds with Matty Selman, a dramatist, and Robert Cohen and Emily Blau Cohen as they discuss how the Mid-century Modern house relates to the Westport arts community and how Barry Blau was inspired to create a dramatic but intimate garden that reflects his ever-evolving tastes.

Regardless of the scale of your garden and the depth of your experience, be prepared to discover how to add new dimensions to your existing landscape and bring it to the next level of intrigue and interest. Blau Gardens has been featured in *Connecticut Cottages and Gardens* magazine and is included in the Smithsonian Archives of American Gardens collection.

Photo by Tim Lentz

Hartford County
Saturday, June 4

Garden of Robin Lensi

The Salsedo Family Garden

★ In addition to the gardens open in nearby Litchfield County, CT (page 63), there is an additional garden open on this date in nearby Dutchess County, NY:

Highgrove Cottage
For garden description and details, see page 157.

BURLINGTON
GARDEN OF ROBIN LENSI

📷 | 🖊 | **NEW**
Hours: 10 a.m. to 4 p.m.

The garden of Robin Lensi (aka lensi designs photography) and Tom Zabel in Burlington, CT started as a blank slate six years ago.

Every landscape is first seen through her lens. As a photographer for the Garden Conservancy a few years ago, and a member of the Connecticut Daylily Society, those many wonderful spaces inspired this one. This creative yardscape is intertwined with color explosions and architectural structures spanning months of viewing beauty incorporating all the possibilities into a personal landscape, that creates "magic" and infuses one with a calm zen-like feeling.

Enamored of all types of plants and with a background in interior design, garden design, and horticulture, there were tons of ideas and a blank slate to begin. The challenges here: the heavy clay soil, a windy site, exceptional water runoff down the mountain, rabbits, and voles. We all know gardens are never stagnant but a constant work in progress, and this one's no different.

As with her passion for cooking, she views the landscape like a layer cake combining large trees and shrubs for color, texture, height, bird habitat, and structure. Then the filling: the perennials that change with the seasons, ending with the icing: the annuals like herbs, dahlias, and zinnias that thrill all summer. Finally, hundreds of bulbs like alliums, tulips, and daffodils that prepare us to be excited when spring beckons us outside again.

This true four-season garden is a passion, including a wide variety of daylilies, hydrangeas, dahlias, roses, grasses, and hostas scattered throughout. Springtime here is for peonies, lilacs, roses, bleeding hearts, nepeta, magnolia, irises, amsonia, spireas, viburnums, and hawthorn trees as the later blooming plants start waking up.

Through this diversity the landscape changes daily—and who knows what next year will reveal, since only Mother Nature will decide?—but they will keep trying to intervene and influence.

— TROWEL TALK—

I've been addicted to gardening since my first home. I've had several properties that were blank slates and hopefully I left my mark and left the land better than I got it.

I love daylilies and alliums and have a large collection of both. I have some unique plants and shrubs that are not common, and I'm always on the hunt for new species or varieties. I have never had any luck with hollyhocks and larkspurs—no clue why!

My favorite garden tool is an auger I just got to help dig holes, and it helped with the 700 bulbs we just planted. I love birds and work to support them in winter and all the rest of the year.

You will find me in the garden every day.

One day I'll sit on the bench I have there. LOL!

— 👍 —

THE SALSEDO FAMILY GARDEN

📷 | ♿ | 🖋

Hours: 10 a.m. to 4 p.m.

Our gardens enjoy a unique location: a hilltop, 1,000 feet above sea level, with a magnificent view of 4,000 acres of watershed and state forest. Beginning in 1977, physical transformations have resulted in stone-walled terraces that render this acre-plus site usable.

The last big change, in 1995, added an expanded backyard terrace with a pool, post-and-beam gardener's tool shed, dwarf conifer collection, vegetable garden, and a collection of hardy chrysanthemums.

The front yard features low-maintenance lawns punctuated by beds of native and exotic trees, shrubs, and perennials. The emphasis here is sustainability with a focus on low maintenance and minimal water requirements.

Litchfield County

Saturday, June 4

★ There are two additional gardens open on this date in nearby Hartford County, CT:
Garden of Robin Lensi
The Salsedo Family Garden
For garden description and details, see page 61.

LITCHFIELD

GLENN HILLMAN

📷 | ♿ partial
Hours: 11 a.m. to 5 p.m.

The garden consists of five garden rooms, each distinctive yet linked together. There are two formal parterres set against the backdrop of the historic 1771 Lynde Lord House.

The upper garden contains a small alpine terrace set within a formal English-style perennial garden with a central pool and a profusion of flowers in a subdued palette.

The lower garden is an herb garden with brick paths, clipped box, and a small central knot garden, with a mixture of herbs and flowers. As the garden has evolved, a second parallel axis and long border have been created, with small trees, shrubs, and perennials.

The newest garden room is a French inspired formal garden and terrace flanked by a more naturalistic planting.

DIGGING DEEPER

Combos for Cohesion, Echoes that Resound
Tovah Martin & Glenn Hillman
Saturday, June 4, 10 a.m. to 11 a.m.

Glenn Hillman's Garden
$30 Garden Conservancy members | $40 General

The moment you begin to create a garden, plants start to interplay. In this Digging Deeper event, we will discuss exploring the dialogues in your garden to the max.

Over the years, Glenn has optimized relationships between the various components of his garden to create harmony on all levels. Hosting an impressive diversity of connoisseur plants, he designs carefully wrought combinations of shrubs, perennials, alpines, and herbs to create a scene with impact and a sense of the past.

Beyond the visual patterns that interplay in the garden, we'll also talk about textural and spatial combinations. We'll even delve into scents as well as discussing components such as pathway choices and elements that speak into the history of gardening, echoing the roots of the house.

In keeping with Tovah's focus on sensory awareness on all levels, we'll plug into all that the garden has to offer. Of course, there will be a walk-through to illustrate our points.

ROXBURY
JAPANESE GARDENS AT CEDAR HILL
📷 | ♿ partial | 🖌
Hours: 10 a.m. to 4 p.m.

This Japanese garden is intended to evoke a sense of serenity, as different rooms invite the visitor to pause and reflect. Stones and ledges throughout reside harmoniously with specimen trees and plantings that marry color, texture, and shape. The water features induce a visual and auditory tranquility, encouraging meditation.

From the teahouse, one has a commanding view of much of the garden with its borrowed Litchfield Hills landscape. Proceed through a stone garden to a series of geometrically patterned orchards and connecting footpaths.

WARREN
MULLA GARDEN
📷 | ♿ partial | 🖌
This garden is open twice this year: June 4 and September 11

Hours: 10 a.m. to 4 p.m.

This garden sits on a clearing atop a granite outcropping overlooking a breathtaking expanse of the Shepaug Reservoir. It is unusual in its structure and content and is truly a collector's playground, consisting of a wide variety of very unusual conifers, trees, shrubs, grasses, and flowering perennials. The beds twirl and dance, creating beautiful flowing shapes and contours. The overall feel and aura are enchanting, with a dueling atmosphere between the formal and informal.

Don't miss the four-square walled Persian garden, whose quadrants are planted with boxwood in the shape of balustrades from the designer's native India.

— TROWEL TALK—

Started container gardening on my parents' balcony in India. Love structure complemented with looseness while arranging plants so there is interest throughout the year.

— 👍 —

Litchfield County

Saturday, June 4

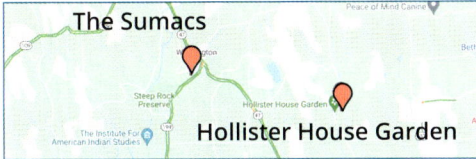

WASHINGTON

HOLLISTER HOUSE GARDEN

📷

300 Nettleton Hollow Road
Washington, CT 06793

Hours: 2022 Special Garden Conservancy Open Days June 4 and June 25, 10 a.m. to 4 p.m.

Otherwise from Friday, April 22, until Saturday, October 8: Wednesday and Friday, 1 p.m. to 4 p.m., and Saturday, 10 a.m. to 4 p.m. Please see page 85 for more information about Hollister House's September 10-11 Garden Study Weekend.

Admission: $5 per person, either by advance registration through the Garden Conservancy's website or at Hollister House.

Situated around an eighteenth-century farmhouse in the Litchfield Hills of northwest Connecticut, this large romantic country garden features exuberant plantings set in rambling formal structure and is noted for its subtle and sometimes surprising color combinations. Reminiscent of such classic English gardens as Great Dixter and Sissinghurst, the garden is divided into a series of rooms that open to vistas over the garden and out onto the natural landscape beyond.

The garden has been a preservation project of the Garden Conservancy since 2005.

THE SUMACS

📷 | ♿ partial | ✒

This garden is open twice this year: June 4 and September 11

Hours: 10 a.m. to 4 p.m.

Set on nine sprawling acres, The Sumacs features a stately home designed by Ehrick Rossiter built in 1894. Rock outcroppings, specimen trees, boxwood hedges, and gardens surround the house.

Within the gates, you will find a formal potager enclosed by a hedge of yews, a cutting garden, orchard, and perennial gardens that have an elegant nod to the classic English garden. The modern elements are brought to life with sculpture, a putting green, and a folly made of wood from the property. Walk through a hidden woodland trail that includes a continued array of specimen trees, shrubs, and shade-loving perennials.

The landscape holds interest throughout the four seasons: spring brings an extensive bulb collection that transitions into a meadow under the apple trees, elaborate tropical planters on the terrace in the summer, and fall is ushered in with a colorful dahlia collection.

New London County

Saturday, June 11

Kentford Farm

STONINGTON

KENTFORD FARM

📷 | ♿ partial | 🌿
Hours: 10 a.m. to 4 p.m.

Kentford Farm is a perennial farm in the making. For 25 years, Paul Coutu and William Turner have been creating grass pathways and planting beds. The farm dates back to 1727, and the previous owner started planting in 1945.

Fifty-foot weeping cherries, a Norway spruce, copper beech, and blue Atlas cedar, to name a few, dot this six-acre garden. There is a walk-in root cellar built into the hillside, and stone walls surround the whole property.

For more information, visit www.kentfordfarm.com

DIGGING DEEPER

Foxgloves at Kentford Farm
Paul Coutu
Saturday, June 11, 4 p.m. to 6 p.m.

Kentford Farm
$30 Garden Conservancy members
$40 General

Every other year, there is an invasion of foxglove (*Digitalis*) that explodes with color in June at Kentford Farm. Come and see these beloved biennials, learn how they came to be, and if they are friend or foe.

Starting with one plant, there are now hundreds dotting this six acre garden. These naturalized beauties will make your heart beat faster.

Photo by Paul Coutu

Fairfield County
Sunday, June 12

Ken Eisold's Garden
Inwood Cottage Garden
Garden of Allison Bourke
Greens Farms Botanical Gardens
Chelmsford

FAIRFIELD
INWOOD COTTAGE GARDEN

📷 | ♿ partial | 🌿
Hours: 10 a.m. to 4 p.m.

The property is 1.25 acres and offers a wide variety of soil and light conditions. The garden's perimeter is defined by old growth trees, with varying light conditions throughout the property. We have sunny areas, dry shade, wetland, and full shade as well. We use native plant material, including perennials, evergreens, and deciduous plants to add seasonal variety and texture.

We focus on winter-hardy plant material and use boxwood, yews, azaleas, and rhododendrons for the foundation and perimeter plantings. For the tree mid-story, we have added dogwood, Eastern red cedar, and river birch. We have an allée of beautybush and enjoy the aroma of the harlequin glorybower.

We have a significant bulb collection, starting early with snowdrops, crocus, daffodils, and some wetland-loving bulbs. We have a pergola with a wisteria and enjoy climbing hydrangeas on tree trunks

as well as our three-story stone chimney. We refer to that as our "bird hotel." We love native understory plantings, including fern and mayapple, and have used liriope in mass plantings.

Summertime is lush with daylily and hydrangea, and we have a full pollinator garden including Joe pye weed, butterfly weed, mallow, and sedum. The season comes to a close with Montauk daisy and aster. We have a pond and a pool as very distinct water features.

GREENWICH
CHELMSFORD

📷 | 🌿
Hours: 10 a.m. to 4 p.m.

This ten-acre property was designed variously by Warren Manning and Bryant Fleming (both formerly of the offices of Fredrick Law Olmstead) and Charles Gillette.

The gardens were created in the early 1900s for Blanche Ferry Hooker, daughter of the founder of the Ferry Seed Company, and a competent plantswoman in her own right.

The property comprises a swale, 0.5 mile of shaded walking trails, perennial beds, a root cellar, a knot garden, a 100-foot-long folly of rose-clad stone arches, a dogwood grove, and a riverbank fern garden.

📷 Photos permitted   ♿ Partially accessible   **NEW** garden or section   🌿 Nature-friendly

GREENWICH
GARDEN OF ALLISON BOURKE

🖋

Hours: 10 a.m. to 4 p.m.

The owner of this 3.5-acre property is a hands-on gardener who designed the garden herself, often using her backhoe to make her ideas a reality.

There is an 80-foot-long mixed border as well as beds of choice and unusual shade-loving varieties, a vegetable/flower garden, more than 100 peonies for cutting, a greenhouse, and many raised beds used for propagation and experimentation. Add to these an extensive compost area and beehives.

RIDGEFIELD
KEN EISOLD'S GARDEN

📷 | ♿ partial

Hours: 10 a.m. to 4 p.m.

This extensive garden on four acres is designed to enhance the features of the landscape: a large open field, a stream, and woodlands.

The garden includes a perennial border, a woodland path with two rustic bridges, a shrub border, a grass garden, and a grove of conifers. A gazebo, pergola, several terraces, and a sculpture provide focal points.

WESTPORT
GREENS FARMS BOTANICAL GARDENS

📷 | NEW

Hours: 10 a.m. to 4 p.m.

This nearly three-acre garden is a combination of three formal perennial rooms that are behind a stone wall and surrounded entirely by 30-foot 'Green Giant' arborvitae.

Each room has a unique personality and flows easily to the next, ending in a sculpted hornbeam allée. There are white perennial gardens throughout the pool area. The highly fragrant roses bloom all summer. A newly added zen garden features miniature perennial trees and unique plantings.

There are numerous key viewing locations throughout the property. One of the key features of the garden is an apple and pear espalier orchard behind the pool house. The property is tiered and has beautiful perennial flowers and trees on all levels with more than 70 multi colored and varietal peonies and more than 100 hydrangeas in varying colors and provenance.

Hartford County
Sunday, June 19

★ There is another garden open on this date in nearby Tolland County, CT:
Bear Run
For garden descriptions and details, see page 73.

GLASTONBURY
THE MURRAY GARDENS

📷 | 🖋
Hours: 10 a.m. to 4 p.m.

This property is a two-acre collection of gardens carved out of a woodland setting punctuated by unusual and native trees.

The front yard features three long blooming perennial borders, a hydrangea bed, and a small pond with a weeping maple water sculpture that gently rains all day. Also in front is a bank of Carpet Flower roses, as well as a naturalized woodland garden, where you can enjoy a myriad of shade and woodland plants and sculpture surprises with soft music in the background.

The backyard has several gardens built into the pool deck and a formal triangle garden containing Knock Out roses,

Oriental lilies, and coleus inside a boxwood border. Daylily beds run along an old stone wall beside a large perennial garden and patio. Curved steps ascend from there to a 50-foot rose bed.

Finally, the sunken garden features a waterfall running from a little upper pond to the fishpond below, surrounded by a spectacular *Heptacodium* tree, several large Japanese maples, and a collection of miniature conifers. Watching over the pond is a six-foot frog sitting on a stone bench.

Litchfield County

Sunday, June 19

CORNWALL BRIDGE

DEBBY AND BART JONES' GARDEN

📷 | ♿ partial | 🖊

Hours: 10 a.m. to 4 p.m.

 In 2000, when Debby and Bart bought their classic Greek Revival house, built by Colonel Dwight Wellington Pierce circa 1836, there were jagged topless spires of 50-foot spruce trees behind the house that had been ravaged by the tornado of 1989. These used to shade a small existing garden.

Debby, a painter with strong feelings about order and geometry, knew little about gardening but cobbled together a "loose" plan for the space. Bart cleared away the vast overgrown riffraff of multiflora rose and wild honeysuckle blanketing the back yard, and together they created gentle meandering paths out of flat stones collected from the adjoining field and circled them around the unsightly stumps, camouflaging them as well as they could

with climbing roses, lilacs, magnolias, and fragrant English cottage garden perennials: clematis, foxgloves, delphiniums.

Each year they try to add a new project: a stonewall fountain, long beautiful beds of teeny spring narcissi, followed by summer nepeta, a crab apple allée, a wisteria-covered pergola, and a topiary barberry alligator, to name a few.

Across the street is an orchard, a small kitchen garden, beehives, and an old dairy barn that is listed on the Connecticut Register of Historic Places.

— TROWEL TALK—

It seems that every time a plant crops up I think it might be my "favorite" plant (with the exception of the weeds of course).

I love hellebores because they are early, have no diseases, and play well in the garden with others, causing no problems whatsoever. But I also adore roses and clematis, which are total problem children needing special attention every time I look at them.

One of my favorite garden "musts" is my Gardener's Hollow Leg which attaches to my waist and is a receptacle for weeds, which saves trips back and forth to my wheelbarrow.

— 👍 —

LAKEVILLE
JUNIPER LEDGE

📷 | ♿ partial
Hours: 10 a.m. to 4 p.m.

Juniper Ledge garden faces south on a gently sloping hillside. It's a garden for meandering; one is often presented with choices of going this way or that way. There are benches along the way for resting and appreciating the views, sometimes of distant hills. A tennis pavilion is a larger, shaded rest spot. There's even a secluded meditation garden hidden away.

Recent changes include eliminating areas of lawn, replacing it in front with mixed shrubs and flowering plants, and, in a quarter-acre south of the residence, with a tended, but natural, meadow. An experiment with NoMow grass in the lilac walk has been successful, so we are extending its use to several other areas.

We've further provided privacy for swimmers and loungers with planted berms. Invasives on the way to the guesthouse are being replaced with mostly native shrubs, defining a pathway.

— TROWEL TALK—

My first garden came with a house I bought in New Jersey. While the rose garden was then in heavy shade, it had prosperous knotweed. Luckily I have none in Connecticut.

I do have acanthus, which I found at the Beatrix Farrand garden in Hyde Park. Many visitors have not seen it before.

— 👍 —

SHARON
GARDEN OF LEE LINK

📷 | 🌿
Hours: 10 a.m. to 4 p.m.

Three stone walls climb up a hillside, at the top of which is a greenhouse containing a wide spectrum of succulents and tropical plants. Within the last few years, the former perennial border was replaced with a new hardscape and three kousa, or Korean, dogwoods set off by a hardscape of gravel and cobble stones.

A perennial border is now behind the greenhouse consolidating all the hard work. A woodland garden edges the ridge line. Throughout there are a lot of potted plants from the greenhouse in the courtyards. One level has a fishpond, which reflects a winter conservatory attached to the house.

WEST CORNWALL
GARDEN OF JANE GARMEY

📷 | ♿ | 🌿
Hours: 11 a.m. to 4 p.m.

An idiosyncratic garden designed by and belonging to garden writer Jane Garmey, whose most recent book is *City Green: The Public Gardens of New York*.

The garden, which surrounds an 1827 house, has evolved gradually over the past eighteen years and is fronted by huge maple trees and bordered by traditional stone walls.

Full of structure, its main features are a narrow water rill framed by a high hornbeam hedge; two long beds, planted for drama and height with shrubs, perennials, grasses, and annuals;

an enclosed kitchen/picking garden intersected by brick paths, a terrace filled with container plants that opens onto a formal boxwood gravel parterre; and a birdhouse village that floats above a glade of giant *Petasites japonicus*.

GARDEN OF MICHAEL TRAPP

📷

Hours: 10 a.m. to 4 p.m.

This intimate Old World-style garden is replete with cobbled paths, terraced gardens, raised perennial beds, and reflecting pools. Overlooking the Housatonic River, the property has a distinct French/Italian flavor.

ROXANA ROBINSON—TREETOP

📷 | 🖋

Hours: 10 a.m. to 4 p.m.

On the grounds of a family Arts and Crafts house built in 1928 is an idiosyncratic hillside garden incorporating granite ledge, steep ravines, placid greensward, and a wooded slope leading down to a lake.

The gardens themselves are separated into two areas. First the well-mannered, level terrain of "Sissinghurst," with a decorous palette of blues, pinks, silvers, and purples, stone paths, and emerald lawn. Then "Margaritaville," a wild and rocky ravine with a riot of giant ferns, orange Tithonia, scarlet crocosmia, red salvias, and orange asclepias.

Around the gardens are deep woods full of ferns and birches; within the garden is a small homemade frog pond. Here nature plays a larger part than nurture. At the front of the house is a fine view of the lake. The owner's grandfather was a nature writer, her parents were birdwatchers, and the owner writes about the natural world in her novels.

The gardens are an attempt to make peace between the wild and the domestic, a response to the powerful surrounding landscape of dense woodlands, steep hillsides, boulders, and ravines.

Tolland County
Sunday, June 19

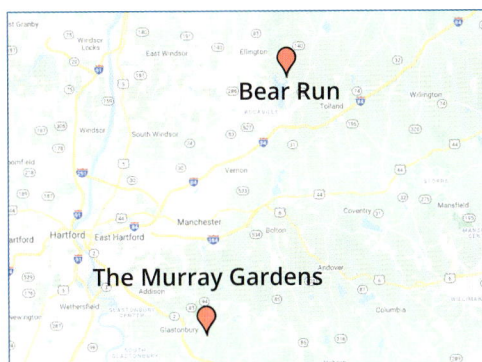

★ There is another garden open on this date in nearby Hartford County, CT:
The Murray Gardens
For garden descriptions and details, see page 69.

TOLLAND

BEAR RUN

📷 | ⚡ | NEW
Hours: 10 a.m. to 4 p.m.

Welcome to the Salsbury's Bear Run, 6.5 partially accessible wooded acres above Lake Shenipsit where the magic begins at the bottom of the driveway, with various lilies and grasses, rhus and fothergilla, periwinkle, leucothoe, oakleaf hydrangea, hellebores, ligularia, and the new witch hazel grove above the mailbox.

Stroll up the Eastern white pine, oak, maple, and beech driveway to greet Great Kneeling Bear with his attendants of sedums, bayberry, andromeda, microbiota, and a Japanese snowdrop; on the left, the three apple trees shade daylilies, catmint, foxglove, yarrow, and spiraea.

Pass by the rose of Sharon, chamaecyparis, varied perennials, two weigela through an arbor overflowing with clematis; pass by the winterberry tree, inkberry and pinky winky and salvia into a peaceful patio garden overseen by 3 ascending stone walls (carved into solid ledge). Here reside banks of perennials, holly, roses, chamaecyparis, boxwoods, mountain laurel, hypericum, butterfly maple, birch, hornbeam, a golden chain tree, and more.

Round the greenhouse, advance up the stone walk past heptacodium, hellebores, European ginger, roses, and the gorgeous stewartia, whose springtime white blossoms are to die for.

Passing under the sun porch, view the massive hydrangea wall on the right, and to the left, (after passing by the 'Delaware Valley' white azaleas, hydrangeas, and Virginia sweet spire) at the bottom of the Hosta Walk resides Reginald the Frog Prince whose three-foot tongue devours all mosquitoes! (If you want a closer look, mind the rough steps.) In front of Reggie are native New England perennials and shrubs.

Moving past the first of the eight raised vegetable beds (we attempt to grow 50 percent of our winter food), rounding the curve guarded by the bear pumping well water, look west past the ginkgo tree with its crescent of peonies, to the heart of the garden, the compost shed with its removable center frame—this is where our fundamental work takes place! As you admire Mama Bear and her climbing cubs, opposite the two teenage boys trying to impress each other, you'll note the mukdenia, helleborus, and andromeda.

Walking north, past the mountain laurel and three Japanese willows, take the center steps through the raised beds to the upper terrace and firepit. Here, view the variety of shrubs and perennials, the redbud, columbine, astilbe, ajuga, and clethra.

Continuing your tour on the driveway, view the smoke bushes just NE of the three Japanese maples. At our front door, take in the azaleas, roses, 'Little Gem' cotoneaster, ladies mantle, red twig dogwood, goats' beard, the new espalier we're now training, and our prize flower, the black cohosh (2)— not to mention the remaining three bears!

Concluding your tour, continue along the driveway past the rose field and sedums, beech plum shrubs, ninebark, and, to the right, a dozen different groundcovers, shrubs, evergreens, and perennials. Thank you for visiting our gardens!

Litchfield County

Saturday, June 25

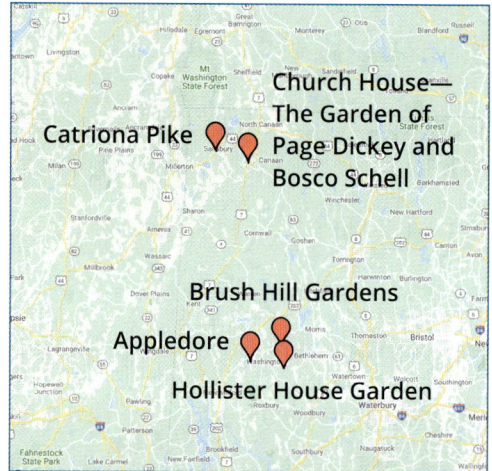

FALLS VILLAGE

CHURCH HOUSE—THE GARDEN OF PAGE DICKEY AND BOSCO SCHELL

📷 | ♿ partial | 🖋

Hours: 10 a.m. to 4 p.m.

The garden here is smaller and simpler than the one we had at Duck Hill, but with a few echoes: a patterned cutting garden, a small greenhouse, a young orchard.

Mixed borders of flowers run along the front of the house beneath three shadblows. A summer garden of hydrangeas, burnets, and roses surrounds our saltwater pool. Mowed paths strike off through meadows that surround the house, leading to trails in our woods, on the west side high and rocky with limestone outcroppings, on the east side, low, damp, and fern-filled.

Best of all, perhaps, is the view beyond the garden, fields, and forest of the Berkshire hills.

SALISBURY

CATRIONA PIKE

📷 | ♿ | ✒ | NEW

Hours: 10 a.m. to 4 p.m.

Inspired by the English Arts & Crafts movement, this garden was started from a completely blank canvas in 2013 by its owners, themselves two English transplants.

The garden is first and foremost a family garden, home to children and a pack of dogs. The overriding goal has always been to re-create the atmosphere of the owner's grandmother's garden, with perhaps different plantings but the same effect of exploding borders within a year-round green framework of hedges, boxwoods, and trees.

Divided into a series of garden rooms leading out and away from the house with areas gradually becoming less formal to blur with its boundaries, the garden now includes mass spring bulb plantings, summer and fall perennial borders, and the use of trees to create extraordinary seasonal displays.

There is also a large vegetable and flower garden, supporting a thriving cut-flower business. The design, the majority of the planting, and all subsequent maintenance has been undertaken by the owners. The garden is still very much a work in progress.

While one half of the couple thinks they surely must be done, the other will say they are completely on track with the original ten-year plan, it's just now a twenty-year plan!

— TROWEL TALK—

I grew up in England surrounded by gardeners. Everyone I knew gardened. I assumed that if you lived in a house you had a garden and were thus a gardener.

My first garden was a 4 by 2 allotment-style bed at my boarding school when I was eight. I remember having a lot of pansies, marigolds, and lettuce—an accidental devotee of the potager!

When I moved to the US 24 years ago, it came as a shock that people had yards and not gardens. Yards seemed to be something to manage and control, whereas gardens are to be grown, nurtured, and celebrated. And as my husband has discovered to his dismay, gardens are never finished!

Impossible to say what my favorite plant is. So many from home I wish I could grow here—ironically the one I miss most from England is the "weed" cow parsley.

And the one plant I cannot grow here, despite many attempts and to much heartbreak, are roses. I am the caretaker of the North-East chapter of the David Austin Graveyard!

— 👍 —

WASHINGTON

BRUSH HILL GARDENS

📷 | ♿ partial | 🌿

This garden is open twice this year:
June 25 and September 11.

Hours: 10 a.m. to 4 p.m.

Take a virtual tour of Brush Hill Gardens at www.brushhillgardens.com for a preview of many different areas, including the Moon Garden planted in yellows and purples, the Rose Walk, the Peony and Wheelbarrow borders, the Serpentine Garden with its garden folly, and up through the Arch into the Woodland Walk with its series of cascading pools and rills.

Each area is adorned with structures designed and built by Charles. The garden has been featured in many articles and books, including Rosemary Verey's book *Secret Gardens* and the HGTV series "A Gardener's Diary." Barbara's new book, *Heroes of Horticulture: Americans Who Transformed the Landscape*, and her first book, *Rosemary Verey: The Life and Lessons of a Legendary Gardener*, will be available for sale.

PRESERVATION PARTNER

HOLLISTER HOUSE GARDEN

📷

300 Nettleton Hollow Road
Washington, CT 06793

Hours:
2022 Special Garden Conservancy Open Days June 4 and June 25, 10 a.m. to 4 p.m.

Otherwise from Friday, April 22, until Saturday, October 8: Wednesday and Friday, 1 p.m. to 4 p.m., and Saturday, 10 a.m. to 4 p.m. Please see page 85 for more information about Hollister House's September 10-11 Garden Study Weekend.

Admission: $5 per person, either by advance registration through the Garden Conservancy's website or at Hollister House.

Situated around an eighteenth-century farmhouse in the Litchfield Hills of northwest Connecticut, this large romantic country garden features exuberant plantings set in rambling formal structure and is noted for its subtle and sometimes surprising color combinations. Reminiscent of such classic English gardens as Great Dixter and Sissinghurst, the garden is divided into a series of rooms that open to vistas over the garden and out onto the natural landscape beyond.

The garden has been a preservation project of the Garden Conservancy since 2005.

WASHINGTON DEPOT

APPLEDORE

📷 | 🖋

Hours: 10 a.m. to 3 p.m.

Created on the site of an old farm, Appledore has grown over two decades into a multi-acre informal garden of overflowing beds, meandering paths, and unexpected destinations.

It delights in all seasons and reflects my passion for interesting trees, shrubs, and perennials. I have never had a plan — the garden has evolved organically by choosing what strikes my fancy and planting with an aesthetic of wild abundance. While much is unusual, there are plenty of old favorites.

Over time, I have come to pay more attention to the garden as habitat—a pesticide-free home for birds, bugs, and pollinators—along with moles, voles, rabbits, and the occasional errant bear.

— TROWEL TALK—

I am a self taught gardener—lots of mistakes along the way. This is my first garden ... every year I plant a new bed and say, "this is my last."

But it never is.

— 👍 —

Litchfield County

Saturday, July 23

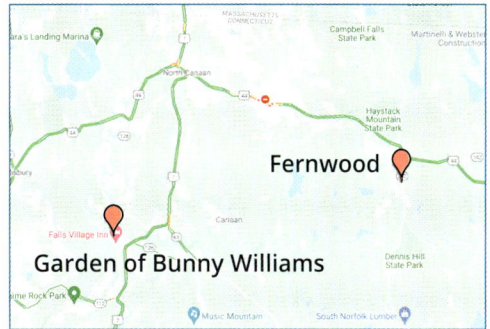

Fernwood

Garden of Bunny Williams

FALLS VILLAGE

GARDEN OF BUNNY WILLIAMS

📷 | ♿ partial | 🖋

This garden is open twice this year:
April 30 and July 23

Hours:
Morning session: 10 a.m. to 1 p.m.
Afternoon session: 1 p.m. to 4 p.m.

Interior designer and garden book author Bunny Williams's intensively planted fifteen-acre estate has a sunken garden with twin perennial borders surrounding a fishpond, a seasonally changing parterre garden, a year-round conservatory filled with tender plants, a large vegetable garden with flowers and herbs, a woodland garden with meandering paths, and a pond with a waterfall.

There is also a working greenhouse and an aviary with unusual chickens, an apple orchard with mature trees, a rustic Greek Revival-style poolhouse folly, and a swimming pool with eighteenth-century French coping.

NORFOLK
FERNWOOD

📷 | ♿ partial
Hours: 10 a.m. to 4 p.m.

The garden was originally designed when the house was built in 1908. Both are in the English Arts & Crafts style.

The garden was an early design by Marian Coffin. We have an early working plan dated 1908, as well as photographs of the garden that were published in the magazine *Country Life in America* in 1922.

Virtually everything had been lost and we based our re-creation on the original layout, but we have taken some liberties. It appears that the large double border was never executed, but we have attempted one, in addition to reinstalling the smaller square upper part of the garden.

Litchfield County
Sunday, July 31

★ There are two additional gardens open on this date in nearby Dutchess County, NY:
Garden of Belinda and Stephen Kaye, Millbrook, NY
Neverest, Wassaic, NY
For garden description and details, see page 182.

KENT
SCULPTUREDALE

📷 | ♿ partial | 🖋
Hours: 10 a.m. to 4 p.m.

Sculpturedale is a garden of four acres surrounding a house built in 1776 with barns and outbuildings.

After the usual brambles had been cleared in successive years starting in 1993, the land indicated what would best suit its areas. Some sun, some shade, some wet, some dry, each area has been planted around existing features of rocks, walls, stumps, buildings, banks, marsh, woods, pond, lawn.

Originally designed to showcase sculptures

that were made here, the garden has developed into its own self, where a large variety of perennials, shrubs, and trees are planted to enjoy in all seasons. No deer fencing and no irrigation mean natives and organics rule, and all work is done by the owners.

Visitors are invited to walk the paths established throughout, to enjoy the life-size steel sculpture, and to visit the studio where the sculpture is constructed. In this late summer, angelica, clethra, ligularia, *Hydrangea tardiva*, cardinal flower, kirengeshoma, nicotiana, and many more are highlights. A very unique treehouse and a tropical island are not to be missed.

New Haven County
Sunday, August 7

MERIDEN
GEORGE TRECINA

📷 | ♿ partial | 🌿

This garden is open twice this year: August 7 and September 10

Hours: 10 a.m. to 4 p.m.

We are back after a two-year absence! During that time there has been a renewed emphasis on perennials, with six new varieties strategically spotted throughout the gardens.

Lawn removal continues in favor of more garden space and pea stone. This garden is known primarily for its hundreds of container plantings (332 last season) including window boxes, hanging baskets, and both permanent and shifting urns. We use hardy shrubs and perennials as well as annuals and tropicals in the containers.

Expect to see phormiums, a new collection of brugmansias, many cannas, and both common and unusual annuals and vines. Don't overlook the garden framework of mature trees, dwarf conifers, and hedges as well as various hardscape features, including two fountains. Some plants will be available for sale.

GARDEN EXTRAS

Sunday, August 7, 1 p.m.

Diverse and Versatile Succulents— extracted from a seminar presented at the 2022 Connecticut Flower & Garden Show.

— TROWEL TALK—

I like most plants, but I find the cacti and succulents most compelling, especially the agaves.

They don't need much attention but always attract attention.

— 👍 —

NORTHFORD
REEDS GAP WEST RESIDENCE
📷 | 🌱
Hours: 10 a.m. to 4 p.m.

The gardens are those of landscape designer Donna Christensen. She and her husband, David, live and work in an old apple barn on the property. They own a design/build landscape company and have collected many large specimen trees and shrubs, which have been assembled in several different gardens throughout the four acres.

The front half of the property includes a two-acre pond with a gazebo, a large waterfall, and a Japanese-style garden with stone bridge. The barn home is surrounded by stone walls, terraces, pool, and other water features, and flowering perennial and annual gardens.

Fairfield County
Saturday, August 27

Old Barlow's Carriage House and Garden

InSitu

★In addition to the gardens in Litchfield County, CT (page 82), there is also a garden open in nearby Westchester County, NY: **Perrin Garden, South Salem, NY** *For garden descriptions and details, see page 191.*

REDDING
INSITU
📷
Hours: 10 a.m. to 4 p.m.

Nestled in the pastoral countryside of Redding, CT, surrounded by 300 protected acres of rock ledges, dense forest, grasslands, and meandering streams, InSitu is a 24-acre sculpture garden where nature and art dramatically intersect.

Owner Michael Marocco, actively involved with the skillful team of designers, craftsmen, and plantsmen, has created a richly composed showcase of architecture, horticulture, and sculpture, harmoniously woven together in a series of 27 garden rooms. The stone, cedar, oak, and rich palette of deep reds and browns integrate InSitu's houses and outbuildings seamlessly into the landscape.

📷 Photos permitted   🦿 Partially accessible   **NEW** garden or section   🌱 Nature-friendly

The sequence of distinctive garden rooms artfully incorporates native meadows, deciduous trees, flowering plants, grasses, arbors, water features, berms, and terraces, all elegantly connected by lawn, stone, and woodland pathways.

Marocco's internationally curated sculpture collection flourishes in concordance with these masterfully styled spaces. Two unique structures—The Sanctuary, a striking stone, chapel-like space emerging from the side of a hill, and Pulpitum, a sculptural observation tower— offer sweeping vistas of the inspiring oasis.

The gardens at InSitu were designed in collaboration with Richard Hartlage. They were installed and are meticulously cared for by John and Andrew Kuczo. InSitu has been featured in numerous publications, including the National Garden Conservancy's book *Outstanding American Gardens: A Celebration: 25 Years of the Garden Conservancy* (2015), a portrait of 50 of America's most beautiful gardens.

with naturalistic drifts of plantings. This reflects a move away from the formal design structure and toward a more sustainable, biodiverse and natural style of gardening.

RIDGEFIELD
OLD BARLOW'S CARRIAGE HOUSE
AND GARDEN

📷 | ♿ | 🖋

Hours: 10 a.m. to 4 p.m.

In the cottage garden of this classic carriage house, garden historian Julia Cencebaugh Kloth has put her knowledge into practice, combining her love of plants with an exuberantly layered aesthetic.

Her fragrant plantings are a riot of color and abound with old-fashioned favorites. Clipped box balls march through at intervals, echoing the hedges in the formal garden beyond. The approach to the woodland walk is more loosely structured

Litchfield County

Saturday, August 27

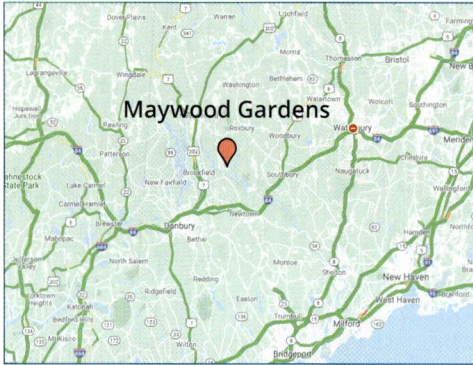
Maywood Gardens

BRIDGEWATER
MAYWOOD GARDENS

📷 | 🌱
Hours: 10 a.m. to 2 p.m.

This private estate features a sunken perennial garden protected by ten-foot stone walls, a gazebo garden planted with flowers and shrubs to attract butterflies and hummingbirds, a rose garden planted in a French design pattern encircled by hemlocks, a woodland path populated by mature beech and cherry trees, as well as viburnum and rhododendrons.

A ledge garden on an exposed hillside, a bed of heather, a white garden, herb garden, ornamental kitchen garden, and a 4,000-square-foot greenhouse give visitors a richly varied tour.

New Haven County

Saturday, September 10

Garden of David & Janet Andrews
George Trecina
Garden of Susan & Richard Kaminski

CHESHIRE
GARDEN OF DAVID & JANET ANDREWS

📷 | ♿ partial
Hours: 10 a.m. to 4 p.m.

The focal point of this half-acre corner lot is a rock-lined stream guarded by a massive weeping willow. A rich variety of perennials and annuals fill the stream's valley with something in bloom from April through October. Plantings are designed to shrug off the raging torrent that comes after heavy rains.

Above the stream, stone walls provide a backdrop for a classic border garden. A bluestone walk and a third level of plantings sit above the walls in front of a typical suburban Colonial home. All this creates a dramatic tableau viewed from the 300 feet of street frontage. The striking view encourages many of the hundred or more people who walk by daily to stop and admire.

On the south side of the yard, a stone

📷 Photos permitted   ♿ Partially accessible   **NEW** garden or section   🌱 Nature-friendly

path wanders between a mass of ferns and a raised rock garden. A long row of rhododendron and azaleas creates the transition from the stream into the backyard. A dramatic, abstract ten-foot carving comes into view before you reach a lawn that flows around a large deck.

A mature Kousa dogwood sits beneath a canopy of tall hardwoods that provide the shade for a woodland area where a wide variety of perennials take turns showing off blooms. A network of river stone paths wind past numerous birdhouses and whimsical recycled household items. The main attraction in the back is a dramatic twelve-foot oak stump carving. Its theme is the various woodland creatures that inhabit the area.

A river stone path on the north side then leads to the front after passing below a tall oak, twelve-foot high rhododendrons, a magnolia, and a small grove of gray birch. Together, they create shade for a garden featuring a variety of unusual hosta.

MERIDEN
GEORGE TRECINA

◉ | ♿ partial | 🖋
This garden is open twice this year: August 7 and September 10

Hours: 10 a.m. to 4 p.m.

We are back after a two-year absence! During that time there has been a renewed emphasis on perennials, with six new varieties strategically spotted throughout the gardens. Lawn removal continues in favor of more garden space and pea stone.

This garden is known primarily for its hundreds of container plantings (332 last season) including window boxes, hanging baskets, and both permanent and shifting urns. We use hardy shrubs and perennials as well as annuals and tropicals in the containers. Expect to see phormiums, a new collection of brugmansias, many cannas, and both common and unusual annuals and vines. Don't overlook the garden framework of mature trees, dwarf conifers, and hedges as well as various hardscape features, including two fountains.

Some plants will be available for sale.

GARDEN EXTRAS

Saturday, September 10, 1 p.m.

Overwintering My Tender Plants—the rescuing process in October and November with a view toward spring.

— TROWEL TALK—

I like most plants, but I find the cacti and succulents most compelling, especially the agaves.

They don't need much attention but always attract attention.

— 👍 —

OXFORD
GARDEN OF SUSAN & RICHARD KAMINSKI

◉ | 🖋
Hours: 10 a.m. to 4 p.m.

All aboard! The OSP&C garden railway will be departing shortly. Garden losses caused by serious illness are finally behind us, with 2021 being the year that all targeted recoveries were made; we even snuck in some new additions.

We think the garden has something to

interest just about anyone. It starts with several roadside gardens and a welcoming topiary.

If the railroad is your final destination, be sure to not miss the perennial beds, fairy garden, and goldfish pond in front of the house. Then proceed past the rose and vegetable gardens to the backyard, where there are more perennial beds. Pass into and through the pergola, keeping an eye out for the old men chiseled into the stone wall. Stop and visit the large goldfish pond; it should be easy to spot the fish, but the frogs are more difficult as they are masters of camouflage. Stop at the gazebo for a rest or go directly to the OSP&C by walking over the bridge or walking around the pond.

We added a couple of small gardens to enhance the train shed and we've added a miniature circus. With the circus addition, we now run three trains simultaneously along with a trolley. Check out the various railroad scenes and let your imagination go wild.

We only ask one thing from our guests: please enjoy yourself. (Please note: trains will not be operating in the event of rain and from noon to 1 p.m. to allow for battery recharging.)

— TROWEL TALK—

Hydrangea and *Acer palmatum* jump out as favorites. After a several year hiatus, we tried lupine again. I'll know in the spring if the streak of bad luck is broken.

I actually enjoy weeding but would not attempt it without my trusted Birkenstock kneeler.

— 👍 —

Litchfield County

Sunday, September 11

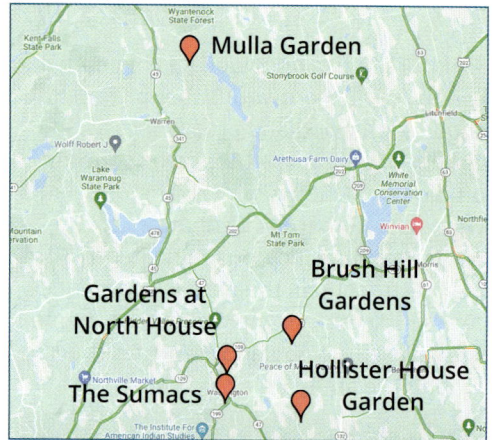

NONPROFIT PARTNER
PRESERVATION PARTNER

HOLLISTER HOUSE
GARDEN

Hollister House Garden, a romantic country garden in the scenic Litchfield County hills of Washington, CT is the creation of American antiques dealer George Schoellkopf.

The garden blends the formal with the informal, the best of twentieth-century English Gardens with an eighteenth-century New England farmstead.

📷 Photos permitted   🧎 Partially accessible   **NEW** garden or section   ➤ Nature-friendly

ANNOUNCING HOLLISTER HOUSE
Garden Study Weekend X

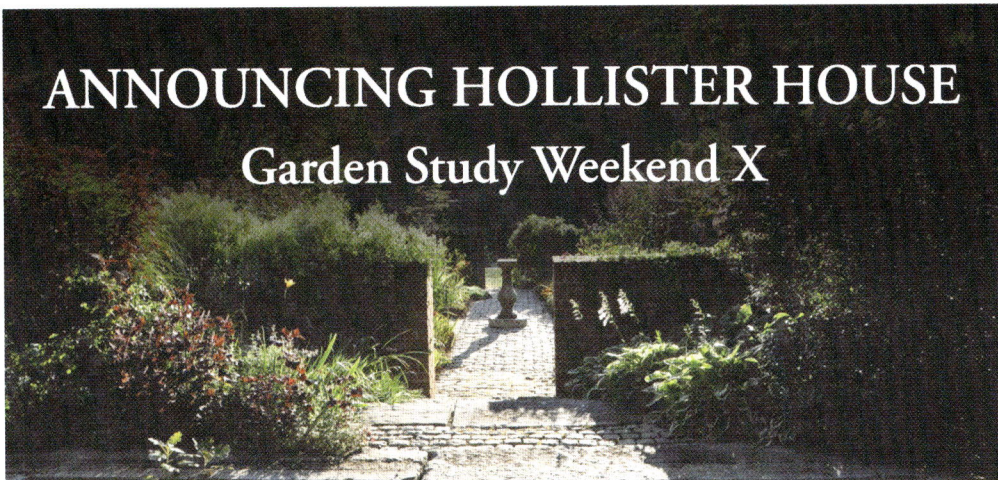

Presented by Hollister House Garden and the Garden Conservancy
September 10-11, 2022

Symposium, Plant Sale & Open Days Garden Tour

Saturday, September 10th
Symposium at the Heritage Hotel, Southbury, CT

Featuring talks by:

Rebecca McMackin - ecologically obsessed garden designer and Director of Horticulture for Brooklyn Bridge Park in New York City

Deborah Nevins - celebrated landscape designer whose work includes the Stavros Niarchos Cultural Center in Athens as well as private gardens.

Helen O'Donnell - horticulturist, gardener, garden designer and propagator of annuals, tender perennials and perennials at Bunker Hill Farm.

Bunny Williams - one of the most talented names in design as well as an accomplished gardener, author of six books and dedicated philanthropist.

The symposium will be moderated by Page Dickey - garden writer, lecturer and designer.

Sunday, September 11th

Garden Conservancy Open Day
will feature private gardens in Litchfield County.

The Sale of Rare and Unusual Plants will open to the public at Hollister House Garden.

For a full schedule of participating gardens, see the Open Days schedule at
www.gardenconservancy.org

For more information and to register for the Saturday program, visit

www.hollisterhousegarden.org
or call *860.868.2200*

At the conclusion of the symposium participants are invited to enjoy cocktails and preview buying at the Sale of Rare and Unusual Plants at Hollister House Garden.

Since 2004, the Garden Conservancy has assisted in the property's transition to nonprofit ownership as a public place for gathering and learning.

Hollisterhousegarden.org

WARREN
MULLA GARDEN
📷 | ♿ partial | 🖋
This garden is open twice this year: June 4 and September 11

Hours: 10 a.m. to 4 p.m.

This garden sits on a clearing atop a granite outcropping overlooking a breathtaking expanse of the Shepaug Reservoir.

It is unusual in its structure and content and is truly a collector's playground, consisting of a wide variety of very unusual conifers, trees, shrubs, grasses, and flowering perennials. The beds twirl and dance, creating beautiful flowing shapes and contours. The overall feel and aura are enchanting, with a dueling atmosphere between the formal and informal.

Don't miss the four-square walled Persian garden, whose quadrants are planted with boxwood in the shape of balustrades from the designer's native India.

— TROWEL TALK—

Started container gardening on my parents' balcony in India.

Love structure complemented with looseness while arranging plants so there is interest throughout the year.

— 👍 —

WASHINGTON
BRUSH HILL GARDENS
📷 | ♿ partial | 🖋
This garden is open twice this year: June 25 and September 11

Hours: 10 a.m. to 4 p.m.

Take a virtual tour of Brush Hill Gardens at www.brushhillgardens.com for a preview of many different areas, including the Moon Garden planted in yellows and purples, the Rose Walk, the Peony and Wheelbarrow borders, the Serpentine Garden with its garden folly, and up through the Arch into the Woodland Walk with its series of cascading pools and rills.

Each area is adorned with structures designed and built by Charles. The garden has been featured in many articles and books, including Rosemary Verey's book *Secret Gardens* and the HGTV series "A Gardener's Diary." Barbara's new book, *Heroes of Horticulture: Americans Who Transformed the Landscape*, and her first book, *Rosemary Verey: The Life and Lessons of a Legendary Gardener*, will be available for sale.

GARDENS AT NORTH HOUSE
📷 | **NEW**
Hours: 10 a.m. to 4 p.m.

Located on a charming country road, the 1930's cottage style house and gardens sit on nearly four terraced acres.

A naturally fed pond at the top of the property overflows into a rocky waterway surrounded by wetland gardens. The pea stone motor court with large shaped boxwoods is reminiscent of the Cotswolds.

The original bluestone terrace in back

is packed with creeping thyme and decorative boxwoods overlooks a nice distant view. Stone steps through pachysandra lead to the terraced pool featuring antique curbing around the patio and pool house.

THE SUMACS

📷 | ♿ partial | 🦅

This garden is open twice this year:
June 4 and September 11

Hours: 10 a.m. to 4 p.m.

Set on nine sprawling acres, The Sumacs features a stately home designed by Ehrick Rossiter built in 1894. Rock outcroppings, specimen trees, boxwood hedges, and gardens surround the house.

Within the gates, you will find a formal potager enclosed by a hedge of yews, a cutting garden, orchard, and perennial gardens that have an elegant nod to the classic English garden. The modern elements are brought to life with sculpture, a putting green, and a folly made of wood from the property. Walk through a hidden woodland trail that includes a continued array of specimen trees, shrubs, and shade-loving perennials.

The landscape holds interest throughout the four seasons: spring brings an extensive bulb collection that transitions into a meadow under the apple trees, elaborate tropical planters on the terrace in the summer, and fall is ushered in with a colorful dahlia collection.

PRESERVATION PARTNER
HOLLISTER HOUSE GARDEN

📷
300 Nettleton Hollow Road
Washington, CT 06793

Hours:
2022 Special Garden Conservancy Open Days June 4 and June 25, 10 a.m. to 4 p.m.

Otherwise from Friday, April 22, until Saturday, October 8: Wednesday and Friday, 1 p.m. to 4 p.m., and Saturday, 10 a.m. to 4 p.m. Please see page 85 for more information about Hollister House's September 10-11 Garden Study Weekend.

Admission: $5 per person, either by advance registration through the Garden Conservancy's website or at Hollister House.

Situated around an eighteenth-century farmhouse in the Litchfield Hills of northwest Connecticut, this large romantic country garden features exuberant plantings set in rambling formal structure and is noted for its subtle and sometimes surprising color combinations. Reminiscent of such classic English gardens as Great Dixter and Sissinghurst, the garden is divided into a series of rooms that open to vistas over the garden and out onto the natural landscape beyond.

The garden has been a preservation project of the Garden Conservancy since 2005.

Fairfield County
Saturday, September 17

There is another garden open on this date in nearby Westchester County, NY:
West Lane Farm, South Salem, NY
For garden descriptions and details, see page 194.

GREENWICH
SLEEPY CAT FARM

📷

This garden is open twice this year:
May 21 and September 17

Hours:
Morning session 10 a.m. to 1 p.m.
Afternoon 1 p.m. to 4 p.m.

The thirteen acres of Sleepy Cat Farm have evolved over the last 25 years in close collaboration between the present owner and Virginia-based landscape architect Charles J. Stick.

The landscape bordering Lake Avenue includes an extensive greenhouse and potager. The "Barn," distinguished by its half-timbered French Normandy vocabulary, is surrounded by thyme-covered terraces, providing an elegant stage set for a fine collection of garden ornament, sculpture, and boxwood topiary.

The visitor's experience of the garden unfolds as pathways lead from garden room to garden room in a carefully orchestrated series of discoveries. The central portion of the garden is distinguished by two parallel garden spaces; the first is dominated by a long reflecting pool, terminated on the north end by a wisteria-covered arbor, and on the south end by a pebble mosaic terrace and fountain basin.

One of the great surprises of the tour is the adjacent garden space. Bordered by a precisely clipped hornbeam hedge, the green architecture of this room is meant to frame the view to the Chinese pavilion (or "ting"—a place to stop and take in the view) positioned on a small island in the middle of a pond teeming with koi. The north end of this garden is terminated by an impressively scaled statue of Atlas.

The heart of the original six acres is most joyfully experienced along the "Golden Path," a granite dust pathway that leads from the main house and formal terraces on top of the hill, out into the New England landscape. As it winds through the oak and beech woodland, one encounters fountains, statuary, an iris garden traversed by a Japanese spirit bridge and planted with 10,000 Japanese iris, and finally a rustic stone grotto.

The woodland stream is bordered by native azaleas and a collection of spring flowering trees and bulbs, all planted for enjoyment throughout the year. The most recent additions to the property include a limonaia used for the winter storage of citrus trees, a new fruit orchard, and a sacred woodland grove that is enjoyed from a series of pathways radiating from a newly planted meadow.

The southern expansion of the property over the past three years has added a new dimension to the overall landscape experience of Sleepy Cat Farm. A recent addition to the garden is an English-style perennial border directly across from the koi pond and, directly below, a viewing path framed by a wisteria arbor. This border is surrounded by decorative stone walls covered with hydrangea, climbing roses, clematis, and boxwood. It consists of four linear beds around a central axis of lawn pathway and features a mixed shrub and perennial border containing a succession of bloom through the seasons.

The iris garden was completed last year with many more Japanese iris cultivars added, as well as a winding bamboo railway path leading to it, featuring a fragrant Korean spice viburnum border interspersed with spring bulbs and fall blooming kirengeshoma. The garden is now bordered by a ring of bright red Cornus 'Arctic Fire' against a backdrop of topiaries Ilex glabra.

In addition, seven new pieces of art have been installed in various spots along the paths.

WESTON
GARDEN OF FRANCES PALMER

Hours: 12 p.m. to 4 p.m.

Adjacent to Frances Palmer's pottery studio is her large cutting garden, which supplies myriad blooms from early spring through frost. Frances grows "Alice in Wonderland flowers." They inspire her ceramics and photography.

Her garden is especially known for its dahlias; she plants more than 100 different shapes-from the smallest "pom" to the largest dinner plate varieties. Colors and textures abound, dahlias interweave with tomatoes, zinnias, amaranth, sunflowers, and herbs. September is the height of the garden's abundance.

DIGGING DEEPER

Growing, Cutting, and Arranging: Flowers for the Garden and Home
Frances Palmer
Saturday, September 17,
10 a.m. to 12 p.m.

The Garden of Frances Palmer

Please join Frances Palmer for a Digging Deeper session in her two cutting gardens for an informal talk about heirloom dahlias and the rest of the flowers she grows for cutting and arranging.

Over cake and coffee, participants will engage in a lively conversation about how Frances' ceramics and flowers intertwine.

Books and puzzles will be available for sale during both the Digging Deeper and Open Garden portion of the day.

Photo by Frances Palmer

WESTPORT
PROSPECT GARDENS WESTPORT

📷 | ♿ partial | 🪶
Hours: 10 a.m. to 4 p.m.

Prospect Gardens Westport dates back to 1874, when the current house was the original Victorian farmhouse for an onion farm that fronted Prospect Road and ran down to the current swampy Aspetuck Land Trust.

Through a series of abutting property acquisitions over the past twenty years, the property is now a contiguous eight-acre arboretum-style garden and includes collections, gardens, open lawns, and winding pathways leading from one area to the next, allowing the visitor a three-dimensional experience of being "in" the gardens.

Some of the property's key features include a Mediterranean graveled entry garden, two orchards, a stone-tiered vegetable garden, berry houses (blueberries, raspberries), a sunny perennial garden, a shady woodland walk, a conifer collection, numerous flowering shrub and grass borders, a Japanese-inspired meditation garden (all

surrounding a tennis court), two pools, and an internationally renowned sculpture.

The newest addition is the one-acre flowering meadow. Mature deciduous and evergreen trees create a sweeping canvas and provide a sense of scale, shape, and texture reflective of the owners' contemporary style and sense of design.

Fairfield County
Sunday, September 18

Blau House & Gardens

WESTPORT
BLAU HOUSE & GARDENS

📷 | ♿ partial | 🪶
This garden is open twice this year: May 29 and September 18

Hours: 10 a.m. to 4 p.m.

These two acres of formal and informal gardens were developed over 50 years by Barry Blau and include many mature specimens, especially rhododendron groves planted below towering oaks and surrounding a Mid-century Modern house.

An allée of pollarded crab apples leads to a Neptune fountain circle surrounded by columnar Norway spruce. Bamboo groves form a backdrop to the Asian garden with a large Buddha, waterfalls, and stream with water lilies and water iris, and a grass garden.

A sunken rose garden is framed by stone retaining walls with boxwood parterre and fountain pools. A folly of astilbe-filled terraced beds is surrounded by stone retaining walls and steps. Lilacs, roses, and lilies are in other areas.

The house also includes front-entry sedum terraces, a roof deck with a commanding view of the gardens, and a skylit pool room and mezzanine filled with interior plants. Features incorporated throughout the garden include paths and walks, benches, ornamental gates, trellis, stone retaining walls, and sculptures.

Urns and planters filled with annuals punctuate the gardens and have been graciously funded by Bartlett Connecticut Arborists office in Monroe, CT.

BARTLETT
BARTLETT
TREE EXPERTS
SCIENTIFIC TREE CARE SINCE 1907

NOTES

Cummer Museum Garden - Jacksonville, FL
Photo by Brian Jones

Florida

Jacksonville
Saturday, March 26

JACKSONVILLE

NONPROFIT PARTNER

CUMMER MUSEUM OF ART & GARDENS

Cummer Museum of Art & Gardens
829 Riverside Ave
Jacksonville, FL 32204

Hours: 11 a.m. to 4 p.m.

★ Start your day at the Cummer Museum of Art & Gardens, 829 Riverside Avenue, Jacksonville, 11 a.m. to 4 p.m. Tickets, maps, and directions to other Open Days gardens in Jacksonville will be given at this location.

The Cummer Gardens, acknowledged by the National Register of Historic Places, have a fascinating history and bear the imprint of some of the foremost names in landscape design and horticulture, including Ossian Cole Simonds, Ellen Biddle Shipman, Thomas Meehan and Sons, and the fabled Olmsted firm.

The Museum's 2.5 acres of historic gardens are unique examples of early twentieth-century garden design, featuring reflecting pools, fountains, arbors, antique ornaments, and sculptures.

The majestic Cummer Oak has a canopy of more than 150 feet and is one of the oldest trees in Jacksonville.

Come Take a Moment

Located in Jacksonville, Florida, the Cummer Museum of Art & Gardens is committed to engaging and inspiring through the arts, gardens, and education.

+ LEARN MORE AT CUMMERMUSEUM.ORG

CUMMER MUSEUM

GARDEN OF ANN HICKS

Hours: 12 p.m. to 4 p.m.

In 1991, two riverfront properties and houses were joined, creating one family house and garden.

Mary Palmer Dargan of Dargan Landscape Architects (Atlanta, Georgia) was engaged to integrate the grounds. In keeping with the formal Colonial Revival style of the "new" house, Dargan created terraces and private garden rooms on the front, shaded side of the property. A walk through an arched pergola along the side of the property opens to a sunny, expansive view of the St. Johns River.

A classical arbor with limestone columns overlooks an oval lawn and a lovely terraced parterre rose garden, reached by a set of English steps. Judy Drake and Gerry Crouch of Sunscapes Landscape Design installed the garden in 1995 and have maintained and augmented it for twenty years.

LANAKILA GARDENS

🖋 | NEW

Hours: 12 p.m. to 4 p.m.

This Mandarin river property hosts a collection of organically maintained gardens across 2.5 acres.

Lanakila Gardens includes a flood-adaptive river garden, a formal garden under ancient live oak canopy, a tropical permaculture food forest, a seasonal vegetable kitchen garden, and a micro cut flower farm for sales to local florists. All annuals are grown from seed in-house, allowing us to drastically expand upon the typical Northeast Florida plant palette.

These biodiverse planting schemes bolster local ecology, mitigate pest pressure, and provide a dynamic succession of edible and ornamental displays. Our focus on soil health, biodiverse planting schemes, and ecological design strives to display best organic practices for a regenerative landscape in northeast Florida.

Garden of Ann Hicks - Jacksonville, FL
Photo by Ann Hicks

NOTES

Hummer Haven - Elburn, IL
Photo by Dee Raimondi

Illinois

ILLINOIS

Far Western Suburbs
Sunday, May 8

ELBURN
HUMMER HAVEN

📷 | 🖋

Hours: 10 a.m. to 4 p.m.

The entire property is always a riot of color; it begins in early spring with tens of thousands of blooming bulbs starting with eranthis, crocus, snow drops, rock iris, scillas, muscari, tulips, hyacinths, and chionodoxa; we continue with fritillaria, corydalis, camassia and others. The most notable bulbs are the extensive varieties of daffodils/narcissi that begin with the earliest bloomers and extend to the latest bloomers. To complement the spring bulbs, we have flowering perennials, shrubs, and trees.

During the summer and continuing through autumn there is always something blooming; there are many species of perennials, lilies, bulbs, and shrubs, and we have a number of unusual plants that are normally found in other climates. There are three landscaped ponds with waterfalls, the largest has a stream that leads to a quarry type pond. One hundred and twenty tons of quarry rock were used in building the ponds. The ponds are home to koi, frogs, dragonflies, damselflies, and waterlilies.

Our gardens are host to butterflies, birds, amphibians, a colony of bats, and other wildlife. The back gardens are interlaced with winding stone paths, where we are continually adding new plantings. For those who enjoy bird watching, we have an assortment of birds that frequent the gardens; in addition to the usual backyard birds, we have Baltimore and orchard orioles, ruby-throated hummingbirds, scarlet tanagers, indigo buntings, kingfisher, white- and red-breasted nuthatches, rose-breasted grosbeak, Tennessee warblers, wrens, tufted titmouse, hawks, turkey vultures, several species of woodpeckers, numerous varieties of finches, along with many other birds that are attracted to the ponds and gardens.

We have been a Certified National Wildlife Habitat since 1991 and are a certified Monarch Waystation and a Xerces Society Pollinator Habitat. Come and enjoy all that our gardens and ponds have to offer.

— TROWEL TALK—

My favorite plant is the trumpet lily because of the fragrance, and if they grew here my favorite would be a gardenia.

My first garden was a small area around the patio of my first apartment, where I grew a few vegetables. I have zero luck with impatiens, they always languish and die, yet I have no problem with plants that are difficult, unusual, and/or not supposed to grow in our area.

My favorite tool is a good sturdy sharp trowel.

The past few years I've been raising monarchs; the caterpillars eat a lot of milkweed leaves, which means having milkweed plants growing in odd areas in the gardens. There are many late night runs bringing in leaves, and I can only imagine what the neighbors think of these late night excursions.

— 👍 —

NOTES

Maine

MAINE

York
Saturday, June 25
Sunday, June 26

Braveboat Harbor Farm

YORK

BRAVEBOAT HARBOR FARM

📷 | ♿ partial | 🌿
Hours: 10 a.m. to 4 p.m.

This garden has been evolving over the last 75 years. It surrounds and complements a Georgian-style stone house.

There are formal and informal borders, a vegetable garden, orchard, and collections of various flowering trees and shrubs.

Apples and pears are espaliered on the house and along the walls of the formal front garden.

Water features include a pond in the woodland garden, a farm pond with rustic bridge, and the Atlantic Ocean.

This treasure is protected by a sculpted arborvitae hedge on the northwest, a mature stand of hickory on the northeast, and an extensive screen of old lilacs on the southeast.

Ongoing projects include expanding the collection of magnolias and rhododendrons, a new shrub border in the old orchard, a woodland walk, a summerhouse with views to the pond and the sea, and the constant refreshing of the front walled garden.

Braveboat Harbor Farm
Photo by Brian Jones

NOTES

Landscape Designer Andrew Grossman's Display Gardens - Seekonk, MA
Photo by Andrew Grossman

Massachusetts

MASSACHUSETTS

Middlesex County
Sunday, May 15

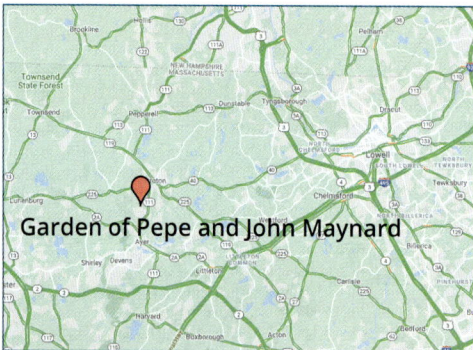

Garden of Pepe and John Maynard

GROTON
GARDEN OF PEPE AND JOHN MAYNARD
📷 | ♿ partial | 🖋
Hours: 10 a.m. to 4 p.m.

Our place, currently about 25 acres, was originally part of a much larger property, most of which was placed under conservation in 2006. We were attracted to it by the sweeping views to the west and the protection offered by hundreds of acres of surrounding fields and woodland, all protected from development.

Starting in the nineteenth century, successive large country houses had been built on the site, surrounded by the formal, high-maintenance gardens of the day. The last of these rather grand houses was demolished in the 1960s. The succeeding generation of the previous owning family was more interested in breeding Black

Angus than in horticulture. As a result the formal gardens had succumbed to neglect, bittersweet, and browsing deer by the time we purchased the property in 2007. At that time we had no interest in restoring formal gardens.

Our first steps were to plant an allée of small sugar maples along the lane leading to our barn, and to fence a small nursery area where we could stockpile plants and grow them safe from deer. We dithered about building a deer fence around more of the property, fearing it would interfere with the view, but finally fenced about fifteen acres. The fence enabled us to begin planting to create informal, naturalistic grounds using native plant material as much as possible. While the nursery is now empty and the maples in the allée have reached eight inches diameter, all the plantings are still young and have only begun to mature. Nonetheless we believe the grounds have grown in enough to reward unhurried exploration with a wide variety of trees and shrubs, and, in the spring, extensive plantings of daffodils and other bulbs.

The surrounding areas under conservation are open for walks, and a few remaining Black Angus add interest to the landscape. In the summer of 2020 an energetic couple working for us decided to clear out a small formal garden neglected for 25 years and overgrown to the point of invisibility. An exceptional stonemason rebuilt the dry stone walls over the winter and we began replanting in the early summer of 2021. An exceptionally wet summer helped to get new perennials established. We are hoping it will look presentable by 2022.

📷 Photos permitted   ♿ Partially accessible   **NEW** garden or section   🖋 Nature-friendly

Worcester County

Sunday, May 15

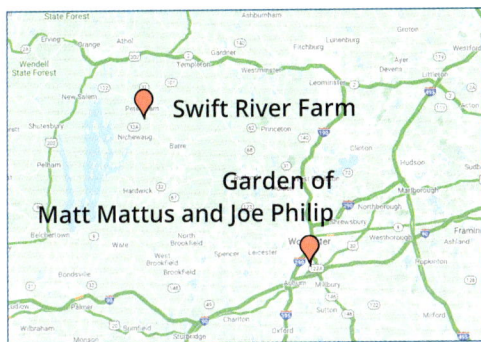

Swift River Farm

Garden of Matt Mattus and Joe Philip

PETERSHAM

SWIFT RIVER FARM

📷

Hours: 10 a.m. to 4 p.m.

A woodland garden screens the house from the road and continues along the north side of the house with many spring ephemerals and flowering trees, ending in a small collection of tree peonies.

A stone walkway leads past a tulip border to a small perennial garden enclosed by a box hedge. Further on is a water garden with a gazebo that overlooks a koi pond. A small herb garden behind the house leads out through a set of clematis arbors to another perennial garden. Next to the greenhouse is a rock garden and beyond it a spring garden with primulas, spring bulbs, and species peonies.

The rock garden looks out on a large meadow designed by Gordon Hayward with a mix of nectar-rich perennials and grasses. Paths through the meadow lead to an apple orchard and a vegetable/cutting garden.

WORCESTER

GARDEN OF MATT MATTUS AND JOE PHILIP

📷 | ♿ | NEW

Hours: 10 a.m. to 4 p.m.

Matt's garden is a mature, third-generation family property in a suburban neighborhood. It contains many tall trees (now more than 90 feet tall) planted in the 1920s by his grandfather and father. "The garden is an ongoing restoration project" says Matt. "I've never opened it up for tours as I've always believed that it was more of a small collector's garden than one that is 'tour-worthy', yet I know that most visitors enjoy the casual atmosphere, and the 'down the rabbit hole-ness' of a true collector's garden!"

Expect to see collections of interesting plants and greenhouse projects, sweet peas, stone and gravel paths, boxwood and hornbeam hedges, garden rooms, and even a small 100-year-old goldfish pond.

Charming and picturesque as a small English garden and as horticulturally interesting as a botanic garden, this 1.5 acres is essentially a home garden, yet one that has recently been featured in *Martha Stewart Living*, *Better Homes and Gardens*, and other magazines. Matt Mattus, whose blog is Growingwithplants.com, is the author of *Mastering the Art of Vegetable Gardening* (2019) and *Mastering the Art of Growing Flowers* (2020).

GARDEN EXTRAS

10 a.m. to 4 p.m. Plant and book sale

📷 Photos permitted   ♿ Partially accessible   NEW garden or section   🌿 Nature-friendly

Greater Boston
Sunday, May 22

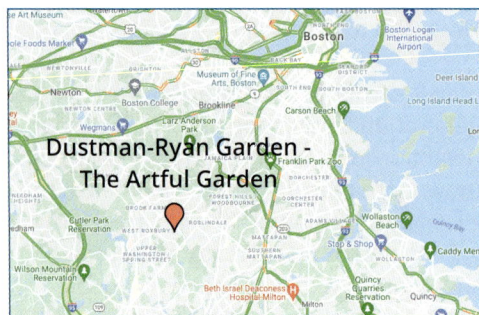

WEST ROXBURY
DUSTMAN-RYAN GARDEN -
THE ARTFUL GARDEN

📷 | ♿ partial

Hours: 10 a.m. to 4 p.m.

This garden reflects the creative efforts of a mighty team: Christie Dustman, professional garden designer, and Patti Ryan, a professional furniture maker. In their own personal garden, these two artists have let nothing hinder their zeal for plants, stone, and whimsy.

The garden is in its eleventh season, and its transformation was done in phases, keeping only a privet hedge and one andromeda. The garden uses plants and objects as sculptures in an array of vignettes and intentional views. By showcasing some plants and objects against a background of other plants and elements, this garden has many levels of complexity and interest.

The owners are members of the Conifer Society, and you will find more than 50 different conifers, as well as rare and unusual plants. It is the reclaimed and castoff items used as art and decoration,

like basketball hoops and organ pipes, that often command the most "ooohs and ahhhs."

photo by Lisa Kessler

Norfolk County
Sunday, May 22

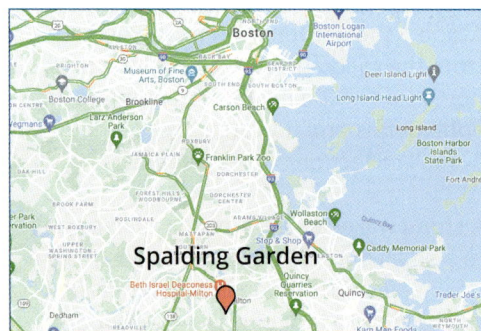

MILTON
SPALDING GARDEN

Hours: 10 a.m. to 2 p.m.

Designed by renowned landscape architect Fletcher Steele in 1924, the Spalding Garden was rescued from demolition in 2005 by the Milton Garden Club. A cultural landscape report was commissioned, and preservation efforts began shortly thereafter and continue at present.

📷 Photos permitted   ♿ Partially accessible   NEW garden or section   🌿 Nature-friendly

The garden, as it remains, stands on half an acre and includes formal gardens bordered by mature boxwoods, a perennial garden, a bowling green, and much of the original brickwork.

In acquiring the garden, it has been the Milton Garden Club's mission to create a pilot project to demonstrate the importance of saving local period landscape from development, to educate the public, and to adopt sustainable practices that set community standards for gardening and preservation.

DIGGING DEEPER

Croquet and Cocktails: Preserving and Restoring Sporting Greens
Georgia Lee
Sunday, May 22 from 12 p.m. to 2 p.m.

The Spalding Garden
$30 Garden Conservancy members |
$40 General

Join us for Croquet and Cocktails on a Historic Sporting Green.

Spalding Garden's formal bowling green was designed with leisure in mind. As preservationists, we hope to not only maintain the beauty and integrity of

our historic garden, but also to utilize the garden for its original purpose: pleasure and entertaining among friends.

Please join us for cocktails and croquet at Spalding Garden. You are invited to step back in time for a leisurely afternoon of sport and conversation. Guests will be served tea, champagne and light bites and learn about the garden and its charismatic designer, Fletcher Steel.

Following a garden tour, guests are invited to join us for a rousing croquet match. White attire and hats are encouraged. Come to play, stay to make new friends.

Photo by Georgia Lee

Berkshires
Saturday, June 11

1391 Barnum Street

★There are two additional gardens open on this date in nearby Columbia and Dutchess Counties, NY:

Garden of Helen Bodian, Millerton, NY
Heaven's Gate, Ancram, NY
Hyland/Wente Garden, Millerton, NY
Katie Ridder and Peter Pennoyer, Millbrook, NY
For garden description and details,
see page 161.

SHEFFIELD
1391 BARNUM STREET
📷 | ♿ partial | 🏹
Hours: 10 a.m. to 4 p.m.

The first garden you see while walking up the driveway is the "Rabbit Garden," so named for the wooden rabbit in its midst. The chainsaw-carved animal is one of many on the property. Under the crabapple tree is a primrose garden. Walking up the stairs toward the house gives you your first view of the pond and waterfall area. From the deck, a series of stone steps and landings leads down past a rock garden to the patio and pond, home to goldfish, frogs, and a shy turtle.

The patio fronts a mixed border of perennials, shrubs, and trees. From the

screened-in porch the pond and waterfall can be seen and heard. The woodland garden behind the house, with its winding paths and many shade plantings, is a cool retreat. The paths in the woodland wind around an array of hostas, hydrangeas, and other shade plants.

— TROWEL TALK—

I have been gardening on my two-plus acre spot for the past 40-plus years. For most of the time I did it myself with help from my husband. For the past eight years I have had a helper for three hours a week.

When I started I knew nothing about gardening, and over time as I learned more and matured in my taste, I have edited my garden for aesthetic reasons and ease of care (more shrubs).

— 👍 —

Bristol County
Saturday, June 11

★ There is another garden open on this date in nearby Kent County, RI:

Villa Kunterbunt, East Greenwich, RI
For garden descriptions and details, see page 208.

REHOBOTH
MCILWAIN GARDEN

Hours: 10 a.m. to 4 p.m.

This garden abuts a golf course, providing expansive views in the English landscape tradition. Optimal plantings have been chosen for the range of challenging ecosystems from rocky/dry soil to windy sites with wet soil.

A cluster of trees with filtered sunlight hosts rhododendrons, azalea, pieris, enkiantus, hellebores, and more. Most of the garden enjoys full sun. This is a garden for all seasons, with the blossoms of the Okame cherries and saucer and star magnolias ushering in early spring, followed soon thereafter by daffodils, grape hyacinth, Spanish bluebells, ground phlox, and PJM azalea.

Early May sees the arrival of tulips, azalea, and the sweetly fragrant *Viburnum carlessii*, lilies of the valley, and lilacs soon

thereafter. By mid-May the bearded iris have opened their blooms, along with the chives, allium, bleeding heart, and rhododendrons.

In June this is followed in swift succession by dogwoods, Virginia magnolia with lemon-scented blossoms, peonies, Dutch iris and gumpo azalea, coral bells, catmint, campanula, clematis climbing on roses and *geranium biokovo*. By late June summer has arrived with hydrangea, roses, foxgloves, garden phlox, daisies, veronica, lavender, astilbe, blue salvia, anise hyssop, and Russian sage.

Fall comes with assorted mums, dahlias, anemone, and flaming fall foliage of various Japanese maples along with red berries on the viburnum, holly trees, and winterberry. The red-twig dogwood shrubs maintain winter interest along with the topiary boxwood and mottled bark of the stewartii tree.

An herb garden with armillary sphere underplanted with alpine strawberries is flanked by a blueberry/raspberry patch, pergola, and roses.

SEEKONK
LANDSCAPE DESIGNER ANDREW GROSSMAN'S DISPLAY GARDENS

📷 | ♿ partial
This garden host is presenting a Digging Deeper program August 6, see page 115.

Hours: 10 a.m. to 4 p.m.

My gardens, which border the Martin Wildlife Refuge and the Runnins River, showcase a wide variety of perennials, shrubs, and grasses.

The property includes a blue-and-white

garden, a hot-colored garden with a checkerboard thyme patio, a cottage garden planted with roses and other old-fashioned favorites, and a rustic pond surrounded by bog plantings.

There is also a cutting garden currently planted with tea roses and dinner plate dahlias. The property is featured in the March/April 2016 issue of *Design New England* and was a finalist in HGTV's "Gorgeous Gardens" competition.

— TROWEL TALK—

My favorite plants vary depending on the season, but I probably get the most joy from my collection of dinner plate dahlias. For some strange reason, I can't seem to grow monkshood (*Aconitum*) here, which is a shame, as their striking flower spikes would be a perfect addition to my blue-and-white garden.

My first garden was in the backyard of my childhood home in Providence, RI. I didn't have my own garden again until I purchased this house in 1998.

My favorite tool is a small hand hoe with an angled blade perfect for weeding.

— 👍 —

Marblehead
Sunday, July 24

Seaside Farm

Glass House Gardens

MARBLEHEAD
SEASIDE FARM

📷

Hours: 10 a.m. to 4 p.m.

This two-acre site on Peach's Point overlooking Doliber Cove has a rich garden history. During the early 1900s it was an Italianate formal garden with pools, formal rose garden, and statuary, part of an enormous estate owned by yachtsman Francis Crowninshield and his heiress, historical preservationist wife, Louise du Pont Crowninshield.

The current owners bought the property with its overgrown and neglected gardens in 1996. Three years later, after discovering the property's rich landscape history, the owners hired Doug Jones from Boston's Keith LeBlanc Landscape Architecture firm to restore the gardens. Based on period black-and-white photographs from 1937, new replicated iron railings were installed, caved-in concrete pools were rebuilt, and old roses were planted to re-create the garden.

The original house no longer exists, thus

certain landscape transitions presented challenges that have been handled delicately. The new house sits on the water, and the gardens surrounding it have been done in a more contemporary style. The property has some enormous beeches that date to the original period.

— TROWEL TALK—

We have a love for jade plants we keep and propagate in our greenhouse. We bonsai many types of plants.

— 👍 —

SWAMPSCOTT
GLASS HOUSE GARDENS

📷 | ♿ partial | 🖋

Hours: 10 a.m. to 4 p.m.

The Glass House is a modernist home designed in 1957 by Martin Bloom, a Harvard graduate and student of Walter Gropius, the founder of the Bauhaus School. Carefully sited on an acre of wooded grounds, the house interacts with the landscape through walls of glass, framing views and blurring the boundary between indoors and outdoors.

There are five distinct outdoor gardens/ spaces wrapping around the house. The unassuming front yard garden gives way to a planting of bamboo anchoring the elevated deck. The back of the house has a rocky outcrop garden framed by mature trees. A bend in a stone path surprises a visitor with a moon gate that leads to two distinct courtyard gardens where conifers have the presence of living sculptures throughout the changing seasons.

The close interaction of the house and the gardens was recently captured in a piece by Tovah Martin featured in the March/ April 2021 issue of *New England Home Magazine*.

Bristol County
Saturday, August 6

DIGGING DEEPER

Digging Deeper: The Low Maintenance Garden
Andrew Grossman
Saturday, August 6,
11 a.m. to 12:30 p.m.

Landscape Designer
Andrew Grossman's Display Gardens,
Seekonk, MA
$30 Garden Conservancy members
$40 General

While many people admire the "English garden look," the almost daily care such plantings require can be daunting. By judiciously selecting and grouping shrubs, perennials, and a smattering of annuals, however, it is possible to create a low-maintenance version of this classic style. I will teach you how to easily re-create the look at your own home as we tour the newest addition to my property, a swimming pool garden brimming with lush plantings and summer color.

Photo by Andrew Grossman

Greater Boston
Saturday, September 17

Gardens at Clock Barn
Home of Maureen & Mike Ruettgers

CARLISLE
GARDENS AT CLOCK BARN
HOME OF MAUREEN & MIKE RUETTGERS

📷 | ♿ partial
Hours: 10 a.m. to 4 p.m.

The Ruettgers family has been gardening here for nearly 40 years, although their house and drying barn date to 1790.

Entering the gardens through an arched gate, explore the old barn with trays full of herbs and flowers from the adjacent cutting garden. These trays were built as a 1930s WPA Project for drying digitalis leaves used medicinally.

East of the barn are beds of flowers, vegetables, and herbs that are rotated throughout the season. An adjacent Belgian fence espalier encloses a garden room displaying calendulas, *Verbena bonariensis*, other herbs, and ornamental vegetables.

Beyond the cordon of pears is the new fall border featuring *Salvia madrensis*, tithonia, Abyssinian banana, and many dahlias. Near the center of the property, a grape arbor leads to a walled garden with four quadrants anchored by antique roses.

Mixed borders there feature sweeps of nasturtiums, 'Amistad' & 'Indigo Spires' salvia, 'Prairie Sun' rudbeckia, heleniums, and edible herbs. A second tier is flanked by two reflecting pools ringed by *Allium lusitanicum* and herbal tapestries.

The greenhouse and potting area is filled with scented geraniums, succulents, gingers, bay, and rosemary varietals.

Beyond, a canopy of 100-year-old oaks shades woodland gardens. Favorite woodland plantings include *Paeonia japonica* and *P. obovata*, anemones, epimediums, *Kirengeshoma palmata*, and hosta from the garden of Francis Williams. Look for the new tree fort, a koi pond, sculptures, and choice specimens of dogwood, magnolia, and maple. Pass through a hornbeam arch to the Clock Barn.

Up on the patio at the house, investigate a collection of Italian pots and troughs filled with favorite specimens, then go around the corner to discover the secret garden.

GARDEN EXTRAS

Exhibition

**Dig for Victory:
Victory Gardens Now and Then**
10 a.m. to 4 p.m.

Gardens have provided not only a balm for the soul but also a joyful point of light during times of uncertainty.

This reflective exhibit explores the connections between the Victory Gardens of WW2 and the COVID-19 pandemic, two events that brought about a resurgence of interest not only in gardening but also in other important gardening traditions such as food preservation and canning.

Enjoy a display of historic artifacts that connects gardeners of the present to the gardens and gardeners of the past. This Garden Extra made possible with the assistance of the Carlisle Garden Club and Historical Society.

*Gardens at Clock Barn
Photo by Brian Jones*

The Garden at Glen Eagles - St. Louis, Missouri

Missouri

MISSOURI

St. Louis
Saturday, June 4

COMING SOON

This year, we are pleased to have the Open Days program returning to St. Louis.

Enjoy this extraordinary opportunity to visit several of the Gateway to the West's finest gardens at the height of the spring season.

Details will be announced soon. Event registration, garden descriptions, photographs, and more information can be found at

gardenconservancy.org/opendays

NOTES

Garden of Maude & John Odgers - Peterborough, NH
Photo by Maude Odgers

New Hampshire

NEW HAMPSHIRE

Monadnock Region
Saturday, June 25

★There is another garden open on this date in the nearby Upper Valley region, VT: **Gordon & Mary Hayward's Garden, Westminster West, VT** *For garden descriptions and details, see page 222.*

Gardens of Maude & John Odgers

The Gardens at Beechwood Farm

PETERBOROUGH
GARDENS OF MAUDE & JOHN ODGERS

📷 | ♿ partial
Hours: 10 a.m. to 4 p.m.

Maude is drawn to using unusual combinations of trees, shrubs, perennials, and annuals in creating interesting textures and harmony of color, light, movement, and design. Her gardens draw inspiration from English border gardens, and her work as an artist. For her, gardening is painting in motion.

A soft palette and flowing shapes are used to create a sense of serenity. Stone walls and granite pieces complement the New England countryside.

Maude and John cleared this land more than 40 years ago, designing and building everything themselves—from the house, with an attached garden room, to a small post-and-beam barn (now garden shed), arbors, unusual undulating wooden fences with moon gates, a bluestone patio that emulates the gardens' shapes, an enclosed raised-bed vegetable garden, a frog pond—along with the many garden beds that envelop their home. Their garden has been featured in numerous publications.

DIGGING DEEPER

An Artist's Garden: A Living Tapestry
Maude Odgers
Saturday, June 25, 4 p.m. to 6 p.m.

The Gardens of Maude & John Odgers
$30 Garden Conservancy members
$40 General

In this intimate one-hour workshop, designer Maude Odgers will walk us through her renowned, deeply personal garden, revealing how her lifelong work

---

as an artist has influenced her unique approach to garden design.

A passionate plant collector with an eye for the unusual, Maude is drawn to plants, shrubs, and trees with interesting foliage and texture-elements which weave strong and subtle forms together creating living tapestries. Using her own evolving landscape as illustration, she'll discuss her method of garden composition and highlight the subtle details that enhance a garden's structure, theme, and impact, both visually and spiritually.

For more than 40 years Maude has worked and reworked this land that she and her husband cleared and planted, and upon which they built their home. Her gardens consist of many meandering mixed borders (influenced by English gardens), several woodland gardens, an herb garden, a garden with a pond, an orchard, and a small unique raised-bed vegetable garden. Her garden has been featured in numerous garden journals.

Photo by Maude & John Odgers

TEMPLE
THE GARDENS AT BEECHWOOD FARM
📷 | 🖎 | **NEW**
Hours: 10 a.m. to 4 p.m.

The gardens of Beechwood Farm are nestled in the side of Temple Mountain with many spectacular views reminiscent of those in the English Cotswolds.

This was originally an old dairy farm, and we are blessed with wide open expanses of fields, providing ever-changing views. We have expanded the original garden of my mother, Gertrude, to many other gardens, including the fountain, front entrance, right bank, crescent, kitchen (which has nothing to do with vegetables; rather it is viewed from the kitchen), dish, gazebo garden by the lower pond, and most recently Greg's Garden by the upper pond and the Boatique Tomato Garden, which is planted in a handcrafted red boat. The gardens all include water features.

The colors used throughout are bold and dynamic. Of particular note, these gardens include 20 out of the "22 Colorful Shrubs" featured in the October 2020 issue of *Better Homes and Gardens*. The diversity of foliage attracts a broad array of birds, butterflies, and pollinators. Some favorites are the hummingbirds, cardinals, herons, robins, blue birds, finches, and Baltimore orioles.

— TROWEL TALK—

That I ended up loving gardening is a surprise. As a child, I hated weeding. Today, I find it a type of meditation. Now, the very first garden that I tended has multiplied in size and become a true passion.

Each year, the planting of my favorite flower has become a larger endeavor; this fall we planted more than 2,000 tulip bulbs.

— 👍 —

Mountsier Garden - Nutley, NJ
Photo by Graeme Hardie

New Jersey

NEW JERSEY

Essex County
Saturday, April 16

NUTLEY
THE MOUNTSIER GARDEN

📷 | ♿ partial | 🌱

This garden is open four times this year:
April 16, May 15, June 4, and September 10.

Hours: 10 a.m. to 4 p.m.

A garden for all seasons that has been created and fine tuned for more than two decades and now encompasses two acres. Owners Silas Montsier and Graeme Hardie have collaborated with noted landscape designer and friend Richard Hartlage, and the result is a feast for the eyes and for the senses.

Principally a stroll garden, there are numerous focal points, small rooms, seating areas, private nooks, and impressive vistas. Drifts of variegated hakonechloa soften the strong architectural underpinnings of the garden, and many of the brilliant and original plant combinations will thrill the devoted horticulturist.

A collection of small sculptures, artworks, and commissioned pieces is interspersed throughout as accent points and disarming bits of humor.

From thousands of early spring flowering bulbs to a subtle but glorious display of green on green in the early fall, there is something new to see and enjoy on every visit.

This month: see the daffodils and hellebores at their peak.

📷 Photos permitted   ♿ Partially accessible   **NEW** garden or section   🌱 Nature-friendly

Hunterdon County
Sunday, May 8

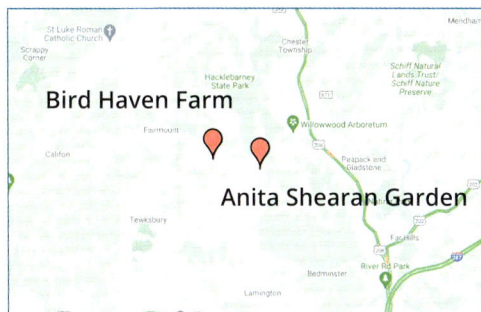

POTTERSVILLE

ANITA SHEARAN GARDEN

📷 | **NEW**

Hours: 10 a.m. to 4 p.m.

We were encouraged to participate in Open Days to illustrate the potential of a small garden. Originally it was intended to only fence the back and plant deer proof plants at the front but this was unsuccessful.

After much deliberation two years ago we decided to fence the front also and install a cattle grid. This is a half-acre garden in the center of a village on a very narrow lot. We have been planting here for five years. The garden was designed to have structure from evergreen hedges and a hornbeam allée providing year-round interest.

There are mass plantings of bulbs that flower in the spring. As the year progresses, the emphasis is on the structure of the garden punctuated by large colorful planters on the terrace. Everything on the property is new with the exception of three old boxwoods that we

relocated and a large tree in the front.

BIRD HAVEN FARM

📷 | 🖋

Hours: 10 a.m. to 4 p.m.

Bird Haven Farm is a celebration of the vision and collector's spirit of Janet Mavec and Wayne Nordberg. The barns, outbuildings, and original nineteenth-century stone house (home of Harriet Stratemeyer Adams, creator of the Nancy Drew mystery stories) have been joined by a contemporary house designed by Smith-Miller + Hawkinson in the 1990s, and more recently by a guest house by Parsons + Fernandez-Casteleiro.

The garden's master plan was completed in 2002 by Fernando Caruncho, lending visual clarity to the cluster of disparate elements. Hardscaping by Dale Booher added clean lines of strategically placed stone walls, evolving Caruncho's concept of a medieval village and a perfect haven for plants.

With an overstory of large mature trees, the 25-acre landscape includes hay meadows, a lush orchard of heirloom apples and other fruit trees, an extensive vegetable and herb garden, and a perennial border designed by Lisa Stamm.

Other features include a meandering woodland walk with cascading ponds, a mixed shrub border, a charming pond hut, as well as a grandchildren's maze garden and elf's stump. Requires a lot of walking.

GARDEN EXTRAS

10 a.m. to 4 p.m. Pop-up sale of Janet Mavec's Orchard Jewelry and plant sale by Atlock Farm.

Somerset County

Sunday, May 8

FAR HILLS

THE HAY HONEY FARM

📷 | 🖌

This garden is open twice this year: May 8 and September 17

Hours: 10 a.m. to 4 p.m.

The Hay Honey Farm's extensive gardens have been carefully added to the landscape since 1989 in a naturalistic manner, with a respect for the history and topography of the site, and consistent with the broader surrounding atmosphere of Pleasant Valley.

The plant collections reflect the diverse interests of the owners and the resident horticulturists and are set within a dwarf conifer/spring bulb garden, a walled perennial border, hosta gardens, meadow, hayfields, a kitchen garden, a woodland garden of rhododendron and companion wild flowers, and a mostly native wild garden, home to a growing assortment of songbirds.

Passaic County
Saturday, May 14

RINGWOOD
RINGWOOD WATER GARDENS

📷 | ♿ | 🌱 | NEW

Hours: 10 a.m. to 4 p.m.

After our children moved out, we turned our backyard, which was a lawn, into a series of water gardens.

As a landscape architect and a lover of plants, I have introduced many different varieties of plants, including perennials, ornamental trees, and many flowering plant materials to my garden.

Recently, we have added an additional piece of land where I am developing a play area for my grandchildren. This area includes paths, a fairy garden, play structures, and more.

> **— TROWEL TALK—**
>
> As my kids grew up and moved out, I turned my backyard into a water garden for me to enjoy!
>
> — 👍 —

WANAQUE
THE SICHAKS' GARDEN

📷 | ♿ | NEW

Hours: 10 a.m. to 4 p.m.

Our garden is on a 2.5-acre lot bordered by natural woodlands with vernal ponds. The tiered garden includes a waterfall, koi pond, bluestone walkways, and arbors, with conditions ranging from full sun to full shade, including a bog garden.

This wide range of lighting and moisture allows for a wide variety of plants, ranging from mature native plants to unusual specimen plants and trees. It is an all season garden with something in bloom from February through November.

The garden was designed with wildlife in mind and has been registered with the National Wildlife Federation for 27 years.

Essex County
Sunday, May 15

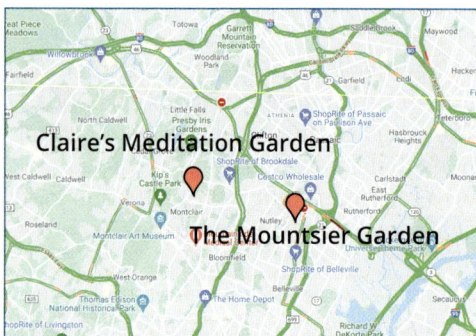

★There are two additional gardens open on this date in nearby Bucks County, PA:
Gardens at Half Moon, New Hope, PA
Paxson Hill Farm, New Hope, PA
For garden description and details, see page 200.

MONTCLAIR
CLAIRE'S MEDITATION GARDEN
📷 | ♿ partial | 🖋
Hours: 10 a.m. to 4 p.m.

Welcome to my garden! There are lots of lovely changes that I've made in the last two years! The front garden now has a nice curving path and new broad steps to the house. You will get to see what I've done with the plantings! Then, follow the brick path around the side of the house and look for the climbing roses, baptisia, smoke bushes, and a Japanese maple.

Open the new gate to a meditation garden—watch the birds at the feeder, notice the Mayan rock wall with its spirit windows surrounding a moon-shaped pond. Enjoy the mounds of Hakone grass, and the clump bamboo, but don't miss the tree bench with the tree's newly made clay animal totems surrounded by hydrangeas,

roses, and hellebores.

Follow the path to the Balinese platform floating in a sea of ferns and daylilies. Take a moment to enjoy the privacy, then walk back to the new deck with its wonderful steel-wire railing.

Come up and see the garden from this vantage point! Welcome to my garden! Iced tea will be served!

> **— TROWEL TALK—**
>
> I love those brazen hussies,tree peonies! They are exquisite and wanton and lush and they make me very happy!
>
> As for lavender—well, it does not like my garden at all! I had one plant that lasted a while. I called it my $500 lavender plant because that's how much money I've spent trying to grow the damn thing!
>
> — 👍 —

NUTLEY
THE MOUNTSIER GARDEN
📷 | ♿ partial | 🖋
This garden is open four times this year: April 16, May 15, June 4, and September 10.

Hours: 10 a.m. to 4 p.m.

A garden for all seasons that has been created and fine tuned for more than two decades and now encompasses two acres. Owners Silas Montsier and Graeme Hardie have collaborated with noted landscape designer and friend Richard Hartlage, and the result is a feast for the eyes and for the senses.

Principally a stroll garden, there are numerous focal points, small rooms,

---

📷 Photos permitted   ♿ Partially accessible   **NEW** garden or section   🖋 Nature-friendly

seating areas, private nooks, and impressive vistas. Drifts of variegated hakonechloa soften the strong architectural underpinnings of the garden, and many of the brilliant and original plant combinations will thrill the devoted horticulturist.

A collection of small sculptures, artworks, and commissioned pieces is interspersed throughout as accent points and disarming bits of humor.

From thousands of early spring flowering bulbs to a subtle but glorious display of green on green in the early fall, there is something new to see and enjoy on every visit.

This month: see the height of tulip season.

Morris County
Sunday, May 15

Jack Lagos

CHATHAM

JACK LAGOS

📷 | ♿

Hours: 10 a.m. to 4 p.m.

I have been developing this one-acre property, which backs onto a lovely wood, for 25 years. The first garden, with an island perennial border, is now one among many. A 100-year-old barn is backdrop for shade-loving plants, and on its sunny sides lie an herb garden and another perennial border.

Ten graceful clematis vines climb beautifully designed lattice fencing which defines the dwarf conifer collection. A woodland garden, my latest project, lies beneath a very large white oak and features a natural rock fountain.

Essex County
Saturday, June 4

NUTLEY
THE MOUNTSIER GARDEN

📷 | ♿ partial | 🌿

This garden is open four times this year:
April 16, May 15, June 4, and September 10.

Hours: 10 a.m. to 4 p.m.

A garden for all seasons that has been created and fine tuned for more than two decades and now encompasses two acres. Owners Silas Montsier and Graeme Hardie have collaborated with noted landscape designer and friend Richard Hartlage, and the result is a feast for the eyes and for the senses.

Principally a stroll garden, there are numerous focal points, small rooms, seating areas, private nooks, and impressive vistas. Drifts of variegated hakonechloa soften the strong architectural underpinnings of the garden, and many of the brilliant and original plant combinations will thrill the devoted horticulturist.

A collection of small sculptures, artworks, and commissioned pieces is interspersed throughout as accent points and disarming

bits of humor.

From thousands of early spring flowering bulbs to a subtle but glorious display of green on green in the early fall, there is something new to see and enjoy on every visit.

This month: see the dogwoods in bloom.

Hunterdon County
Sunday, June 12

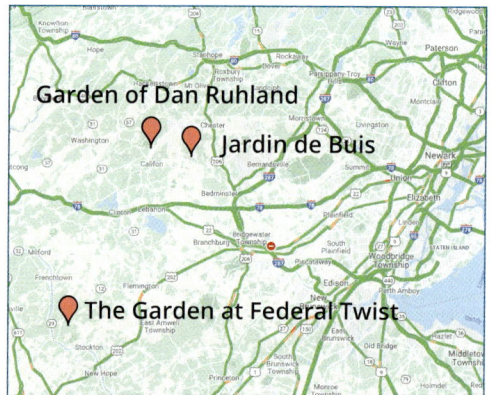

CALIFON
GARDEN OF DAN RUHLAND

📷 | **NEW**
Hours: 10 a.m. to 4 p.m.

Established garden with extensive hardscape, specimen trees, and extensive plantings on a sloped site. Deer fenced. We have been here one year and have added a vegetable garden, some fruit trees, bees, some shade gardens, and we continue to mix in/add our own touches.

📷 Photos permitted   ♿ Partially accessible   **NEW** garden or section   🌿 Nature-friendly

POTTERSVILLE
JARDIN DE BUIS
📷 | ♿ partial | 🌿
Hours: 10 a.m. to 4 p.m.

The gardens and landscape are part of an ongoing project begun in 1992 as a complete renovation and expansion of an eighteenth-century dairy farm on 35 acres.

The original four barns and a single wooded hedgerow were all that was left of the abandoned farm in the heart of deer country. The gardens closest to the barn/house complex were structured around three courtyards formed by the barns, stone walls, and boxwood.

The stone parking court leads to the entry/west courtyard, which is adjacent to the formal sycamore and boxwood garden off the kitchen. Continuing around the house is a thyme garden that leads to the eastern court with the pond and white garden. Moving westward away from the house you encounter the formal French potager surrounded by privet and fence. This vegetable garden was laid out on axis to the north side of an old cowshed and the orangery. The greenhouse was salvaged from Rutgers University and designed around an English-style orangery. It is solar powered and heated, plus the lawn and gardens are all treated organically.

Behind the cowshed is a nursery of boxwood collected from around the world. The overall aesthetic was trying to find a balance between the things we love, the French formal boxwood gardens, English borders, and the informal play of trees and allées that merge the formal grid to a much more informal sense of an American country landscape.

GARDEN EXTRAS

10 a.m. to 4 p.m. Sale of exceptional boxwood cultivars.

STOCKTON
THE GARDEN AT FEDERAL TWIST
📷 | 🌿
Hours: 10 a.m. to 4 p.m.

When we moved into a mid-century house overlooking the woods, I immediately knew only a naturalistic garden would be appropriate to the place.

The garden is hidden. You enter through a woodland garden to the side of the house, where you first glimpse the broader landscape behind: a large, sunny glade. Federal Twist is a landscape garden, and it uses multiple intersecting paths, immersive plantings, and the surrounding tall forest trees to create an illusion of spatial immensity in a relatively small garden. The garden is intended to encourage exploration and attention to detail, and to evoke strong emotion.

Begun as an experiment to explore garden making in the challenging conditions of unimproved, heavy, wet clay, the garden is ecologically similar to a wet prairie and is maintained by cutting and burning. Federal Twist has been featured in the *New York Times, the Financial Times of London, Gardens Illustrated,* and numerous other magazines and books, including Thomas Rainer's and Claudia West's *Planting in a Post-Wild World*, Claire Takács's *Dreamscapes*, and Christopher Wood's *Gardenlust*.

Federal Twist recently appeared in the BBC television series "Monty Don's American

---

Gardens" and in his new book of the same name.

James Golden's own book on the making of the garden—*The View from Federal Twist: A New Way of Thinking about Gardens, Nature and Ourselves*—was published in the UK in October 2021 and in the US in March of this year.

— TROWEL TALK—

James Golden, born in Mississippi though resident in New York City for most of his adult life, was a writer in the corporate world. Nearing retirement, and embarking on what he happily calls *la vita nuova*, he moved to a property in western New Jersey to make a garden.

It was an unusual site for a garden—little more than a derelict wood on heavy, wet clay—but he was taken with the site's emotional power and the intangible qualities of the landscape. When he began the garden, he also began a now well-known blog, The View from Federal Twist.

Fifteen years on, James is a celebrated garden maker and thinker whose garden, Federal Twist, has featured in numerous publications including the *New York Times, Gardens Illustrated, Horticulture, Better Homes and Gardens*, and other magazines and books. After visiting Federal Twist for the BBC Gardener's World series, American Gardens, Monty Don, the British TV gardening guru, said, "after over 50 years of gardening and visiting gardens, it made me rethink what a garden can be and do."

— 👍 —

Bergen County
Saturday, June 25

MAHWAH
SISKO GARDENS
📷 | ✒
Hours: 10 a.m. to 4 p.m.

Paul has been working on this 3.5-acre property for 36 years. The land was completely wooded within 50 feet of all sides of the original home, which years ago was a small farmhouse.

Major tree removal has opened the property to sunlight and sunset views. The fishpond and pool area are surrounded by terraced gardens from relocated stone farm walls that were on the property along with larger stones unearthed from additional construction to the home. The terraces and upper gardens have been planted with mostly perennials and numerous annuals for spring through fall color.

A new raised bed vegetable garden was added to an adjoining plot of land in 2020 which includes a ten-zone drip and spray watering system. All these gardens, as well as additions to the original home and his art studio/barn building have been developed personally by Paul.

With more than 1,000 feet of installed deer fencing and electric driveway gates, the gardens are now much safer from the resident deer population that live within the surrounding forest.

Of note are the numerous contemporary metal sculptures throughout the property which were all created by Paul during his artful career and later.

The Sisko Gardens and Sculpture Site is a premier example of an owner designed, constructed, and maintained sanctuary that should be seen and enjoyed.

— TROWEL TALK—

I like changing the gardens yearly and replenishing the soil with compost. I try different plants yearly and experiment with different ways to support plants as they grow.

On 3.5 acres my front end loader and electric golf/garden cart are indispensable. My favorite hand tools are the Radius tools. They are the best ergonomically shaped tools I've ever used.

— 👍 —

PARAMUS
SHARON MA'S GARDEN
📷 | 🖋 | NEW
Hours: 10 a.m. to 4 p.m.

As an environmentalist, I do everything based on how it impacts our environment, especially when I garden. I have recycled many items which I found that others were no long using, turning them into sculptural accents that I would otherwise have had to purchase.

I created a dynamic mosaic wall mural using broken ceramic pieces. I turned fractured concrete drain pipes into pedestals for potted plants. A large wooden picture frame divides my garden into separate areas without obstructing views. The metal paper rack becomes an artful trellis while large drums become rain barrels to prevent rain water runoff as well as saving money in water bills. Also, please note the exciting greenhouse I had built from recycled thermopane windows a friend gave me.

I am a succulent and cactus collector using many of them to decorate my gardens as they require minimal attention.

I also enjoy creating garden themes. My garden consists of a gnome village rock garden, Venetian garden decorated with numerous succulents, a koi pond with an Asian feel, a tropical corner as well as a fairy garden "Flower Bed." I pride myself in having a large variety of unique plants, many of which I have started from seed or propagated from cuttings.

I hope my garden will inspire my visitors to try many new things with their garden, as gardening is all about self expression. I look forward to your visit.

— TROWEL TALK—

I started my first garden in 2015 and it was a self-watering raised bed for vegetable gardens. I am still learning how to grow Chinese greens such as Chinese broccoli and bok choy because they bolt easily and always get eaten by pests.

My favorite plants are any plants that have fragrance, such as tree peony, peony, and oriental lily.

— 👍 —

WALDWICK
NOEL SCHULZ'S GARDEN

📷 | 🖋 | NEW
Hours: 10 a.m. to 4 p.m.

There's something for everyone on this quarter-acre property, especially if you love rocks!

Many were found on the property, some were donated by neighbors, and the remainder purchased to fill specific requirements (i.e., bluestone for smooth paths, wall rocks, and rocks in the gardens for visual effect).

Wherever feasible, the owner constructed the walls, paths, and naturalistic areas himself as part of his personal design that evolved over the last seven years. They form the backdrop for the color and texture of the plants and shrubs that make up the garden "rooms"—rock garden, woodland shade garden, wildflower garden, crevice garden with water features, and vegetable and fruit garden.

Troughs and pots, filled with flowering annuals, line the patios and walkways. There are several seating areas throughout the property to sit and enjoy the sights.

— TROWEL TALK—

I have been gardening since I was 4 or 5, starting with tomato and root vegetable plants, and helping out at my grandparents' farm.

I acquired my grandfather's pitchfork, but now I use it to turn the compost pile for my flower gardens.

— 👍 —

Hunterdon County

Saturday, August 20

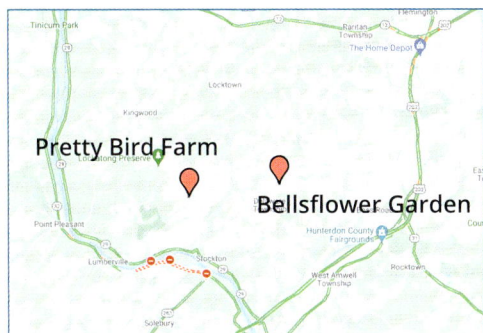

STOCKTON
BELLSFLOWER GARDEN

🖋

Hours: 10 a.m. to 4 p.m.

Bellsflower is a garden of flowers from spring through fall. In 1995, the year following our purchase of the farm, I started garden beds with little knowledge and lots of enthusiasm. Plants were chosen for color and size and often just because they caught an eye at the garden center.

Knowledge came with time. Plants that survived and thrived began to shape the garden. *Phlox subulata* covers large swaths and hangs over stone walls. The pink and yellow of early catmint and allysum signal spring. Irises, roses, and a succession of *Hydrangea arborescens*, *H. paniculata*, and *H. macrophylla* follow.

July and August find crape myrtle and summer phlox in pink, blue, white, and coral. Come September the asters begin, and the final chapter is all about blue, with tall roses adding their exclamation

points and grasses flowing in the breeze. Flowering shrubs and specimen trees bloom from March through September. As the leaves color and fall, the bright holly berries herald winter, when they feed robins as the snow flies.

PRETTY BIRD FARM

🖼 | ♿ partial | 🖋

Hours: 10 a.m. to 4 p.m.

Pretty Bird Farm is a flower and vegetable garden nestled in Delaware Township, one of the most scenic areas of Hunterdon County. Our hillside location overlooks the Rosemont Valley and allows us to be a low water use site.

Our cultivated garden is now about an acre in size and is planted yearly with more than 150 different varieties of annuals, perennials, and vegetables. While our garden has been growing over the last eight years, so has our family, and our vision for the garden has also evolved over this time.

What started as a food garden for just the two of us, our half-acre garden now supports our growing small business. We sell organically grown produce and flowers to the local community and beyond. It has become a sanctuary for local pollinators and as a waystation for migrating monarchs. It has become a place for our young children to grow and learn about the natural world around them. As you wander the grass walkways you may find a secret hideout, a bit of artwork, or a lost toy.

Come visit us in June for a showcase of our Cool Flowers. These are our cut flowers that are planted the previous fall and early March of this year and tucked in under frost cloth and mulch to bring them into bloom in May—the time of year most people in our 6B hardiness zone are just planting things in the ground.

Visit in August to see the garden in full bloom! We plant thousands of milkweed plants and other pollinator host plants each year. Expect it to be full of butterflies! August is also the peak for tomatoes, and we will offer tasting of our ripe and ready heirlooms.

Essex County
Saturday, September 10

NUTLEY
THE MOUNTSIER GARDEN

📷 | ♿ partial | 🖋

This garden is open four times this year: April 16, May 15, June 4, and September 10.

Hours: 10 a.m. to 4 p.m.

A garden for all seasons that has been created and fine tuned for more than two decades and now encompasses two acres. Owners Silas Montsier and Graeme Hardie have collaborated with noted landscape designer and friend Richard Hartlage, and the result is a feast for the eyes and for the senses.

Principally a stroll garden, there are numerous focal points, small rooms, seating areas, private nooks, and impressive vistas. Drifts of variegated hakonechloa soften the strong architectural underpinnings of the garden, and many of the brilliant and original plant combinations will thrill the devoted horticulturist.

A collection of small sculptures, artworks, and commissioned pieces is interspersed throughout as accent points and disarming

---

bits of humor.

From thousands of early spring flowering bulbs to a subtle but glorious display of green on green in the early fall, there is something new to see and enjoy on every visit.

SHORT HILLS
GREENWOOD GARDENS

PRESERVATION PARTNER

GREENWOOD GARDENS

Since the early twentieth century, Greenwood Gardens has been a private retreat with formal Italianate gardens graced by colorful tiles, rustic stone teahouses, mossy pebbled walks, and vistas stretching for miles into the surrounding wooded hillsides.

Careful preservation work and imaginative horticulture have returned much of the garden to its original Arts and Crafts design.

Greenwood Gardens is endorsed by the Garden Conservancy as a Preservation Project Garden.

DIGGING DEEPER

The History of Greenwood Gardens: Presentation and Guided Walking Tour

Greenwood Gardens
Saturday, September 10,
3 p.m. to 5 p.m.
$30 Garden Conservancy members
$40 General

In 2003, Peter P. Blanchard III and his wife Sofia, set out to fulfill the wishes of Peter's late father, the second of two owners of a 100-year-old, 28-acre property in Short Hills, New Jersey, by turning the former private estate into a public garden, in the process, conserving it for posterity.

What followed was an exercise in perseverance and a labor of love. Today, Greenwood Gardens has undergone significant transformation and has welcomed thousands of visitors since opening to the public in 2013.

This enchanted hideaway features pristine examples of early twentieth-century fountains, garden follies, terraces, grottoes, winding moss-covered paths, allées of London plane and spruce allées, ornamental shrubs, and bucolic ponds, all set amidst one of the most densely populated regions in the country.

The Digging Deeper program at Greenwood will provide both a 16-minute narrated slide presentation—*From Pleasant Days to Greenwood, a Century of Change in the Garden*—followed by a 45-minute guided walking tour of the grounds led by our volunteer docents who will share details of the site's history, landscape, and architecture.

In the process, participants will learn about the impact of two families—the Blanchards and the Days—on the property and how their efforts set the stage for the Greenwood of today. The tour ends with discussion time and Q & A session.

Photo by Greenwood Gardens

wild flowers, and a mostly native wild garden, home to a growing assortment of songbirds.

— TROWEL TALK—

Oh, so many favorite plants! Collections of American holly, rhododendron, hostas, maples, dwarf conifers, oaks, and more. We also enjoy growing many plants from seed.

— 👍 —

THE HAY HONEY FARM

📷 | 🖋

This garden is open twice this year: May 8 and September 17

Hours: 10 a.m. to 4 p.m.

The Hay Honey Farm's extensive gardens have been carefully added to the landscape since 1989 in a naturalistic manner, with a respect for the history and topography of the site, and consistent with the broader surrounding atmosphere of Pleasant Valley.

The plant collections reflect the diverse interests of the owners and the resident horticulturists and are set within a dwarf conifer/spring bulb garden, a walled perennial border, hosta gardens, meadow, hayfields, a kitchen garden, a woodland garden of rhododendron and companion

Garden of Dan Ruhland - Califon, NJ
Photo by Dan Ruhland

NOTES

Hyland & Wente Garden - Millerton, NY
Photo by Larry Wente

New York

NEW YORK

Westchester County

Sunday, April 24

LEWISBORO

THE WHITE GARDEN

📷 | 🖋

Hours: 10 a.m. to 3 p.m.

The native oak-hickory forest provides a "sacred grove" setting for the modern Greek Revival style house, designed by architect Patrick Naggar.

The gardens, designed by Patrick Chassé, ASLA, were completed in 1999. Nearest the house, the gardens are classically inspired, including a theater court, a pergola garden, a nymphaeum, a labyrinth, and additional hidden gardens include a perennial ellipse, an "annual" garden, a conservatory "jungle" garden, and an Asian-inspired moss garden. Several water features accent the landscape, and native plantings dominate in areas outside the central gardens. Many sculptures enrich this landscape

and one can visit a Temple of Apollo on an island in the main pond. In spring, more than 500,000 daffodils bloom in the woodland. Woodland walking paths weave over a meandering brook and through a shady dell.

Several glasshouses can be seen, including a new state-of-the-art greenhouse that supports the gardens. Head gardener Eric Schmidt, who ably orchestrates the rich garden plantings throughout the property, is on hand for questions.

Dutchess County

Saturday, May 7

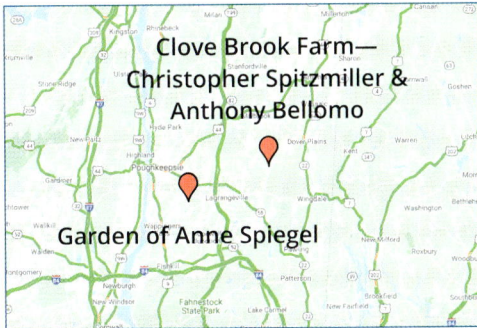

Clove Brook Farm—
Christopher Spitzmiller &
Anthony Bellomo

Garden of Anne Spiegel

MILLBROOK

CLOVE BROOK FARM—CHRISTOPHER SPITZMILLER & ANTHONY BELLOMO

📷 | ♿ partial | 🖋

*This garden is open twice this year:
May 7 and September 24*

Hours: 10 a.m. to 4 p.m.

The garden at Clove Brook Farm was started about seven years ago following a restoration of the historic Greek Revival farmhouse.

The garden has quickly grown into a series of interconnected spaces, beginning with a horseshoe-shaped garden near the house that is surrounded by a clipped hornbeam hedge and anchored by a dovecote. It's this garden where we have a spectacular show of tulips and sweetpeas in spring, followed by towering dahlias in late summer.

A few years ago another large garden "room" was added which centers on an oval swimming pool and neoclassical style pool house. This garden is also bounded by a hornbeam hedge and includes perimeter beds filled with various herbaceous perennials which evolve throughout the growing season, starting with poppies in early spring, then peonies, roses, lilies, and finally dahlias.

Last year my partner, landscape architect Anthony Bellomo, designed and installed a large kitchen garden which we pack with various vegetables. We are both confirmed garden addicts, and in addition to the more formal garden spaces, continue to add informal and naturalistic plantings throughout the property. We've planted several mixed shrub borders studded with drifts of bulbs, embellished our existing orchard, and collected unique sculptures to establish focal points.

There is nothing more satisfying than tending and fostering a garden, and watching it develop and mature. It's all documented in *A Year at Clove Brook Farm* (Rizzoli, 2021, with foreword by Martha Stewart).

📷 Photos permitted   ♿ Partially accessible   **NEW** garden or section   🖋 Nature-friendly

WAPPINGERS FALLS
GARDEN OF ANNE SPIEGEL

📷 | ♿ partial
Hours: 10 a.m. to 4 p.m.

The dramatic natural setting of this rock garden is the first thing visitors notice. The massive and beautiful outcrop has been enhanced by a series of stonewalled raised beds constructed on stepped ledges and cliffs and planted with choice specimens.

Included in the extensive screes and sand beds will be found alpines on many a rock gardener's wish list: astragalus, oxytropis, and penstemon are exceptionally well represented, but the list could go on. The north end of the garden had to be rebuilt after the tornado of 2000; the south end has been extended and developed into a series of tufa and crevice beds which have reached the top of the cliff, and the natural crevices on the back of the cliff are now being planted.

The sunny and windy garden is never watered because of an inadequate well, and there is continuing experimentation with xerophytic and drought-tolerant plants. There is also a separate fenced stream garden, home to plants that like wet feet, and a new area beyond the north end of the cliff is being developed for hellebores and other shade lovers.

This garden is a testament to both Nature and Nurture: the site is spectacular, but the dedicated hand of the gardener is everywhere adeptly and discreetly in evidence.

The garden received the prestigious Linc and Timmy Foster Millstream Garden Award in 2011 from the National Rock Garden Society.

Eastern Long Island
Saturday, May 7

Garden of Marshall Watson

Glade Garden—Abby Jane Brody

The Garden of Dianne B.

Biercuk & Luckey Garden

EAST HAMPTON
GARDEN OF MARSHALL WATSON

♿ partial | 🪶
Hours: 10 a.m. to 4 p.m.

Set on a bluff overlooking Gardiner's Bay, this home maintains two gardens.

One is a thoroughfare for a large herd of hungry deer and faces punishing ocean winds and salt, and one is partially fenced and partially walled. The entire property is transitioning to fully organic.

The Charlestonian gates welcome you to the interior designer's garden. A gravel forecourt bordered by a holly stilt hedge, rhododendron bed, and gated potager features a wisteria-draped carriage house/potting shed and a neoclassic gazebo which overlooks the walled garden. Note the log-rounds walkway built from cherry and oak trees felled by Hurricane Sandy.

📷 Photos permitted   ♿ Partially accessible   **NEW** garden or section   🪶 Nature-friendly

A gentle fountain greets you as you circle around the organic vegetable garden and ascend the Italian-inspired circular stairs.

The gazebo is surrounded by cascading maples and a unique euonymus groundcover where variegated irises and allium pop through. As you proceed along the formal gravel entrance, flanked by boxwood and agapanthus, the first of many pear and apple espaliers appears. A *Chionanthus virginicus* bush and a golden climbing rose are set amongst topiary lilacs.

The reflecting pool is flanked by two Hakuro-nishiki willow standards which frame the federal doorway of the Greek revival-style house. Versailles boxes are filled with David Austin tree roses and fig topiaries. A shade garden beneath a magnolia draws your eye up the hydrangea allée interspersed with pink, white, and blue hydrangea (almost patriotic.)

Beyond the Chippendale gates lies the sea garden, where boxwood, sarcococca, Sargenti cherries, and osmanthus shelter peonies, asters, irises, tamarix, lambs-ear, and other deer-resistant varieties. A sea pebble-walk leads to a large marble table around which comfortable chairs are placed to enjoy the expansive water views.

Though Italian influenced in the clipped evergreens and statuary, French influenced in the potager and espaliered trees, English influenced in the blowsy borders and variety of plants, and colonial influenced by its symmetry and formality, it is essentially a new American garden in its eclectic unity. And with many places to sit, lounge, rest, eat, and relax, it is ultimately a comfortable garden.

GLADE GARDEN—ABBY JANE BRODY

📷 | ♿ partial
Hours: 10 a.m. to 4 p.m.

Rare and unusual (and some not so) ornamental trees and shrubs and shade-loving perennials form the understory and groundcover in this niche carved in native woodland over a 35-year period.

This is a playground for an ardent gardener and plant collector, and plants that do not meet high standards of performance quickly give way to others waiting in the wings.

Planted for year-round interest, in midspring camellias that rise above carpets of hellebores, woodland phlox, wood anemones, and minor bulbs capture the most attention, and are succeeded by epimedium, daphne, fragrant rhododendrons, species peonies, and more.

During the summer, color and fragrance are provided by a progression of hydrangeas, Asiatic and American clethra, crape myrtles, and a range of stewartia, together with the newest treasure, a purple-leaved *Styrax japonicus*.

GARDEN EXTRAS

10 a.m. to 4 p.m. Plant sale.

— TROWEL TALK—

Plant collector, especially woodies. Botanizing in Europe, Mexico, and China. Influenced by visiting gardens and nurseries in UK and Europe.

Garden columnist for local paper for

18 years. Work on Village community gardens, including curator of Mimi Meehan Native Plant Garden.

— 👍 —

THE GARDEN OF DIANNE B.

📷 | 🖋

Hours: 10 a.m. to 3 p.m.

A nearly century old classic pink magnolia regularly stops traffic here on Davids Lane, so in an ideal world it will be in fulsome bloom on this Spring Open Day.

Between climate change and hungry critters, one can't promise anything, but surely there will be many and various fritillary, trillium, lots of blue spring "little" bulbs, and at least a few precious jack-in-the-pulpits from Dianne's extensive collection.

This is a layered garden that mixes it all up. At least twenty diverse Japanese maples mingle with symbols and sculptures that pop up among twisted trees, weepers, and odd woodland plants.

Dianne labels herself a "garden stylist" as her modus operandi: weaving together texture, accessories, color, patterns, and layered shapes that echo her twentieth-century career in fashion. Her garden provides the zing for her blog, Dirtier, which is the progeny of her '90s gardening book, *Dirt* (still available at Amazon.com).

WAINSCOTT

BIERCUK & LUCKEY GARDEN

📷 | 🖋

Hours: 10 a.m. to 4 p.m.

Our four-season woodland garden under a high oak canopy shelters a collection of rhododendrons, camellias, azaleas, kalmia, pieris, understory trees, perennials, bulbs, and tropicals in season. A mostly sunny rear corner contains a pool designed as a pond with a waterfall and is surrounded with plantings that peak mid-July through October. Winding paths and stone walls enhance a sense of depth and elevation change on a mostly flat acre. There is something in bloom every season.

Greene County
Sunday, May 8

Westchester County
Saturday, May 14

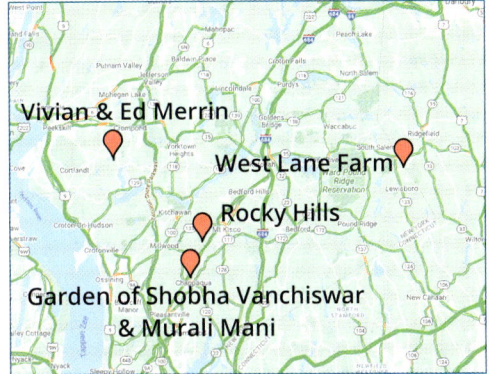

CORNWALLVILLE
GREENE BEE GREENHOUSE

📷 | ♿ partial | 🖋

Hours: 10 a.m. to 4 p.m.

Greene Bee Greenhouse is a nursery and budding arboretum located in the beautiful foothills of the Catskills. Visitors have the unusual opportunity to explore the extensive woody plant collections and established gardens on the surrounding grounds and seefirsthand what the nursery's offerings look like when planted in the landscape.

The owners, Eli and Briana, are passionate horticulturists whose love of plants informs the myriad and diverse selection and nursery inventory. At Greene Bee Greenhouse, the philosophy is to grow responsibly, and being mindful land stewards is paramount.

Greene Bee only cultivates and sells plants that coexist peacefully with the indigenous species of this region (both native and non-native), while simultaneously striving to showcase broad and unique variety.

CHAPPAQUA
GARDEN OF SHOBHA VANCHISWAR & MURALI MANI

📷 | ♿ partial | 🖋

Hours: 10 a.m. to 4 p.m.

This modestly sized, organically maintained garden won the 2007 Golden Trowel award from *Garden Design* magazine.

It features a cottage garden of bulbs and perennials, a Belgian fence espalier of fruit trees, a grape arbor, an herb garden, a checkerboard garden, and a "meadow" with naturalized bulbs, native plants, a Domenico Belli sculpture, and a greenhouse.

There are many European touches, like rose arbors, window boxes, a fountain, and Anduze pots. There is also a terrace with a wisteria-covered pergola for outdoor dining.

A vertical garden of mostly ferns and

heuchera, inspired by Patrick Blanc, was installed five springs ago. It has been a steep learning curve and we are still learning! This wall has become quite the attraction.

Modest in size, our garden is rich in detail and has a great deal of visual appeal. This garden was featured in the 2010 "Best of" issue of *Westchester Home* magazine, and hosted a well received "Wilding Walls, Fruiting Fences" Digging Deeper in 2021.

— TROWEL TALK—

Both my garden and myself are like the little engine that could. "We think we can" is our motto and keeps us chugging.

I have never had much luck with eremerus. I console myself with the thought that I've saved myself lots of money that's better spent on other plants.

— 👍 —

CORTLANDT MANOR
VIVIAN & ED MERRIN

📷 | ♿ partial
Hours: 10 a.m. to 4 p.m.

The Merrins are proud to announce the first Amazonica lilies grown in a private garden, three to four feet in diameter, with three- to four-inch edges.

The Merrin garden has been featured in several books and magazines; the most spectacular is Dominique Browning's *The New Garden Paradise: Great Private Gardens of the World*. The garden has been done with the expertise of Patrick Chassé.

A dramatic lookout made of glass and wood allows visitors to survey the property and its lake. Mixed borders flow in and out of the six- or seven-acre garden, containing indigenous plants as well as species and rare cultivars. These include rare trees, hundreds of hellebores, twenty-five magnolias, a garden of giant bamboo, a large and beautifully designed succulent garden, a cactus garden, and the Stumpery (what a wonder to come out of Hurricane Sandy).

On a pond with a "pond house" is a paradise of lotus, 500 of them. More than 300 mountain laurels surround the garden, in a planting that makes them part of the total landscape. Rare tropical plants, all of which are on display during the summer months, are kept in four greenhouse structures. These include rare orchids, three gardenia trees of various sizes, many hibiscuses, some unique, and various other unusual tropical plants.

Also our stream garden now has an entrance with 1,500 blue balloon flowers of a delicious blue, and 1,500 red *Primula* near the stream. Our large vegetable garden has many rare and Asian plants. We have also just redone our cut leaf Japanese maple garden; it is glorious. Plus, many more sights to see.

📷 Photos permitted   ♿ Partially accessible   **NEW** garden or section   ➤ Nature-friendly

MOUNT KISCO
ROCKY HILLS

📷 | ♿ partial
Hours: 10 a.m. to 4 p.m.

At Rocky Hills, planting among the stone walls began in the 1950s by William and Henriette Suhr, whose legacy is continued by current owners Barbara and Rick Romeo.

You will find mature specimens of black walnut and ash, complemented by weeping beech, dawn redwood, stewartia, dogwood, and an impressive collection of magnolias and conifers. Tree peonies and an extensive planting of rhododendrons and azaleas compete for attention with the carpet of bulbs throughout the thirteen acres.

Most impressive in May and June are the forget-me-nots, which are allowed full freedom throughout the garden. Starting on the hillside meadow, clouds of perfect blue flowers appear among an ever-expanding rock garden, through the hills and terraces, walls and paths, and fern woodlands, finding good company with self-sown Primula along the natural brook that serves as the heart of the garden.

SOUTH SALEM
WEST LANE FARM

📷 | 🌱
*This garden is open twice this year:
May 14 and September 17.*

Hours: 10 a.m. to 5 p.m.

I began working with owner John Papa in 2018, providing design and consultation on land use for the 21-acre property. Plans are in the works to create a sanctuary/farm that allows for innovative environmental land/farm use benefiting the community by combining arts and sciences with horticulture and education.
                              —Laura Tuttle Stabell

West Lane Farm has a balance of lawns and gardens, woodlands, and wetlands. Meadows create a tapestry of flowers utilized by the bees tended by beekeeper Tony Steger.

Sculptures by Suzanne Benton have been installed in the main "community gathering" garden, designed by Laura Tuttle Stabell. Areas for growing food, native, medicinal, cut flower, and pollinator plants have been started.

Farmer Joe Alvarez's storage container LED farm is up and running, providing microgreens.

GARDEN EXTRAS

10 a.m. to 5 p.m. Sale of rare native plants, cut flowers, microgreens, honey, and candles.

Dutchess County

Sunday, May 15

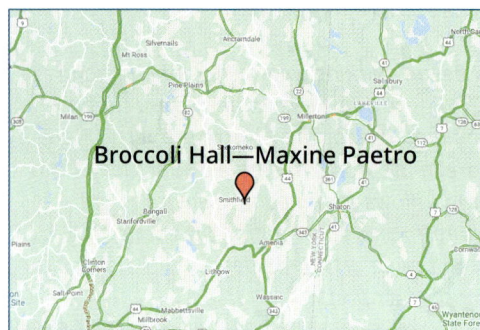

Broccoli Hall—Maxine Paetro

AMENIA

BROCCOLI HALL—MAXINE PAETRO

📷 | ♿ partial | 🖋

Hours: 10 a.m. to 4 p.m.

Visitors to Broccoli Hall describe this English-style cottage garden as "incredible," "inspirational," "magical"—and they come back again and again. Starting in 1985 with 1.5 acres of bare earth, Maxine Paetro collaborated with horticulturist Tim Steinhoff to create a series of enchanting garden rooms.

Broccoli Hall offers an apple tunnel; a brick courtyard; a lavish display of spring bulbs blooming with crabapples in May; an extensive border of irises, peonies, and old shrub roses flowering in June; a tree house with long views; and a secret woodland garden with a teddy bears' picnic.

We have some whimsical rustic carvings by woodsman/artisan Hoppy Quick: new bears, new stairs, new chairs, and some exceptionally charming bird feeders. Photos and magazine stories about

Broccoli Hall can be viewed at www.broccolihall.com.

In 2010, Broccoli Hall was expanded to five acres and two new mud ponds were installed. This is where we began a breeding program—but we don't sell our fish. To see the "elusive kishusui" project in progress, go to www.kishusui.com. We look forward to seeing you in the garden in 2022!

Ulster County
Sunday, May 15

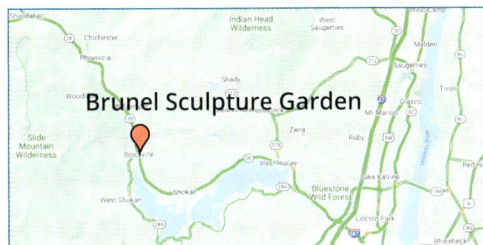

BOICEVILLE
BRUNEL SCULPTURE GARDEN

📷 | 🖋

Hours: 10 a.m. to 4 p.m.

Multifaceted garden with terrain changes, several garden rooms spanning various sun and shade areas, and a slew of unusual specimen fruit trees, vines, and shrubs that combine to create a magical garden environment on 1.3 compact acres planted between and among a collection of century-old figurative and narrative concrete statuary.

The Alsatian-style house is surrounded by pea gravel and bluestone pathways through iris, geranium, lilies, and European hornbeam. Prized tree peonies lead the way to a formal boxwood herb garden with phlox and foxglove which then transitions to a rhododendron slope underplanted with hellebores and other groundcovers.

Up the white pine root stairs is a level sunny garden with several pollinator beds, a hardy kiwi pergola and the newest additions—two Czech crevice gardens and a native plants bed devoted to attracting pollinators. The native plant pollinator garden at the front of the visitor center is in full glory in late summer and early fall.

Eastern Long Island
Sunday, May 22

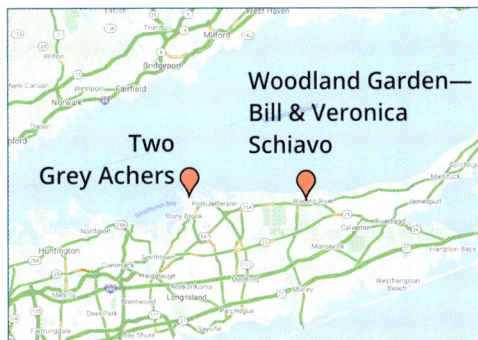

OLD FIELD
TWO GREY ACHERS

📷 | ♿ partial | 🖋

Hours: 12 p.m. to 4 p.m.

This garden was designed by its owners to provide beauty and interest in every season. Adjacent to Conscience Bay on Long Island's North Shore, the mild maritime microclimate is reflected in the broad range of taxa thriving on this intensively planted site.

A remarkable collection of choice conifers, rhododendrons, azaleas, Japanese maples, and other companions amassed over three decades creates a year-round tapestry of color, texture, and form.

Come, enjoy, and find specific ideas for stunning, hardworking woody plants to add to your own garden.

GARDEN EXTRAS

see next page

📷 Photos permitted   ♿ Partially accessible   **NEW** garden or section   🖋 Nature-friendly

GARDEN EXTRAS

Noon to 4 p.m. Your garden host will lead a special tour focusing on the use of woody plants for year-round interest.

— TROWEL TALK—

Aging gracefully we hope, along with plant material in a well established landscape.

All planning, design, and installation done by owners. Short on annuals, perennials—mostly woody ornamentals. Water feature.

Favorite plants are conifers due to their year-round contribution to the palette of colors.

— 👍 —

WADING RIVER
WOODLAND GARDEN—BILL & VERONICA SCHIAVO

📷 | 🖊

Hours: 10 a.m. to 4 p.m.

Our property is a heavily wooded acre and a half comprising one large pond, three small ponds, and two streams.

The main area on which our house is situated is ringed with twelve- to fifteen-foot rhododendrons and other flowering shrubs. The terrain was re-landscaped over time to make it both lawn-less and deer resistant, with many varieties of plants.

A recently added feature is a shade and fern garden in the front woods that provides a lush setting surrounding a stone patio used for bird watching and relaxation. There is also a nature trail that meanders from the top of the front woods and ultimately runs parallel to the 75-foot stream and waterfall that ends by the front door.

Behind the house are two ponds, the largest of which is densely surrounded by trees and ornamental grasses and highlighted by a Japanese red maple that drapes over a waterfall at the bottom of a 40-foot stream emerging from the woods.

In addition, our woodland garden is a National Wildlife Federation Certified Wildlife Habitat. The property abounds with wild turkeys, deer, a wide variety of birds, and the occasional fox. The landscape design was developed with serenity, meditation, and harmony in mind.

Dutchess County

Saturday, June 4

★ There are five additional gardens open on this date in nearby Litchfield County, CT:
Glenn Hillman, Litchfield, CT
Japanese Gardens at Cedar Hill, Roxbury, CT
Mulla Garden, Warren, CT
Hollister House Garden, Washington, CT
The Sumacs, Washington, CT
For garden description and details, see page 63.

different levels. A peach and apple espalier is featured against the charming cottage. The views show the magnificent landscape of the Smithfield Valley, not a house in sight.

— TROWEL TALK—

I retired to the Hudson Valley and when I bought my house which I named Highgrove Cottage (hope Prince Charles doesn't mind), I inherited a beautiful perennial garden which I have been redesigning every year.

I love color and try to awaken these flowers every two to three weeks so I get a nice delightful array. However, I don't have luck with *Crocosmia lucifer* and have to replant them every year for I love the way they look with the Russian sage.

— 👍 —

MILLERTON
HIGHGROVE COTTAGE

📷 | ♿ partial
Hours: 10 a.m. to 4 p.m.

Barbara's garden, atop the beautiful Smithfield Valley in the heart of the Millbrook Hunt Country, is exhibited in vibrant colors in her perennial landscape around her cottage.

Her fashion background shows in the mix of color from an array of roses, crocosmia, Russian sage, *Allium* 'Globemaster', lilies, phlox, and many more among stone and cast-iron sculptures and stone walls on

Nassau County
Sunday, June 5

GLEN COVE
KIPPEN HILL

📷 | ♿ partial

Hours: 10 a.m. to 4 p.m.

Kippen Hill is a twelve-year-old garden that encompasses five smaller gardens situated on 1.5 acres. The variegated garden grows 'Dragon's Eye' pine and Japanese forest grass, variegated hosta and acuba. A formal garden of English-style borders with a central-axis bubbler fountain is the anchor to the site.

An Asian garden with an aviary pagoda is home for our Asian-native egg-laying hens. Coltsfoot from the Humes Japanese Stroll Garden and black bamboo are featured here, along with a majestic centenary boulevard cedar that was planted when the house was first built in 1910.

A small vegetable garden with heirloom tomatoes hosts a collection of nineteenth-century American garden equipment. The roomy front lawn is planted with ornamental papyrus in paisley-patterned beds, surrounded by English-style borders.

A Lord and Burnham greenhouse dating to 1925 was rescued and restored from a famed Gold Coast estate about seven years ago by Dean and Jonathan. This outbuilding doubles as a site for our collection of tropicals, including bananas and orchids, as well as a dining room for guests during all four seasons.

LOCUST VALLEY
CAROL & JIM LARGE'S GARDEN

📷 | ♿ partial | 🖋

Hours: 10 a.m. to 4 p.m.

This garden truly reflects the personality of its owners, having been redesigned and altered over their 30 years of ownership.

The bones of the original garden were designed through Innocenti and Webel in the late 1930s around a much older frame farmhouse that was moved to the site and altered in 1936 by architect Bradley Delahanty.

The property encompasses ten acres of mature woodlands, streams, ponds, and fields placed in a framework of Long Island's signature rhododendron, mountain laurel, and azalea. There are several more formal garden areas planted with specimen woody plants, herb and perennial gardens, lawns, and terraces.

> **— TROWEL TALK—**
>
> I am a plant lover, our garden contains plants that I have brought and bought at auctions and trips to nurseries near and far. I am continually adding new areas of interest and making more work for myself and a project every year or two.

I particularly love sharing with other garden- and plant-loving members of my family and friends, helping my children who like to garden develop and plan their gardens.

There are many rhododendron and pieris in this garden, and I particularly like mountain laurel. Although we live in a great place for growing it, I have had mixed luck in getting it to establish.

— 👍 —

OYSTER BAY
THE BARNYARD

📷

Hours: 10 a.m. to 4 p.m.

The Barnyard is tucked behind the main road and up a narrow, wooded driveway that opens up to a great lawn. This leads to a 1700s converted barn/house at the upper part of the property.

Though we renovated the barn for a growing family more than 40 years ago, it wasn't until the last renovation in 2011 that the feature backyard landscape really evolved from what was a play area, driveway, and some old building foundations. Though confined in area and quite terraced, the finished product presents a very unique and sculptured backyard garden.

It features a channeled and woodland stream that flows over two waterfalls and ultimately into an old foundation reservoir. The natural and formal are made to blend perfectly as if they've existed there for years. In this small-space, outdoor living environment on many different levels are nestled numerous examples of choice

plants, amid interesting configurations of native boulders. At each level are different refreshing sounds of water and a new and unusual plant to complement every niche.

As the landscape continues to mature and evolve, it becomes even better and more "fun" for this horticulturist.

PORT WASHINGTON
THE GARDENS AT SANDS LIGHT

📷 | ♿ partial | ✎
Hours: 10 a.m. to 4 p.m.

The Gardens at Sands Light are located on the waterfront estate of a former Vanderbilt mansion and nineteenth-century lighthouse and cottage, providing a unique and dramatic setting.

The French château–inspired residence provides a grand centerpiece for the four-acre garden, the creation of a passionate plantswoman and artist. The garden will take you from a mixed woodland and stream to a beachside marble temple, large shrub and perennial borders to formal knot garden, and cactus garden onto a large private beach.

A strolling garden, designed to provide privacy and to entertain, joins quiet alcoves as well as spacious terraces and outdoor living arrangements. A lush summer display is achieved by the addition of more than 100 containers, sporting vibrant colored annuals and large tropicals.

The extensive collections include specimen plants with unique habits and variegations, orchids and rare tropical plants, as well as peacocks, koi, and tortoises.

Westchester County

Sunday, June 5

Garden of Michael and Suzanne Inglis

PLEASANTVILLE

GARDEN OF MICHAEL AND SUZANNE INGLIS

📷 | ♿ partial

Hours: 10 a.m. to 4 p.m.

Nearly three-quarters of an acre are nestled into the valley with a small stream. This mature shrub and perennial garden borrows from its surroundings and yet remains an idyllic private space.

The garden was completely designed and planted by the owner in the last 20 years. There are full-sun perennial beds, a wisteria arbor, climbing roses, clematis, butterfly garden, and two shade gardens. Most of the plants are deer resistant.

Columbia County

Saturday, June 11

★ There are three additional gardens open on this date in nearby Berkshire County, MA:

1391 Barnum Street, Sheffield, MA
For garden description and details, see page 112.

and Dutchess County, NY:

Hyland/Wente Garden, Millerton, NY
Katie Ridder and Peter Pennoyer, Millbrook, NY
For garden description and details, see page 161.

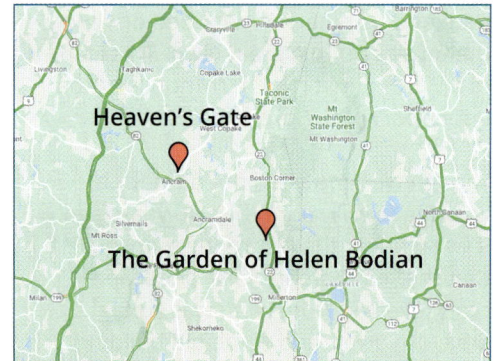

Heaven's Gate

The Garden of Helen Bodian

ANCRAM

HEAVEN'S GATE

📷 | ♿ partial

Hours: 10 a.m. to 4 p.m.

The gardens surrounding Betzie's old Ancram farmhouse were designed as a series of wanderings of garden rooms— each with a specific purpose and sense of enclosure.

Yet, Betzie's style is untraditional and

playful, more natural and almost jungle-like—punctuated by texture, size, shape, and color.

MILLERTON
THE GARDEN OF HELEN BODIAN

📷 | ♿ partial | 🌿
Hours: 10 a.m. to 4 p.m.

When a site opened for a large rock garden, Helen Bodian began a two-decade excursion into garden making, in the process satisfying an interest both in botanical diversity and in creating spaces with a welcoming ambience and interest for every season.

One challenge at the outset was to find a way to display the plants she began collecting and propagating, yet at the same time have the arrangement agree with a sprawling, northeast landscape.

The result is an informal overall scheme with paths cutting through fields, around a pond, up to forest trails and connecting four distinct gardens with each other: a large rock garden cut into a hillside next to the house; a romantic perennial garden squared off between hornbeam and mixed shrub hedges; a gravel garden adjacent to the greenhouse displaying a collection of tender salvias; and an ornamental kitchen garden with kale, amaranth and cardoon for structure and a scattering of annual flowers, for color.

Dutchess County
Saturday, June 11

Hyland/Wente Garden

Katie Ridder & Peter Pennoyer

MILLBROOK
KATIE RIDDER & PETER PENNOYER

♿ partial | 🌿
Hours: 10 a.m. to 4 p.m.

Our hornbeam-enclosed flower garden with formal bluestone paths frames fourteen flowerbeds and was inspired by Wave Hill in the Bronx. The garden is centered on a small terrace with fountain bowl and a wisteria-draped pergola.

Our house, designed by my husband, Peter Pennoyer, faces directly onto the garden with a mudroom in the form of a small temple aligning with the central path. The beds feature fastigiate beech, dwarf conifers, grasses, annuals, and ever-developing unusual combinations.

Our landscape architect, Edmund Hollander, designed our property with simple hedgerows and trees, reserving the flower garden and woodland path for me to unleash a less disciplined approach. Our land runs the length of an old farm stone wall. The principal elements align from east to west: meadow, flower garden, greenhouse, woodland path, cutting garden, and, finally, the corn field of the neighboring farm.

MILLERTON

HYLAND/WENTE GARDEN

📷 | ♿

Hours: 10 a.m. to 2 p.m.

The property consists of a modern barn-like structure located on rolling farmland overlooking Indian Mountain and Indian Lake.

The house has eight doors leading to a series of distinct gardens, intentionally blurring house and gardens. Emphasizing grasses, textures, colors, and plant combinations, the gardens blend with surrounding wildflower meadows and are designed for interest in all seasons. There is a rill with bamboo, a secret garden, a pool garden, a garden of solar panels, and a wooded walk down to Indian Lake.

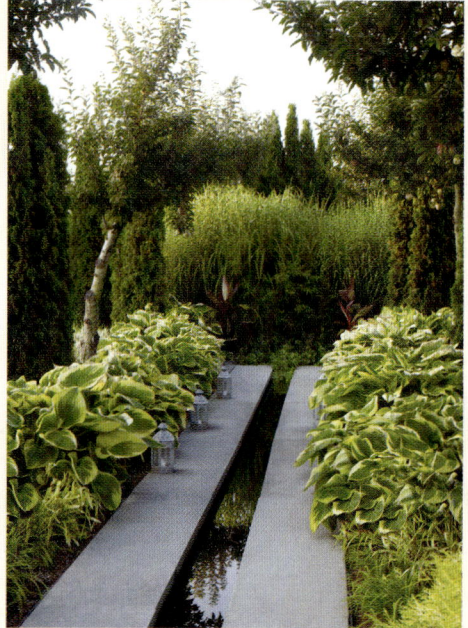

well as garden and larger agrarian landscape. The mass plantings, varied grid, and occasional strong verticals of the garden suggest the patterns of the surrounding agricultural fields and farm complexes.

Emphasizing grasses, textures, colors, and plant combinations, the gardens are designed for interest in all seasons.

Photo by John Hyland

Columbia County
Saturday, June 18

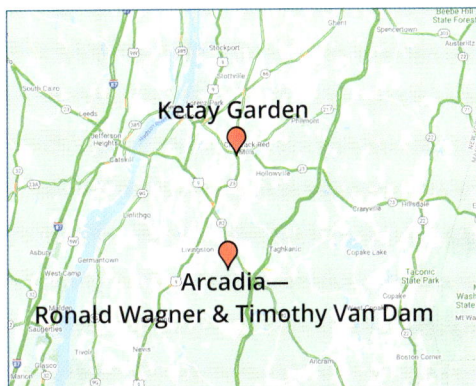

CLAVERACK
KETAY GARDEN

📷 | ♿

Hours: 10 a.m. to 4 p.m.

An allée of large maples and oak, bordered by meadows on either side, forms the entrance to the gardens which surround the house. A large garden in front of the house and a smaller one behind lead down to a meadow in the distance framed by views of the Catskill Mountains.

The front garden is bordered by a semicircle of forsythia that shields the garden from the road. An iron, circular bench surrounds an oak tree and is a great place to sit in spring when the irises and redbud are in bloom.

The garden behind the house has a large pergola off the house, which is covered with yellow trumpet vine and looks over the garden and meadow beyond. From this garden, a curving mown path leads down the hill, through the meadow, and then along the side of the property bordered by our homage to Tuscany: a line of tall narrow Irish juniper, which can, when you squint, look like a row of cypress. In the distance are the barn and the Catskill Mountains.

A smaller rustic pergola is set away from the house with a stone terrace to the side. Two Adirondack chairs sit there for anyone who wishes to watch the sunset or just enjoy the breeze on the meadow. The walled bocce court with its row of Adirondack chairs added not long ago, has become a favorite late afternoon gathering spot.

WEST TAGHKANIC
ARCADIA—
RONALD WAGNER & TIMOTHY VAN DAM
📷 | ♿
Hours: 10 a.m. to 4 p.m.

Our 1840 Greek Revival-style farmhouse is set in a pastoral landscape of 28 acres. An avenue of sweet gum trees lining the formal driveway is planted in forced perspective to visually extend the approach to the house.

The gently rolling hillside is punctuated by a magnificent grove of black locust trees and a grove of deciduous conifers, including bald cypress, metasequoia, and larch trees. A wildflower meadow rises to the north, a new pentagram-shaped grove of gingko trees can be reached by a mown path leading through the meadow, another path leads through the forest beyond.

The informal plantings include the lilac border, rhododendron, mountain laurel, and hydrangea beds. A large pond is the

focus of surrounding naturalistic plantings of daylilies, rudbeckia, Japanese iris, and swamp azalea, giving views of the wetland beyond. Symmetrical twin terraces at the house feature a wisteria arbor–covered stone dining table on the south and perennial border of peonies and roses on the north.

A new stumpery bed of ferns and shade-loving woodland plants has been created to line the service drive to the south.

Saratoga Springs
Saturday, June 18

Winterberry Cottage Garden

Foxglove—
Sarah Patterson's Garden

A Place to Nest—Moe's Garden

Dalton
Garden

Susie
Kane-Kettlewell's
Garden

MIDDLE GROVE
DALTON GARDEN

📷 | ♿ partial
Hours: 10 a.m. to 4 p.m.

Our 2.5-acre garden is located in a serene woodland setting surrounding our home in Middle Grove, NY. Mature trees and shrubs of various forms frame the house and provide vertical accents. Their strength is balanced by the softer contours of the many perennials growing in the garden.

Sitting areas are found throughout, allowing the visitor to rest and enjoy varied views of the garden. Pause and reflect as you listen to the sound of the waterfall at the pond or sit and relax in the swinging basket chairs.

Wander the garden paths where you will find large collections of native plants (trillium, clintonia, ferns, arisaema), shade perennials (astilbe, heuchera, primula,

cimicifuga, hosta), shrubs (peonies, hydrangea, viburnum, rhododendron), and trees (Japanese maple, dogwood, miniature ginkgo). Newer plantings include over 40 cultivars of David Austin roses.

Adding interest are a small pond and numerous statues, urns, and other ornaments (collected over years of travel) reflecting the theme of the area in which they are located. The garden includes an extensive hosta collection in addition to our own hybridized seedlings.

— TROWEL TALK—

Meg— My first garden was a 10' x 60' vegetable garden. I wanted to grow vegetables to can and freeze for the winter.

I was new to gardening and planted 60 tomato plants. I had no idea of the yield I would receive. I canned and canned and froze and gave away tomatoes. I had tomatoes everywhere, I learned quickly that year to reduce, drastically, the number of tomato plants for the following year.

My favorite gardening tool is the Korean Ho-Mi digger. It is simply the best weeder that I have ever used.

—👍—

SARATOGA SPRINGS
A PLACE TO NEST—MOE'S GARDEN
📷 | ♿ partial | ✒
Hours: 10 a.m. to 4 p.m.

Our gardens are on a small city lot. We have utilized the space for small shrubs, perennials, herbs, and vegetables, with very little lawn. We have introduced various plants of our interest: some from grandparents, some from other gardeners, and some from childhood memories of lilacs, violets, and lily of the valley. I feel that in sharing plants, your garden flourishes.

We created raised beds for quite an array of vegetables, and then intermingled tomatoes with perennials. I really enjoy collecting my own seeds and find that the plants do even better the following season, acclimating to their own environment.

It is such a pleasure sitting on the front porch, and walkers will comment on how beautiful the gardens are. I am grateful to be able to share this with them.

— TROWEL TALK—

I make a strong effort to maintain organic gardening, permaculture, and pollinators, and try to utilize the small area to have shrubs, perennials, and vegetables.

My goals are to every year expand my knowledge of plants and our relationship with them.

— 👍 —

FOXGLOVE—
SARAH PATTERSON'S GARDEN
📷 | ✒
Hours: 10 a.m. to 4 p.m.

Nestled among a growing city, Foxglove Garden is an escape from it all. It is not a formal garden, just meandering paths past the many varieties of trees and evergreens, such as *Malus*, *Magnolia*, *Styrax obassia*, *Cornus florida*, and *Ilex* 'Mary Holman'.

Among the trees are shrubs and herbaceous plants, some of my favorites being viburnum, ilex, hydrangea, hosta, peonies, *Alchemilla mollis*, geraniums, ferns, and of course, digitalis.

I started creating the garden in 2008, each year redesigning and tweaking. My hope is that as you wander the garden, you are able to let go of the world outside and feel a sense of peace and calm.

— TROWEL TALK—

My first garden was part of the sixteen acres I grew up on. It was an old-growth woodland full of native wildflowers and large beech trees. It is where my love of shade gardening started.

— 👍 —

📷 Photos permitted   ♿ Partially accessible   NEW garden or section   ✒ Nature-friendly

WINTERBERRY COTTAGE GARDEN

📷 | ♿ | 🍃

Hours: 10 a.m. to 4 p.m.

In Saratoga Springs, behind a small West Side cottage named Winterberry, is this truly secret sanctuary, with an entrance featuring a line of hydrangeas backed by arborvitae and pachysandra that opens up to perennial gardens, raised beds for vegetables, a wildflower space, and a forest corner.

The garden is designed to be environmentally friendly with bark chip paths that can be renewed; decomposed chips go on the flower beds. Chemical products are kept to a minimum. The flowers and shrubs are selected with the color scheme of blue-green, chartreuse, and red and white. Love of color also has brought yellow, pink, and other colors into the garden.

There are a variety of places for sitting in the old garden furniture placed along the walkways and on the patios. Viewing the garden from many angles and being immersed in plants and flowers is very important to the Moodys, who hope visitors feel free to sit in these spaces.

SCHUYLERVILLE

SUSIE KANE-KETTLEWELL'S GARDEN

📷 | ♿

Hours: 10 a.m. to 4 p.m.

These gardens have changed somewhat since I last showed the garden for the Conservatory tour, but they still include the formal parterre.

I have teamed up with my partner, Paul Schneider, an avid horticulturist and sculptor. With his help we have been able to make more use of the property by opening up beds and growing the more unusual or rare plants that we find.

The rock gardens and containers holding rock garden plants and rocks are multiplying rapidly and being placed throughout the garden beds along with Paul's sculptures and make for a more interesting overall effect.

Westchester County

Saturday, June 18

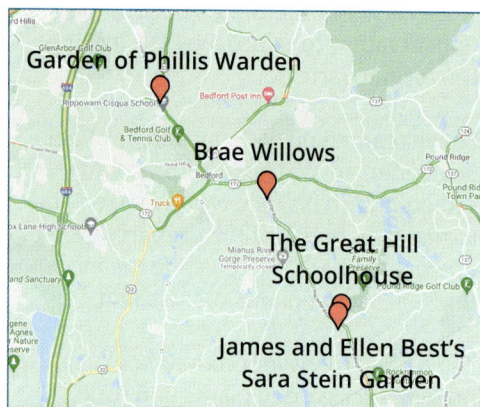

BEDFORD

BRAE WILLOWS

📷 | ♿ partial
Hours: 10 a.m. to 4 p.m.

Brae Willows, a one-acre garden, began its infancy in June 1967 as an open, barren piece of land with three rhododendrons and a smattering of mature trees. It was completely designed and planted by the owner, who also helps with the maintenance.

The division of the property by a small seasonal creek, which winds its way through to the Mianus River bordering the back of the property, created the biggest challenge to the owner. Unifying the two sides was accomplished through careful use of trees, shrubs, and bridges.

Because of the river, the water table is in places only several feet from the surface of the ground. Careful planning was needed to use plant material that was visually stimulating without having it look like wetlands.

The varied and extensive use of conifers makes for seclusion, surprise, serenity, and year-round beauty. There is no downtime here. Meticulous attention has been paid to detail. Arbors and five natural stone garden paths leave you wondering what lies beyond. Ornate iron gates beckon your entry. A secluded patio, bird baths, and cement and decorative iron planters add to the total enchantment. Benches, strategically placed, beg you to linger awhile. Three bridges invite you across the creek.

Walk under an iron arbor, down a stone path flanked by a perennial and shrub garden, open a small picket gate, and you find yourself looking at a view of the river. Curved stone walls gently frame the two patios, and a large stone arbor welcomes you into the main part of the garden. A high tsuga hedge frames the gravel driveway.

A new "hidden garden" was created in 2021. Though small in size—10 feet wide by 90 feet long—it is filled with diversified hardscape elements and tall, narrow taxus. This captivating and tranquil setting brings a sense of peacefulness. A vista of the gardens can be seen from the covered porch.

— TROWEL TALK—

Have been gardening since I was eleven. Have never taken "it can't be done" as an answer. This is my first garden as an adult ... so 53 years. Learned by trial and error, reading, talking to knowledgeable people, and some courses.

My favorite garden tool is the hedge

📷 Photos permitted   ♿ Partially accessible   **NEW** garden or section   🌱 Nature-friendly

pruners I have that I can extend the handle.

Saw a bunch of "twigs" lying on the ground behind the hemlocks in the pachysandra. Lifted it up to toss it and to my surprise, there were five baby chipmunks. So tiny their eyes were still closed. Put the twigs back and every three or four days checked on them.

Two weeks passed and they started to look a little different from chipmunks. In fact they were baby rabbits. A short time later they were having a grand time in the gardens. Was fascinating to see them grow from infancy to adulthood. I knew they would eventually destroy things but what a treat and surprise they were.

Loved it.

— 👍 —

BEDFORD
THE GREAT HILL SCHOOLHOUSE
📷 | 🖋 | NEW
Hours: 10 a.m. to 4 p.m.

The Great Hill Schoolhouse is a historic property on two acres that is owned by landscape designer John Holm and industrial designer Harry Allen. The original structure served as a local school house for a century until the 1940s.

Over the last 20 years, John has replaced lawn, pachysandra, and foundation plantings with native (mostly) trees, shrubs, perennials, grasses, and sedges. It's a sustainable landscape that draws inspiration from natural plant communities with great emphasis on structure, texture, and movement. In fall, plants are left to provide winter interest

and to provide habitat for overwintering insect sustenance for birds.

Much of the garden's character comes from the juxtaposition of the loose, flowing nature of the meadow-style planting against structural elements such as hedges, rock walls, and mature boxwoods. The crisp edging of the path that takes you through the garden offsets the organic elements.

The house is set underneath a copse of mature sugar maples that provide shade for a woodland garden and a patio with potted Japanese maples. There is also a crevice style rock garden with a collection of alpines, desert plants, and troughs.

— TROWEL TALK—
John Holm's career in landscape design started at the New York Botanical Garden's School of Horticulture. His first job out of school-was working for Martha Stewart as head gardener on her estate in Bedford.
In 2016 he founded John Holm Landscape Design and has been working on a variety of independent projects since.

— 👍 —

BEDFORD HILLS
GARDEN OF PHILLIS WARDEN
📷 | 🖋
This garden is open twice this year: June 18 and August 6

Hours: 10 a.m. to 4 p.m.

This garden of many facets includes perennial borders, three water gardens, a formal vegetable garden, wildflower garden, fern garden, marsh garden, a tree platform overlooking the marshlands, a woodland walk, a hidden garden, and a formal croquet court.

The garden extends over seven acres, the back four acres of which are a study in what deer do not eat.

POUND RIDGE
JAMES AND ELLEN BEST'S
SARA STEIN GARDEN

📷 | ♿ partial | 🌿
Hours: 10 a.m. to 2 p.m.

This ecological restoration by Sara Stein, the native plant pioneer, spans 5.5 acres and includes upland and wetland meadows, woodlands, and thickets.

Documenting her planting experiences in her books (*Noah's Garden*, *Planting Noah's Garden*, *My Weeds*), she included many native species important to wildlife but not often used in landscaping.

Other features include a stone terrace planted with grasses and sedges, an herb garden within openings in a brick patio, and a planted moss garden and path around the pond. There are numerous paths through the various habitats, all showing a viable, sustainable alternative to the conventional suburban landscape design.

Ellen and James Best acquired the property in 2007 and have been maintaining it since then.

DIGGING DEEPER

**A Rose is Never Just a Rose—
Plants in Community**
Mathew McDowell
Saturday, June 18, 2 p.m. to 4 p.m.

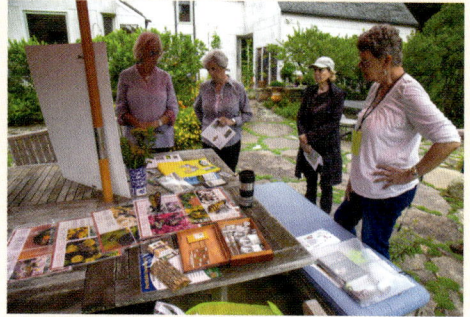

James and Ellen Best's
Sarah Stein Garden
$30 Garden Conservancy members
$40 General

Mathew McDowell is a horticulturist and naturalist who specializes primarily in regional native plants, invasive species management, and designing planted spaces attractive to humans and wildlife.

He's Garden Director of the Leon Levy Native Plant Garden for Bedford Audubon Society and is a Wildflower Island tour guide at Teatown Lake Reservation.

Plants are complicated beings. Each is a product of its own evolutionary history, and most importantly of its relations with the other plants and animals (humans included) with which it shares its habitat.

In this walking guided tour, we'll be exploring the unique adaptations of plants to be found within the Sarah

Stein Garden, many of which might be found growing wild in New York.

In particular, we'll focus on the native species present and their complex interrelationships with local wildlife and each other, as well as threats they're facing.

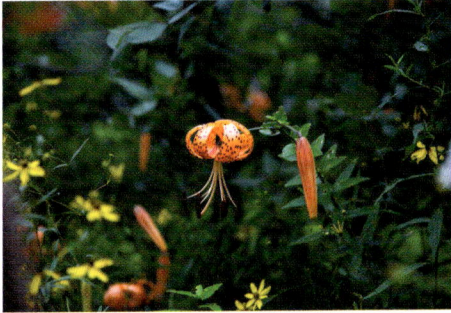

Photos by Phillip Carruthers

Dutchess County
Saturday, June 26

Uplands Farm—
Zibby & Jim Tozer

Squirrel Hall

Lossing Manor

Dappled Berms—
The Garden of Scott VanderHamm

DOVER PLAINS
LOSSING MANOR

📷 | ♿ partial | 🖋

Hours: 10 a.m. to 4 p.m.

The story of the garden at Lossing Manor is one of rescue, along with its house.

A prosperous farm when it was the home of prominent Victorian historian Benson Lossing, the property suffered a long subsequent decline, the lot of too many among upstate New York's treasure trove of eighteenth- and nineteenth-century houses. Before redemption, the garden had languished as a rural equipment dump.

Hedges and boxwoods form symmetrical axes that follow the unusual geometry of the 1806 house, observing Russell Page's dictum that the straight line is a natural complement to plant forms. Within those borders, North American native flowers predominate. Species continue to change, adapting to unusual shifts in weather conditions and the challenge of gardening in the region's heavy clay soils.

— TROWEL TALK—

We let the bees dictate which are the favorite plants.

— 👍 —

MILLBROOK
SQUIRREL HALL
♿ partial | 🌱
Hours: 10 a.m. to 4 p.m.

Squirrel Hall is a surprisingly amusing garden formally designed on a tiny village lot of less than one acre. The rectilinear layout emanates from a central axis defined by an allée of sixteen hornbeams with two niches. The garden is organized into a series of rooms with features usually reserved for larger properties.

The front lawn is small and enclosed by shrubs, low stone walls and driveway steel. Bordering the lawn is a newly created glade. This garden room features trees, shrubs, perennials, grasses, ferns, and bulbs all selected for their interest and suitability for a "wild garden."

A brick walkway through boxwood hedges leads you past the front door to an antique wrought iron gate. Through the gate and down the steps one enters the sunken garden. Here, mammoth hostas, statuary, shrubs, and antique iron seating surround a fountain.

Walking north across the gravel and up the steps leads to a pavilion terrace and

dining courtyard. There one finds more stonework and a massive fireplace. Walk a few more paces east, up three stairs to view and stroll the allée.

Two parterres are east of the allée; an 80-foot long x 16-inch wide yellow-leaf-plant border sits beyond. The apiary on the eastern border is guarded by "Fred," a grand archer. The petite orchard is to the west, and "le shed," a neoclassic folly, resides to the north.

Two entrances, one to the west and one to the east, lead to a woodland stroll featuring hemlocks, shade-loving perennials and shrubs, and "the bungalow."

POUGHKEEPSIE
DAPPLED BERMS—THE GARDEN OF SCOTT VANDERHAMM
📷 | ♿ partial
Hours: 10 a.m. to 4 p.m.

The garden is situated on a one-acre property within a 1950s (IBM-era) suburban community. As a result of the mature trees that dominate the grounds, a shade perennial garden was created and cultivated over 24 seasons of weekend gardening.

The assembled collection of plants, spread throughout numerous beds and man-made berms, relies heavily on the juxtapositions of color, texture, and form to bring interest and natural beauty to the garden.

One of the highlights of the garden is the collection of more than 378 different hosta cultivars numbering more than 643 specimens, all labeled for ease of identification. The garden will host a pop-up plant sale with Adams Fairacre Farms.

Dappled Berms is one of 25 gardens featured in the recently published book by Linda O'Keefe, *Inside Outside: A Sourcebook of Inspired Garden Rooms*.

GARDEN EXTRAS

Adams Fairacre Farms will be on site selling plants during this Open Day.

— TROWEL TALK—

I am a collector at heart, which is why hostas, with their various cultivars/ varieties numbering in the thousands, and the possibility of acquiring many of them appealed to me. I now have some 378 different cultivars.

Sometimes having a clever imaginative name is enough of an incentive for me to purchase a new hosta. Hosta 'Tickle Me Pink' is an example of a hosta whose name initially drew me to the plant but whose physical characteristics (beautiful golden yellow leaves with reddish/ pink petioles) are truly rewarding and a stand-out in the garden.

— 👍 —

STANFORDVILLE

UPLANDS FARM—ZIBBY & JIM TOZER

📷 | ♿

Hours: 10 a.m. to 2 p.m.

Uplands Farm includes a range of gardens in an Arcadian setting. Of special interest is the circular Romantic Garden, with its forget-me-nots, bleeding hearts, blue trapezoidal loveseats, and blue Moorish gate, all by Madison Cox.

The white gate, with its Chippendale-style latticework and its ball and chain, was designed by Charles Stick of Virginia. The Pool Folly, which was inspired by the teahouse at Kykuit, has latticed walls, pagoda lanterns, and an eternity gate. Between two large paddocks, there are arches covered with 'William Baffin' roses, under which nepeta and lavender create a path to a meadow.

The Playhouse and the Tennis Cottage have their own charming gardens. The main garden is a 70-foot herbaceous border filled with flowering perennials, grasses, Alberta spruces, topiaries, and shrubs.

Other gardens dot the larger property of rolling hills, grand old trees, a lush meadow of rye, and paddocks with miniature horses, Babydoll miniature sheep, miniature donkeys, Belted Galloway cows, and two long-haired Myotonic goats.

Delaware County

Saturday, July 9

Cynthia & Charles Bonnes

Henderson Hollow Farm—
Mermer Blakeslee & Eric Hamerstrom

ANDES

CYNTHIA & CHARLES BONNES

📷 | ♿ partial

Hours: 10 a.m. to 4 p.m.

Our garden is on a hillside facing the western Catskills, with four ponds descending toward the mountain view.

Around the house and large barn, part of a former dairy farm, are several formal garden spaces defined by native stone walls. They include a perennial border, a fountain terrace, and a vegetable garden. An allée of Japanese lilacs ascends the hillside, and informal plantings edge two of the ponds and a connecting stream.

Visitors are welcome to bring a blanket and picnic on the lawn or hike the trails on the property.

ROSCOE

HENDERSON HOLLOW FARM—MERMER BLAKESLEE & ERIC HAMERSTROM

📷 | ♿ partial | 🖋

Hours: 10 a.m. to 4 p.m.

Our garden began in 1990 on this defunct farm, taking its form from a dry streambed running down the hillside. The beds are dense, deep, and layered, and the plants are encouraged to retain some of their wildness, often forming drifts from selfsown seedlings.

The stonework is both old and ongoing: a stone bridge, hand-hewn flagstones, stone steps snaking through a swampy meadow. There's rusty metal too. Antique trucks and farm equipment are settled about, and an iron footbridge crosses the streambed.

The garden was featured in *Garden Design* magazine. The house, barns, and front porch are open to all our visitors.

— TROWEL TALK—

Thirty-five years ago when I was a single mom living in a tiny farmhouse, my mother gave me six red pelargoniums she had left over after doing her window boxes. I planted them in the dirt on each side of the front door. From that moment on, I was hooked.

I was a gardener. Even though I don't like red pelargoniums at all, I still find myself touching their leaves on my way by in a nursery. A gesture of recognition.

— 👍 —

Eastern Long Island

Saturday, July 9

The Landcraft Garden Foundation

Previti/Gumpel Garden

Entwood Garden

Garden of Arlene Bujese

BRIDGEHAMPTON

ENTWOOD GARDEN

📷 | ♿

Hours: 10 a.m. to 4 p.m.

Entwood is a seven-acre, parklike walking garden developed over 25 years from a flat potato field into a series of garden rooms, expansive views, specimen plants and trees, and features intended to make it difficult for adults and children to stay inside by providing a sense of peace, wonder, and fun.

Entering through an intimate, densely planted, English-style cottage flower garden, the visitor proceeds under an arbor past the owner's 1860 cottage to view a small, Japanese-style garden and koi pond. A second koi pond lies ahead hidden by a grove of cedars of Lebanon.

Crossing north through the pond on stones set in the water, the visitor enters a large arboretum of unusual cultivars of magnolia, dogwood, sweetgum, Japanese maple, redbud, dove (handkerchief) trees, conifers, and many others. From shaded paths and shade gardens around the perimeter, views reveal a contoured landscape, a gazebo in the distance, and two large ponds.

Looking down from the bridge crossing the first, you notice a wide variety of mature koi, a few of which can be hand fed if you request some koi food from Ed, who has designed and maintained these ponds. Past the bridge, you will approach the gazebo which is set in a circle of maples and surrounded by a secret path intended to delight those young at heart.

Turning right you step onto a zigzag bridge through the "monkey jungle," to the back entrance to the garden. Turning right on the gravel driveway, you will pass dogwood and rhododendron shaded by native black cherry and red cedar.

Following the driveway, you will see a rock garden behind an orchard on your right, with steps leading up to a golf tee, which provides the highest vantage point for the garden. A brief stroll downhill brings you to another large pond with even more colorful koi and most importantly by this time, a sitting area.

From there, paths lead through shade gardens, past a swimming pool, to the last of the koi ponds, and back to your starting point.

📷 Photos permitted   ♿ Partially accessible   **NEW** garden or section   🌱 Nature-friendly

EAST HAMPTON
GARDEN OF ARLENE BUJESE

📷

Hours: 10 a.m. to 4 p.m.

Situated on a sloping half-acre, the landscape comprises four rooms. A flower garden bordered by evergreens surrounds a goldfish pond at the rear of the house. Brick walkways weave throughout.

The front property is terraced into three levels, each with evergreen backdrops to create a "green" environment in winter. More than 20 sculptures are strategically placed around the property, including large works by William King, Hans Van de Bovenkamp, Alfonso Ossorio, Dennis Leri, Arline Wingate, James de Martis, and Calvin Albert.

Favored trees are flowering fruit specimens, conifers, and deciduous trees and shrubs, including a variety of hydrangeas.

The garden has been personally created and maintained by the curator/art dealer over a period of 25 years, with the aim of offering a meditative "walk around sit here and there" environment for all seasons.

PREVITI/GUMPEL GARDEN

📷

Hours: 10 a.m. to 4 p.m.

This garden is a series of rooms. Numerous outdoor sculptures by the owners are scattered throughout.

Paths wind through cedar groves past casual lawns and plantings. There is a sun garden with stone terraces and fountain, a cool and restful shade garden, and a fire pit area.

Go through Pop's Garden to the tented dining area, then to the arbor and two artist's studios, which will be open for viewing, one at ground level and one accessed by a stair tower. Move past the games lawn to the pool area, where you can rest in the shaded pergola at the end of the patio.

MATTITUCK
THE LANDCRAFT GARDEN FOUNDATION
📷 | ♿ | 🖋

Hours: 10 a.m. to 4 p.m.

In 2020, garden owners Dennis Schrader and Bill Smith formed the Landcraft Garden Foundation, a 501(c)(3) not-for-profit foundation. The Landcraft Garden Foundation is dedicated to inspiring, educating, and promoting gardening, horticulture and the preservation of our natural environment.

Our mission is to provide a horticulturally diverse garden that offers knowledge of the plant world and acts as a laboratory for experimenting with horticultural techniques, plant diversity, breeding, and design. Ultimately our goal is to provide the experience of delight that gardens bring to people throughout the world.

Set in the heart of the North Fork's wine region, this four-plus-acre public garden surrounds a restored 1840s farmhouse. In 2008, the house went through a major renovation and the gardens and terraces surrounding it have since been redesigned. The deck, porches, and stone terraces are filled with hundreds of container plantings. There are many perennial and mixed shrub borders throughout the garden that can be accessed by numerous winding paths. Garden rooms, hedged in by hornbeam and boxwood, feature various themed gardens within.

Additionally, there is a vegetable/herb garden, a formal knot garden, several bog plantings, meadow gardens, and a woodland shade area. The garden also features rustic arbors, trellises, stone walls, and a tiki hut that contains a collection of exotic plants.

The newest meadow garden surrounds the "Ruin"—a subterranean stone grotto partially covered with a sedum green roof. The three roundels located in the eastern part of the garden are made from locust wood harvested from the property. The roundels support climbing roses and seasonal exotic vines and are underplanted with a collection of shade-loving plants.

There are many sitting areas to enjoy the views and a natural clay pond with stream and bridge, and other smaller ponds for waterlilies and papyrus. Many of the plantings throughout contain tropicals, subtropicals, tender perennials, and annuals. There are a handful of hardy palms and a large grove of *Musa basjoo*, the hardy banana. The Mediterranean garden, which has collections of subtropical fruits, also contains the bee yard.

The house and gardens are encircled by ten acres of rehabilitated meadows with mowed paths for viewing native plants and wildlife. The meadow contains grasses, perennials, and shrubs that provide a habitat for deer, fox, groundhogs, rabbits, box turtles, wild turkeys, and many other birds and insects.

GARDEN EXTRAS

10 a.m. to 4 p.m. Plant sale.

Eastern Long Island

Saturday, July 16

CUTCHOGUE

CONNI CROSS GARDEN DESIGNER

📷 | ♿ partial

Hours: 10 a.m. to 2 p.m.

This is a 23-year-old garden on approximately five acres. It is three-quarters shade garden with light, sandy soil, designed by garden designer Conni Cross.

An unusual solar house is surrounded by a tufa garden featuring dwarf and miniature conifers and alpines. Look for a waterfall, four ponds, an aviary and barnyard, beautiful stonework, a children's playhouse, natural-style pool, rare plants, lush gardens, and many other unusual garden features.

SOUTHOLD

MAYFIELD

📷 | ♿

Hours: 10 a.m. to 4 p.m.

This lovely expanded cape is sited on 3.5 acres. It includes a pool and outdoor kitchen, and was originally designed by Conni Cross.

A cabana, charming vegetable garden, orchard, and expansive views of woodlands, meadow, and adjacent vineyard complete the picturesque setting.

Mr. Di Maggio received his certificate degree in Landscape Design at the New York Botanical Garden several years ago and continues to collaborate with Ms. Cross on ongoing projects. Both Mr. and Mrs. Di Maggio are very interested in all aspects of design as is evident in both the house and garden.

Columbia County

Sunday, July 24

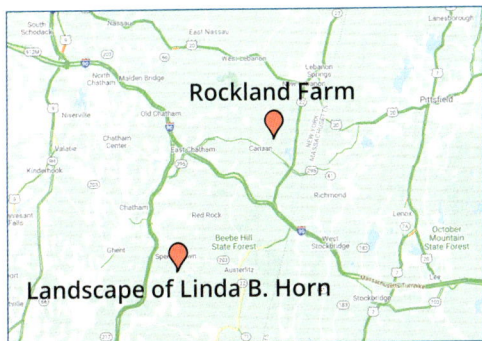

CANAAN
ROCKLAND FARM

📷 | ♿ partial | 🖋

Hours: 10 a.m. to 4 p.m.

The garden comprises a variety of areas that flow one from another over about ten acres of our property. A 450-foot-long rock ledge runs parallel to the front drive and is topped by a dry garden in silver, gray, and blue, with a thyme walk along one edge.

Raised areas on the west side of the house feature exotic and tropical plants, many in containers. Behind the house is a sequence of garden rooms: a lavender garden contained within a raised hornbeam hedge; a perennial garden in pastels surrounding our pool; a water garden, fronted by a white garden and with a shade garden and rhododendron walk behind; a hot sundial and rock garden; and a fenced vegetable and cutting garden.

From here, a hydrangea allée leads to either a lawn—with a seating area nestling within sweeps of perennials on one side and a mixed garden containing a faux-bois set on the other—or to steps up to a small, wooded knoll, where paths offer intermittent views of the garden and the hills beyond and connect a folly, a pet pergola, a water feature, and a stumpery.

Where the garden meets open land, a Tim Prentice kinetic piece snakes its way through the trees, and a massive carved bench in a pine grove overlooks a three-acre lake in the middle-distance.

Our garden has been featured in magazines and in the books *Great Gardens of the Berkshires*, *Private Edens*, and *Private Gardens of the Hudson Valley*.

— TROWEL TALK—

We started this garden with almost no previous experience and have spent 30 years making all the mistakes possible!

— 👍 —

SPENCERTOWN
LANDSCAPE OF LINDA B. HORN

📷 | ♿ partial | 🖋

Hours: 10 a.m. to 2 p.m.

The restoration of my landscape has been the goal for fifteen years of living here after a move from Chicago. There are four restored ecosystems: wetlands, waterfall, domestic area of native grasses, and woodland.

The last section of restoration was started last fall with eliminating dead trees and then new seeding. This year goldenrod was weed-wacked and new trees planted.

The landscape was featured in the September 2017 issue of *New York Cottages & Gardens* with a five-page spread. Native restoration workshops have been held here through the Columbia Land Conservancy, Spencertown Academy, and Berkshire Botanical Garden.

Eastern Long Island

Saturday, July 30

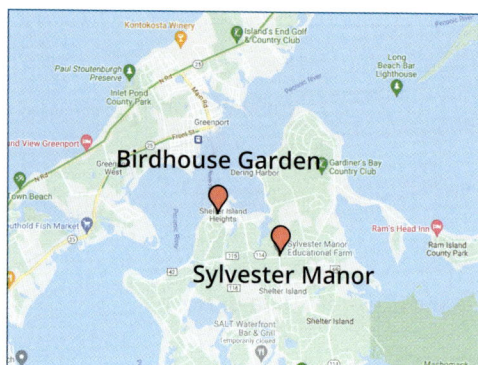

SHELTER ISLAND HEIGHTS
BIRDHOUSE GARDEN

📷 | 🖋

Hours: 10 a.m. to 4 p.m.

Tim Purtell's garden in Shelter Island Heights mixes trees, shrubs, grasses, and flowering perennials with the goal of attracting and supporting wildlife such as bees, butterflies, and birds.

There's no lawn. Instead, the eighteen-year-old landscape is planted predominantly with natives that provide color, texture, and fragrance from March to November. Aside from the pleasures of its natural form, which mimics wilder places but on a small scale, the garden also serves as a model for how home landscapes can help reverse the decline in insect populations.

— TROWEL TALK—

I became interested in plants as a college student. My first garden was an eye-catching combination of cosmos

---

📷 Photos permitted   ♿ Partially accessible   **NEW** garden or section   🖋 Nature-friendly

and poppies planted from seed. A great success! The next year I planted the same seeds and ... nothing happened. I quickly learned a gardening basic: seeds need rain or supplemental water.

I moved on to daylilies, then fell in love with native plants, which have become my passion. Because I have dry, sandy soil, I can't grown many plants (like cardinal flower) that need constant or reasonable moisture. Fortunately, many of my favorite plants (like butterfly weed) prefer dry, sandy soil.

My favorite garden tool is a trowel that belonged to my partner's father.

— 👍 —

SHELTER ISLAND
NEW

**PRESERVATION PARTNER
NONPROFIT PARTNER
SYLVESTER MANOR**

SYLVESTER
MANOR

The lands of Shelter Island's Sylvester Manor were once the hunting, fishing and farming ground of the Indigenous Manhansett People.

The site known today as Sylvester Manor was home to eleven generations of Sylvester descendants. Gifted to the nonprofit organization Sylvester Manor Educational Farm in 2014, the 235-acre historic site is the most intact slaveholding plantation remnant north of Virginia.

Over the past 400 years, Sylvester Manor has been a provisioning plantation, an 18th-century Enlightenment-era farm, and a pioneering food industrialist's summer estate.

Today Sylvester Manor includes the 1737 Manor House, an early colonial formal garden remnant, majestic native and specimen tree groves, creekfront and wetlands, numerous outbuildings, a 19th-century restored windmill, a family cemetery and Afro-Indigenous Burial Ground, and a vegetable and livestock farming operation.

Sylvester Manor was designated a district of national significance on the National Register of Historic Places in 2015.

Hours: The grounds and walking trails are open to the public daily from dawn to dusk, February through December. For more information, please visit www.sylvestermanor.org

Admission: Free. Donations welcome.

DIGGING DEEPER

see next page

**Rooted in Place: Unearthing the
Stories of Sylvester Manor**
Donnamarie Barnes & Sara Gordon
Saturday, July 30, 10 a.m. to 11:30 a.m.

Sylvester Manor
$30 Garden Conservancy members
$40 General

Join Donnamarie Barnes, Director of History and Heritage at Sylvester Manor, and planner Sara Gordon, for a walking tour of the core of this unique northern plantation remnant, owned by a single family of European descent from 1651-2014.

Donnamarie and Sara will describe the challenges inherent in this cultural landscape of great historic significance, where interpretive and restoration opportunities are weighted with a wealth of archaeological and archival materials, extant and yet to be unearthed; and a dearth of references to those who toiled here.

The tour will include the 2-acre formal garden whose establishment is believed to date back to the 1650s, and a burial ground of indentured, enslaved and free people of color where study is underway in partnership with indigenous descendants of Long Island's First Peoples.

Photo courtesy of Sylvestor Manor

Dutchess County

Sunday, July 31

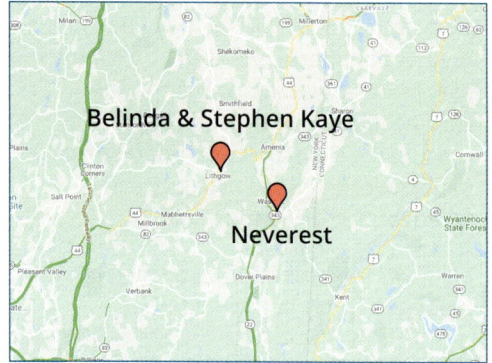

★ There is another garden open on this date in nearby Litchfield County, CT: **Sculpturedale, Kent, CT**
For garden descriptions and details, see page 78.

MILLBROOK

BELINDA & STEPHEN KAYE

📷 | ♿ | 🖋
Hours: 10 a.m. to 4 p.m.

Recently we were able to purchase adjacent property with a pond we'd overlooked for 45 years. Dredging the pond of 100 years of silt was the first improvement we made.

Then aquatic plants went in, including native lotus, which are now rapidly taking over. The shrubby willows we planted around the perimeter attract innumerable birds. The addition of the pond greatly expands the scope of a garden that was originally designed around a lily pool and Carpenter Gothic potting shed at the entryway to our house. Here, an informal

---

📷 Photos permitted   ♿ Partially accessible   **NEW** garden or section   🖋 Nature-friendly

parterre is planted with ornamental vegetables, annuals, and perennials.

Over the years we've added a mini-rock garden/trough collection at the side of the house and a fountain by a local sculptor by the back porch. A shrubbery on a berm between the road and front lawn also evolved to screen out noise and dust. We continue to tweak and upgrade this wild area leading down to a playhouse and a mowed path around the pond.

— TROWEL TALK—

My favorite plant has changed over the years, but right now it's just plain old *Phlox paniculata*. Where I grew up there was a whole hedge of very old white and/or hideous magenta phlox but the perfume was tremendous.

Now there are so many new, gorgeous colors and they all look great together. Perhaps the perfume isn't as good as the old varieties, but it's still the wonderful smell of high summer.

— 👍 —

WASSAIC
NEVEREST
📷 | 🌱
Hours: 10 a.m. to 4 p.m.

Neverest has evolved over sixteen years with the help of our neighbor and garden designer Marsha Kaufman.

We found an old house with a patio, long stone wall, hemlock row, and mostly weeds. The site is shady and steeply sloped. We built stone walls and steps to terrace the land, and added a path with native woodland plants.

Each spring we added perennial beds, then two fountains, a deck, fence, gravel courtyard, bluestone walk, entry garden, screen porch, large vegetable patch (raised beds over concrete slab), and most recently a screen house to protect the berries. The plants selected feature chartreuse and purple, though there are lots of hydrangeas and a rain garden across the road.

Just retired; I expect we'll have new projects.

— TROWEL TALK—

We bought the house nineteen years ago having zero experience gardening. Luckily next door was a garden designer, Marsha Kaufman, who has patiently taught us over many projects. She helped us select plants, which we bravely installed and maintained.

Leo, an architect, obsessed about hardscape (paths & stone walls) and color (much purple & chartreuse).

We retired three years ago, and Ken has expanded the vegetable garden three times. He cooks or cans everything we grow, and we just built a root cellar. Then maybe a greenhouse. Leo is responsible for the cutting garden and its contents.

We put in four trees last summer (oak, sweet-gum, tulip, and catalpa), three fruits a year prior.

— 👍 —

Dutchess County

Saturday, August 6

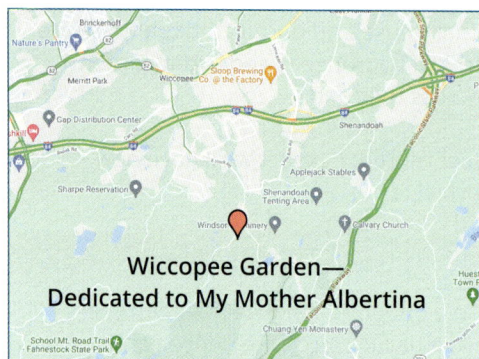

Wiccopee Garden—
Dedicated to My Mother Albertina

★ There are four additional gardens open on this date in nearby Putnam County and Westchester County, NY:

Rumford Hall
Rivermere on the Hudson
The Greneker Retreat
Garden of Bernard Marquez & Tim Fish
For garden description and details,
see page 186.

HOPEWELL JUNCTION

WICCOPEE GARDEN—DEDICATED TO MY MOTHER ALBERTINA

◉ | ♿ partial | **NEW**
Hours: 10 a.m. to 4 p.m.

Situated on Shenandoah Mountain, the downward sloping nature of our property naturally provides a lovely wooded berm that creates a sunken sanctuary, a sacred garden space designed with a sense of balance and harmony that instantly communicates a stillness, tranquility, and peace.

The famous poet Makoto Ooka tells us

Japanese Gardens "ask that you go beyond the garden spiritually, that you look at the garden not merely as an object but also as a path into the realm of Spirit."

To create an oasis of tranquil beauty that combines aesthetic pleasure with sacred, contemplative overtones, several elements are employed and can be found in this garden: STONE, WATER, SHADES OF GREEN (primarily found in evergreens), PLANTS, BAMBOO, MOSS COVERED STONE, and a device known as HIDE AND REVEAL so that every turn of the path shows something new.

At a certain point along the garden path the garden becomes a Japanese Hybrid. I leave behind the variety of red annuals and perennials with touches of yellow gold that I had chosen as the accent color and go "crazy" with color provided by more colorful annuals and perennials in other gardens.

One first encounters a rock garden along the driveway full of all splashes of color often provided by towering cosmos, Knock Out roses, mandevilla, euphorbia, and shasta daisies. There is a black nine-pot stand of interest filled with hibiscus of every color.

The Shed Garden adds interest and returns to the reds and golds of the Japanese Garden. To the left there is a golden Asian Lily Garden surrounded by a large Shade Garden, a Bleeding Heart Garden, an Epimedium Rubrum garden overlooked by a tall ornamental pom pom tree. The gardens outside the gate are also worthy of note, especially in the spring.

Putnam County
Saturday, August 6

Rumford Hall

BREWSTER

RUMFORD HALL

📷 | ♿ partial | 🌱

This garden host is presenting a Digging Deeper program August 27, see page 190.

Hours: 10 a.m. to 4 p.m.

Rumford Hall is a fifteen-acre property with mature plantings and monumental boulders in the foothills of the Appalachians. A stone table near the foxgloves is engraved with the date of the house—1879—and a smokehouse huddles under greenery in a courtyard garden with an old weathered door.

We have boxwood and roses, a plum allée, viburnum room, pergolas, orchard, vegetable garden, fernery, and a pool garden with succulents and grasses. Fences are lined with ninebark, honeysuckle, and tapestry hedges. The ruins on the hill are adjacent to a woodland garden enclosed by stone walls.

Visitors are encouraged to follow the trails that we have signposted in the hills; the forest has a footbridge and a mountain upholstered in moss.

Westchester County

Saturday, August 6

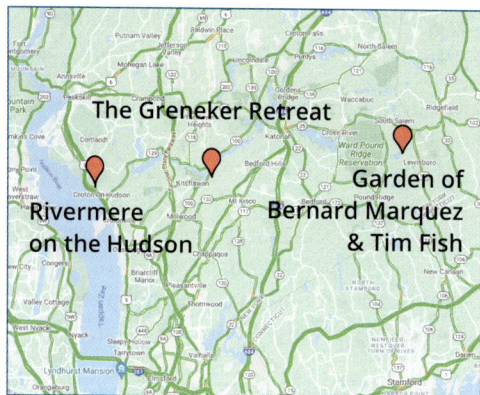

BEDFORD HILLS

GARDEN OF PHILLIS WARDEN

📷 | 🖋

This garden is open twice this year:
June 18 and August 6

Hours: 10 a.m. to 4 p.m.

This garden of many facets includes perennial borders, three water gardens, a formal vegetable garden, wildflower garden, fern garden, marsh garden, a tree platform overlooking the marshlands, a woodland walk, a hidden garden, and a formal croquet court.

The garden extends over seven acres, the back four acres of which are a study in what deer do not eat.

CROTON ON HUDSON

RIVERMERE ON THE HUDSON

📷 | 🕴 partial | 🖋
Hours: 10 a.m. to 4 p.m.

The Rivermere estate overlooks the Hudson River at its widest point and has its own microclimate. The garden offers several vantage points for peaceful reflection and meditation with serene river views: the water garden, the gazebo overlooking the stream-fed duck pond, and the lawn.

A newly planted vineyard with cold hardy grapes is fed by natural water from the pond. A pergola made of natural materials provides a setting for farm-to-table eating in the vineyard. The waterfall garden contains native plants, tropical plants, ayurvedic herbs, and vegetables with medicinal properties.

A small experimental rooftop garden for greens sits atop the peacock house. Flowering trees, daffodils, and seasonal plantings round out the collection.

MOUNT KISCO

THE GRENEKER RETREAT

📷
Hours: 10 a.m. to 4 p.m.

This 1925 home in Mount Kisco is one of five designed and built by Lillian Greneker, whose works are now curated in Harvard's Arthur and Elizabeth Schlesinger Library on the History of Women in America. Her husband, C. P. Greneker, was then director of publicity for the Shubert Theater.

This two-acre property has meandering woodchip trails, two streams, seven small bridges, two "secret" gardens, and a wonderful grove of 24 'Heritage' river birch trees.

📷 Photos permitted   🕴 Partially accessible   **NEW** garden or section   🖋 Nature-friendly

It includes a natural fern garden and other beautiful perennial gardens, created by the owners, that contain astilbe, roses, statuary, a kitchen stone garden, and other whimsical features. The home, on this undulating property, is enchanting.

— TROWEL TALK—

Favorites: astilbe, clethra, bottlebrush buckeye; never had luck with cosmos.

First garden: a small backyard vegetable garden as a child.

— 👍 —

SOUTH SALEM
GARDEN OF BERNARD MARQUEZ & TIM FISH
📷 | ♿ partial
Hours: 10 a.m. to 4 p.m.

The garden, recently featured in *Garden Design* and *Westchester Home* magazines, consists of several garden rooms that flow into each other on different levels.

Existing natural stone outcrops accentuate many of the spaces. Garden compositions utilize conifers and broadleaf evergreens, including a variety of boxwoods, some uncommon in the Northeast. A koi pond, considerable stone work, and views of Pound Ridge Reservation and Lake Kitchawan are highlights.

Annuals, perennials, artifacts, water features, and containers complete the experience. The gardens make creative use of what was difficult terrain.

Columbia County
Sunday, August 14

★ There is another garden open on this date in nearby Greene County, NY: **Abeel House Prairie, Catskill, NY** *For garden descriptions and details, see page 189.*

CLAVERACK
PETER BEVACQUA & STEPHEN KING
📷 | ♿ partial | 🌿
Hours: 10 a.m. to 4 p.m.

We decided to open our garden in August again this year as visitors seemed to really enjoy seeing it in this later season. (In the past, we have always opened our garden in early June.)

In August the summer garden is in full sway with lilies and phlox in bloom in the various borders, and the hydrangea walk is beginning to blossom. Towering forms of *Sylphium perfoliatum*, *Sanguisorbia tenuifolia*, and *Rudbeckia lacinata* command attention in the yew-enclosed Sunk Garden, and in the Nearly Native Garden (the wild garden where the beehives are kept) a sea of Queen Anne's lace, *Rudbeckia triloba*, and the wands of various grasses will prevail.

The garden has been described as magical and "a private world." This may be because of its division into many rooms where one space unfolds upon the next, each with its own sense of individuality and charm, but always with an eye for structure, form, and texture.

The garden has been twice featured in the *New York Times* as well as in *Gardens of the Hudson Valley* (Monacelli Press), *Private Gardens of the Hudson Valley* (Monacelli Press), *Berkshire Living* magazine, *Rose and Ivy* magazine, and *Gardenista*. Bevacqua is a featured designer in *Garden Design Masterclass* (Rizzoli), the soon to be released *My American Garden* (Timber Press) and most recently in *New York Cottages and Gardens*.

HUDSON
VERSAILLES ON HUDSON

📷 | 🖋

Hours: 10 a.m. to 4 p.m.

We wanted to create a garden that looked as if it had been planted when the house was built, in 1901.

The entire land formation presented a real challenge; from the house to the bottom of the garden was a steep 30-foot drop. We needed to create an elegant way to move through the garden, so we carefully designed multi-level stone patios and easy-access stairways to guide you down to the fountain.

We chose a most unexpected plan that would take advantage of the dramatic views of the river, hills, and sunsets. By turning the garden on its axis, we created

the illusion of a massive property with grand, sweeping lawns; long, flowing hydrangea and hornbeam hedges; and architectural boxwood balls. Our fountain and the hornbeam curve are the highlights of this quiet garden, complete with fish, frogs, and water plants.

In the spring and early summer, the garden is predominately green and white, and it turns ever more pink as the summer progresses. In the winter, this garden makes an equally strong statement due to its framing by many evergreens.

Versailles on Hudson offers ever-changing vistas as you walk around the property. From the upper and lower patios, the grand porch, the four staircases, the long lawns and the bubbling fountain, this special garden always delights and soothes the soul.

📷 Photos permitted   🧎 Partially accessible   **NEW** garden or section   🖋 Nature-friendly

Greene County
Sunday, August 14

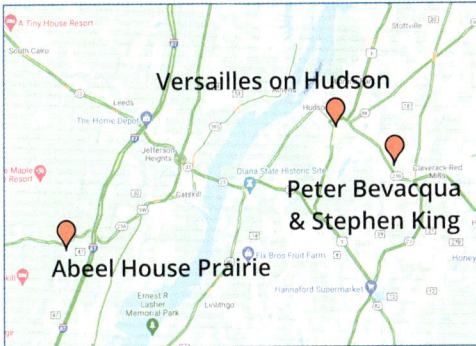

★ There are two additional gardens open on this date in nearby Columbia County, NY:

Peter Bevacqua & Stephen King
Versailles on Hudson
For garden descriptions and details,
see page 187.

CATSKILL
ABEEL HOUSE PRAIRIE

📷 | 🖊

Hours: 10 a.m. to 4 p.m.

The Abeel House Prairie is four acres of wildflowers and native grasses. It blankets a small holler in a secluded valley next to an eighteenth-century Dutch stone house once owned by David Abeel, an early settler in the Hudson Valley.

The owners planted the prairie ten years ago, a decision they regretted almost immediately. Apparently they thought the prairie would be a low-maintenance solution to a brush-covered hillside that was too steep to mow. In hindsight, they say it would've been easier to cut the brush weekly with a pair of hand shears. They learned that establishing

and maintaining a wildflower prairie is a nonstop battle against invasives.

Today, however, the results are magnificent. The prairie is full of more than two dozen varieties of flowers and grasses. Bordered by a small brook and bisected by a short hiking trail, it is an easy walk. While strolling through the prairie you may hear a noticeable buzz—a collective celebration of bees that visit here for one of the finest dining experiences of their lives.

— TROWEL TALK—

I know the names of more weeds than I do flowers. I couldn't tell you the difference between a bougainvillea and a bluebell. In fact, I'm not even sure "bluebell" is a flower at all (although it sounds like it should be, if it isn't).

Truth is—I have less gardening experience than anyone ever in the history of Open Days. Yet I've been told by Master Gardeners that my prairie is remarkable. Go figure.

Come see what hard work and dumb luck can accomplish.

— 👍 —

Putnam County
Saturday, August 27

Rumford Hall

explored with reference to William Morris designs and the artistic origins of the movement.

The garden integrates both formal and naturalistic elements, implementing Arts & Crafts hallmarks such as pergolas, garden rooms, and stone walls. Concept, color, scale, and plant selection will be considered, with an emphasis as well on site considerations and fitting the garden to the contours of the land.

Photo by Jeanne Farewell

BREWSTER
RUMFORD HALL

📷 | ♿ partial | 🖋

DIGGING DEEPER

Developing an Arts & Crafts Garden
Jeanne Farewell
Saturday, August 27, 3 p.m. to 5 p.m.

Rumford Hall
$30 Garden Conservancy members
$40 General

An Arts & Crafts–style home built in 1879 is the inspiration for Jeanne Farewell's garden, which will be

---

Westchester County

Saturday, August 27

★ There are three additional gardens open on this date in nearby Fairfield and Litchfield Counties, CT:

InSitu, Redding, CT
Old Barlow's Carriage House and Garden, Ridgefield, CT
Maywood Gardens, Bridgewater, CT
For garden description and details, see pages 80 and 82.

NORTH SALEM

PERRIN GARDEN

📷 | 🖎
Hours: 10 a.m. to 3 p.m.

A curved driveway partially lined with bottlebrush buckeye and fragrant sumac leads to a rise revealing an English-style country house bordered by an apple orchard to one side, a woodland garden on another side, and a grass meadow in the front.

Visitors pass through a series of beech- and yew-lined courtyards to get to the front door. In the rear, formal gardens

surrounded by stone walls contain mature perennials and provide lovely views of preserved land in the distance. A small brick and flagstone area surrounded by perennials offers an intimate spot for dining under a sweet gum tree.

Below the formal gardens, a transition garden combines native grasses with blueberry bushes and gives way to a wildflower meadow. The property continues to evolve in its incorporation of more and more native plants to provide a habitat for wildlife and a more sustainable landscape for the future.

— TROWEL TALK—

I am committed to using more and more native plants in my garden and enjoy learning and experimenting with what works. My garden is my sanctuary where I go to get away from this crazy world and enjoy the glories of nature.

I believe that to experience the outdoors is important to our mental health and well-being. I hope that more and more people will recognize this and help preserve our beautiful Earth for future generations.

— 👍 —

Eastern Long Island

Saturday, September 17

Marshouse—
Garden of Edwina von Gal

EAST HAMPTON

MARSHOUSE—

GARDEN OF EDWINA VON GAL

📷 | ♿ partial | 🌿

Hours: 10 a.m. to 4 p.m.

My garden is named Marshouse (pronounced Marsh House) because my house is literally in a salt marsh, on stilts. I love the marsh because I am not allowed to touch it. The other, upland side, is where I garden.

The garden is a series of ecosytems, with a meadow at either end, which I have been working on since I moved here in 2003. It was only a year ago (spring 2021) that I finally put deer fencing around about half of it, and now, I am going wild filling it with all the flowering native plants that the deer have eaten out of all our Hamptons wild places. It is very much a work in process, but it always will be. It is my place to experiment; to test ideas about growing native plants, creating habitat, and managing biomass before I try them on my clients, or recommend them to others.

This is where I meet my own commitment to the initiative we recently launched: www.234birds.org. This makes for a lot going on. The four-plus acres contain a variety of gardens in various stages of progress: meadows, meadow-like borders, a woodland, and a moss garden. I do not remove any biomass from the property, so I have explored ingenious ways to use it: log walls from invasive trees, Hugelkulture piles, hay stacks of the meadow cuttings, plus lots of composting.

After all of that, you can, like me, relax with a visit to the marsh over a small boardwalk that leads out to Accabonac Harbor through a magical hummock.

> ## — TROWEL TALK—
>
> After 50 years of gardening I am looking for plants that are not looking for me to fuss over them. That usually means natives.
>
> Beginning gardeners are generally happy to hear me tell them I have killed more plants than they ever will. Plants that are willing give their lives to help us know them better.
>
> — 👍 —

DIGGING DEEPER

**Designing for Nature-Keeping:
A Garden's Commitment without
Losing Its Looks**
Edwina von Gal
Saturday, September 17,
4:30 p.m. to 6 p.m.

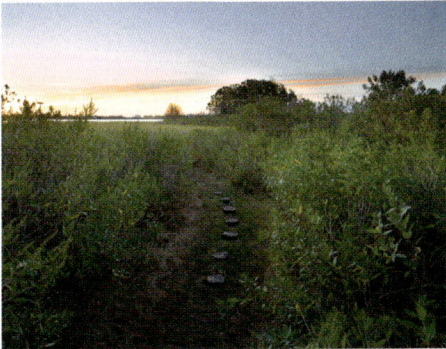

Marshouse—Garden of Edwina von Gal
$30 Garden Conservancy members
$40 General

Join me in a tour of the property
with a discussion about the joys and
challenges of making and keeping a
commitment to toxic-free/nature-based
gardening—how to let nature play a
role and learn to love letting go and
delighting in the results. Talk native
plants and animals with as many local
experts as I can muster.

We will end up with wine and hors
d'oeuvres on my deck overlooking
Accabonac Harbor.

Photo by Allan Pollock-Morris

Ulster County
Saturday, September 17

The Garden of Ann Krupp

SAUGERTIES
ANN KRUPP BRYAN

DIGGING DEEPER

**"When Every Leaf is a Flower": Form
and Color in the Autumn Garden**
Ann Krupp
Saturday, September 17,
5 p.m. to 7 p.m.

The Garden of Ann Krupp
$30 Garden Conservancy members
$40 General

Expand your garden beyond blooms
using the color, structure, and texture
of plants. As a garden designer in the
mid-Hudson Valley, Ann Krupp will

📷 Photos permitted   ♿ Partially accessible   **NEW** garden or section   🌿 Nature-friendly

discuss how she designed, planted, and maintains her own garden to allow foliage to take center stage in sun and shade.

Photo by Ann Krupp Bryan

Westchester County
Saturday, September 17

West Lane Farm

★ There are three additional gardens open on this date in nearby Fairfield County, CT:
Sleepy Cat Farm, Greenwich, CT
Garden of Frances Palmer, Weston, CT
Prospect Gardens Westport, CT
For garden description and details, see page 88.

SOUTH SALEM
WEST LANE FARM

📷 | ➤

This garden is open twice this year: May 14 and September 17.

Hours: 10 a.m. to 5 p.m.

I began working with owner John Papa in 2018, providing design and consultation on land use for the 21-acre property.

Plans are in the works to create a sanctuary/farm that allows for innovative environmental land/farm use benefiting the community by combining arts and sciences with horticulture and education.
—Laura Tuttle Stabell

West Lane Farm has a balance of lawns and gardens, woodlands, and wetlands. Meadows create a tapestry of flowers utilized by the bees tended by beekeeper Tony Steger. Sculptures by Suzanne Benton have been installed in the main "community gathering" garden, designed by Laura Tuttle Stabell.

Areas for growing food, native, medicinal, cut flower, and pollinator plants have been started. Farmer Joe Alvarez's storage container LED farm is up and running, providing microgreens.

GARDEN EXTRAS

10 a.m. to 5 p.m. Sale of rare native plants, cut flowers, microgreens, honey, and candles.

📷 Photos permitted   ♿ Partially accessible   **NEW** garden or section   ➤ Nature-friendly

Dutchess County

Saturday, September 24

MILLBROOK

CLOVE BROOK FARM—CHRISTOPHER SPITZMILLER & ANTHONY BELLOMO

📷 | ♿ partial | 🖋

This garden is open twice this year: May 7 and September 24

Hours: 10 a.m. to 4 p.m.

The garden at Clove Brook Farm was started about seven years ago following a restoration of the historic Greek Revival farmhouse.

The garden has quickly grown into a series of interconnected spaces, beginning with a horseshoe-shaped garden near the house that is surrounded by a clipped hornbeam hedge and anchored by a dovecote. It's this garden where we have a spectacular show of tulips and sweetpeas in spring, followed by towering dahlias in late summer.

A few years ago another large garden "room" was added which centers on an oval

swimming pool and neoclassical style pool house. This garden is also bounded by a hornbeam hedge and includes perimeter beds filled with various herbaceous perennials which evolve throughout the growing season, starting with poppies in early spring, then peonies, roses, lilies, and finally dahlias.

Last year my partner, landscape architect Anthony Bellomo, designed and installed a large kitchen garden which we pack with various vegetables. We are both confirmed garden addicts, and in addition to the more formal garden spaces, continue to add informal and naturalistic plantings throughout the property. We've planted several mixed shrub borders studded with drifts of bulbs, embellished our existing orchard, and collected unique sculptures to establish focal points.

There is nothing more satisfying than tending and fostering a garden, and watching it develop and mature. It's all documented in *A Year at Clove Brook Farm* (Rizzoli, 2021, with foreword by Martha Stewart).

STANFORDVILLE

BEAR CREEK FARM

📷 | ♿ partial | 🖋
Hours: 10 a.m. to 4 p.m.

Acclaimed for flowers both nationally and globally, Bear Creek Farm is considered the premier flower farm in the Northeast.

Realizing nature's capacity to reduce stress and enhance overall wellness, the farm focuses on an innovative approach of integrating growing fields with living spaces.

Each of the meadows and multiple growing

areas has its own aesthetic. The dwellings are careful, award-winning restorations of historic architecture. Both gardens and farm areas are integrated together to form a homogenous feel to the property.

The property invites you through an artful stone-pillared entrance along a long curving driveway framed by lilies, red maples, and river birches. The 150-year-old farmhouse is surrounded by impressive trees, including a 350-year-old sycamore, one of the largest in Dutchess County, dressed with an apron of spirea, as well as towering Norway spruces and unusual dawn redwoods.

Wander among mature ninebark bushes framed by raspberry brambles, with an old trumpet vine and even older tractor-trailer converted to an over-sized flower box. Meander along pathways among crabapple, pear, and Katsura trees. There is a handmade stone grill and various pottery pieces from around the world.

The natural pond, bordered by Little Wappingers Creek, is surrounded by willow bushes and has a grape vine arbor. It is also home to budding patches of milkweed to attract monarch butterflies. A new addition opposite the pond is a mid-century modern pool house.

Of course surrounding everything are the flowers: hundreds of Japanese anemones, thousands of peonies, and acres and acres of dahlias. This eclectic property doesn't have a single description, but rather is filled with a wide range of delights and discoveries.

ELLEN PETERSEN

📷 | 🖋

Hours: 10 a.m. to 4 p.m.

I have been gardening here for 41 years, but, thanks to the help of Danielle Giulian, I continue to make changes, refining the design, renovating older plantings, and beginning new areas. One goal is to have interest every month of the year.

High summer is the start of the dahlias and phlox and other perennials. Our carefully assembled collection of plants includes more natives every year. I love finding interesting native cultivars like *Liquidambar* 'Slender Silhouette' but also enjoy the thrill of searching out exotic rarities.

A meadow of *Sporobolus heterolepsis* (prairie dropseed) frames "Windblown Couch," a sculpture by Vivian Beer. Robert Murray's "Willow" is next to the pond, and "Portal" by Carla Edwards will entice you to take the path up a little hill. There is a beautiful big Franklin blooming behind the house.

While I would definitely not call this a low-maintenance garden, we only occasionally water anything after the second year and fertilize only container plants. Compost suppresses weeds and feeds the soil without making it too rich. In spite of all the very tall perennials, we need very little staking.

The garden was included in Jane Garmey's book, *Private Gardens of the Hudson Valley*.

📷 Photos permitted   ♿ Partially accessible   **NEW** garden or section   🖋 Nature-friendly

Dutchess County

Saturday, October 29
Sunday, October 30

PAWLING
THE BRINE GARDEN—
DUNCAN & JULIA BRINE

📷 | 🖋

Hours: 1 p.m. to 5 p.m.

This naturalistic, six-acre garden connects diverse topographical areas of a former dairy farm.

The garden has an ecological approach; however, it's not purist. Mature native communities of shrubs and trees combine with select non-native plants. Meandering paths join off-site and on-site views.

Duncan Brine and his wife and partner, Julia, are the principal landscape designers at GardenLarge. He's an instructor of naturalistic landscape design at the New York Botanical Garden. Anne Raver, in the *New York Times*, wrote that the Brine Garden is "a dreamlike landscape." In 2010, on the occasion of the garden's twentieth anniversary, Doug Tallamy and his wife visited the Brines. Thomas Christopher recently interviewed Duncan on his podcast, "Growing Greener."

The garden is published in an array of books and magazines, including *Private Gardens of the Hudson Valley* and *Gardens of the Hudson Valley*. Open Day visitors receive a whole property plant list of 178 species. See www.gardenlarge.com for more.

Donald Pell Gardens - Phoenixville, PA
Photo by Donald Pell

Pennsylvania

PENNSYLVANIA

Bucks County
Sunday, May 15

★There are two additional gardens open on this date in nearby Essex County, NJ:
Claire's Meditation Garden, Mountclair, NJ
The Mountsier Garden, Nutley, NJ
For garden description and details, see page 132.

NEW HOPE
GARDENS AT HALF MOON

📷 | ♿ | 🖋

Hours: 10 a.m. to 4 p.m.

Garden owner is a nursery stock broker who also operates a small nursery specializing in grafted conifers. In calling on the trade, I was exposed to a wide variety of unusual trees and shrubs and fell easily into the habit of collecting them.

We purchased this property 40 years ago which included the stone farmhouse, a tenant house, and the ruins of a large barn, but other than a lovely old 'Suffruticosa' boxwood hedge, now gone, was almost completely devoid of any landscaping. Our gardens grew and evolved over the years and are now populated with those plants collected in my travels in combination with selections of other compatible trees and shrubs.

There is also a conifer garden which resulted from a long association with the Iseli Nursery in Oregon, and includes quite a few 40-year-old specimens blended with newer additions.

Throughout the property, keep an eye out for rare and unusual plants that are everywhere and can pop up unexpectedly! Deer found our hostas last year (about 200 of them) that had gone unmolested for years. This spring we replaced them all, changing the aspect of the garden considerably. We hope the garden will, in time, be more interesting and deer resistant, but we'll see!

— TROWEL TALK—

As an 81-year-old gardener I can no longer get down on my hands and knees to weed my gardens and instead use a long-handled Dutch push weeding device. It cuts weeds off below the surface and is fast and efficient.

— 👍 —

PAXSON HILL FARM

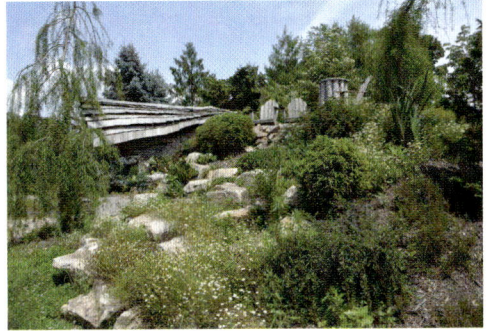

Hours: 10 a.m. to 4 p.m.

Nestled in scenic New Hope, Paxson Hill Farm encompasses 30 acres of imaginative landscapes sure to bring delight to avid gardeners and nature lovers alike.

Winding, naturalistic paths lead you through a variety of ever-evolving gardens inspired by world travels and a keen eye for design. You will find elaborate ponds, a large hedge maze to get lost in, a conifer garden, formal and "not so formal" gardens, and even a Hobbit House.

A true hidden gem and a perfect stop on a tour of Bucks County!

Photos by Bruce Gangawer

📷 Photos permitted   ♿ Partially accessible   **NEW** garden or section   ✒ Nature-friendly

Chester County
Saturday, June 25

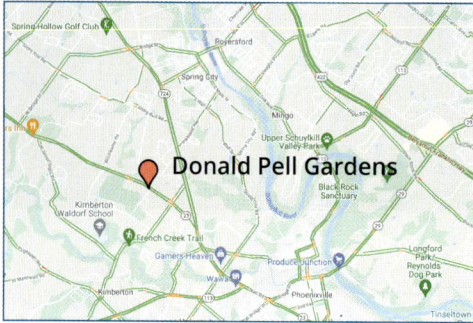

PHOENIXVILLE
DONALD PELL GARDENS

📷 | 🖋

Hours: 10 a.m. to 4 p.m.

Tour the private studio gardens of award-winning garden designer Donald Pell. Since 2008, Pell has been converting this fourteen-acre farm into a lush landscape of naturalistic gardens in the New American style.

The farmhouse, Oval, and woodland gardens focus on exploring the beauty of plants in defined spaces that create an experience of place.

Gravel pathways surrounding a historic stone farmhouse lead visitors through tall blocks of grasses and forbs, providing an intimate reaction to unique plants and novel combinations as they arrive at the rear natural-stone patio with sweeping views south.

Here, viewers overlook the Oval, where large-scale perennial plantings are laid out in block and intermingled compositions to mimic natural habitats while showcasing form, texture, and color.

Monolithic slab steps lead toward the grand American Pecan tree that is the centerpiece of the woodland garden.

— TROWEL TALK—

Picking a favorite plant would be like picking a favorite child. *Bouteloua gracilis* 'Blonde Ambition' has been a very challenging plant. *B. gracilis* grows in dry, rocky soils, but I have had 'Blonde Ambition' in these landscapes and it has performed marginally well. Sometimes in tighter clay, where the throat stays moist, they have done reasonably well, but not always.

As far as tools go, a Hori Hori knife is my favorite.

— 👍 —

NOTES

Blithewold Mansion, Gardens & Arboretum - Bristol, RI
Photo by Blithewold Mansion, Gardens & Arboretum

Rhode Island

RHODE ISLAND

Providence County
June 4 & 5

The Providence Preservation Society (PPS) was established in 1956 to respond to the proposed demolition of a number of 18th- and early 19th-century houses on College Hill.

Unlike many historic preservation organizations which were formed to preserve a particular building, PPS has always been an advocate for neighborhood revitalization. From that small neighborhood group, PPS has grown into a multifaceted citywide preservation and planning organization.

Our mission is to support and advocate for historic preservation, thoughtful design, and people-centered planning. www.pvdpreservation.org

This year, we are pleased to announce Open Days in Providence, Rhode Island in partnership with the Providence Preservation Society.

Enjoy this extraordinary opportunity to visit some of Providence's oldest homes and gardens at the height of the spring season.

Details will be announced in late winter. Event registration, house and garden descriptions, photographs, and more information will be available at https://www.providencehousetour.com/

Lloyd Avenue - Providence, RI
Photos by Warren Jagger Photography

Kent County

Saturday, June 11

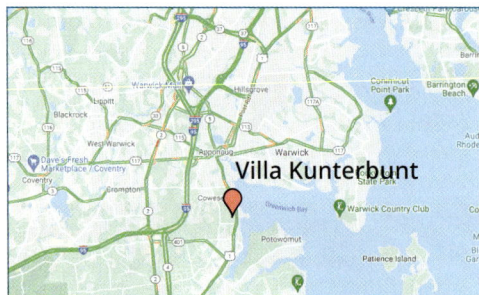

Villa Kunterbunt

★ There are two additional gardens open on this date in nearby Bristol County, MA:
Landscape Designer Andrew Grossman's Display Gardens, Seekonk, MA
McIlwain Garden, Rehoboth, MA
For garden description and details, see page 113.

EAST GREENWICH

VILLA KUNTERBUNT

📷 | 🕊

Hours: 10 a.m. to 4 p.m.

A 1915 Arts & Crafts house is surrounded by a variety of gardens and borders. The main garden, designed by Andrew Grossman, is a formal four-square garden.

This garden is inspired by the large farmhouse kitchen gardens of Switzerland and southern Germany. The garden features wooden fences, arbors, and a main gate. Pea stone walkways separate the brick-lined geometrically arranged beds.

This property also features a large koi pond, also designed by Andrew Grossman, which attracts frogs and dragonflies. There is a large stone wall with beds in front of it

featuring a variety of ferns and perennials. Plantings are chosen mostly to attract pollinators since the garden owners are also beekeepers.

— TROWEL TALK—

One of my favorite plants is anise hyssop because it attracts so many pollinators. I am also partial to old-fashioned roses although they are very labor intensive. I never had luck with delphiniums and lupines—probably because our summers are too humid.

My favorite garden tool is the Felco clipper!

My first garden was probably my grandmother's (and mother's) in Germany.

—👍—

Photo by Doris Kirchner

📷 Photos permitted   ♿ Partially accessible   **NEW** garden or section   🕊 Nature-friendly

Newport
Saturday, June 18

Blithewold Mansion,
Gardens & Arboretum

BRISTOL

NONPROFIT PARTNER

**BLITHEWOLD MANSION,
GARDENS & ARBORETUM**

BLITHEWOLD
MANSION, GARDENS & ARBORETUM

101 Ferry Road
Bristol, RI 02809
📷 | ♿ partial | 🪶

Hours: Tuesday - Saturday: 10 a.m.
to 4 p.m.; (3 p.m. Sundays. Open on
most Monday holidays. Closed July 4,
November 24, December 24 and 25.

Admission: Adults $16; Child 6-17 $6;
Military and Student $11

Blithewold is a 33-acre summer
estate in Bristol, RI, with grand views
of Narragansett Bay. It is nationally
significant in American history as one of
the most fully developed and authentic
examples of the Country Place era.

The property features a 45-room
mansion filled with family heirlooms
and framed by a series of lovely gardens
that range in character from mysterious
to exotic and from poetic to practical.
An exceptional collection of rare and
unusual plants, specimen trees, an
accessible greenhouse, and whimsical
stonework project a character that
is romantic, fresh, and inspiring-and
unique to Blithewold.

Our mission is to preserve New
England's finest garden estate through
excellence in horticulture and historic
preservation, and by our example to
teach and inspire others.

www.blithewold.org

DIGGING DEEPER

**Landscape in Translation:
Arts & Crafts Ideals
in the 21st Century**
Gail Read and Betsy Ekholm
Saturday, June 18, 1 p.m. to 3 p.m.

Blithewold, Bristol, RI
$30 Garden Conservancy
and Blithewold members
$40 General

With sweeping views of the Narragansett

Bay, Blithewold was created as a seaside summer retreat in the 1890s and remained in the same family for almost 100 years. Today, this 33-acre estate still evokes the romance of the Country Place era.

Explore this landscape and its rich history, along with the ideas of the Arts & Crafts movement in a walking tour with Blithewold's horticulturists Gail Read and Garden Manager Betsy Ekholm. They will discuss the particular joys and challenges of preserving a living landscape, and how Blithewold has decided to honor its history and the collector's spirit of the early owners by embracing new plant species, thus keeping the gardens fresh and inviting.

Photo by Blithewold Mansion, Gardens, & Arboretum

Little Compton

Sunday, July 17

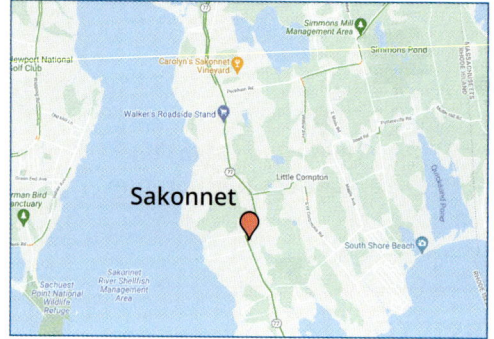

LITTLE COMPTON

SAKONNET

Hours: 9 a.m. to 5:30 p.m.

Sakonnet Garden is a hidden exotic garden embedded within a native coastal fields landscape, a long-term project of John Gwynne and Mikel Folcarelli.

This ongoing experiment in design, scale, and plantings began as an acre-sized spring woodland garden and is subdivided into spaces separated by high windbreak hedges and stone walls that enable growing of many Zone 7 plants. Each space has its own mood and horticultural objective.

These woodland areas are very different in summer—mostly shady and green, but with the "subtropical quadrant" at peak of exuberance. Open for the first time for the Garden Conservancy, a new "pollinator plus" summer garden is a colorful walk-through perennial border conceived as a biodiversity maze. Thousands of flowers produce nectar for butterflies, bees, especially native bees, and other insects important for pollination.

Clipped topiary ilex begins to mimic the Nupé house posts from Ghana.

★ Please note that Sakonnet Garden manages registration for this event and Open Days tickets are not accepted. More information is available at www. gardenconservancy.org/opendays.

NOTES

_____

_____

_____

_____

_____

_____

_____

_____

_____

_____

_____

_____

_____

_____

_____

_____

_____

_____

_____

_____

_____

_____

_____

Forty Oaks Farm - Campobello, SC
Photo by Betty Montgomery

South Carolina

SOUTH CAROLINA

Spartanburg
Saturday, April 9

CAMPOBELLO
FORTY OAKS FARM
📷 | NEW
Hours: 10 a.m. to 4 p.m.

Betty has been a hands-on gardener for almost 50 years. She has learned to know and love plants of all shapes and sizes. She has traveled extensively to different gardens in Europe and Asia and learned to love and appreciate all kinds of gardens.

Betty is a syndicated columnist for *USA Today* and local papers and has authored two books, *How to Grow, Cultivate and Enjoy Hydrangeas* and *A Four Season Southern Garden*.

Betty tends a five-acre garden that features all kinds of plants. She started out with mainly woody plants and grew into bulbs and perennials. Her garden is a wonderland of azaleas when it is open this year.

SPARTANBURG
MEEKS GARDEN
📷 | NEW
Hours: 10 a.m. to 4 p.m.

In mid-April you will be seeing a garden covered in moss and blooming azaleas. Many different varieties of native plants will be showing their blooms, and the ferns will be showing their new fiddleheads.

Many maples will be leafing out and also showing their blooms, and you may even see some wildlife and migrating birds, especially moving along a wide and expansive creek. Several other water features highlight the property.

Charleston

Saturday, May 28
Saturday, June 4

Hours: 9 a.m. to 2 p.m.

COMING SOON

This year, we are pleased to have the Open Days program returning to Charleston. Enjoy this extraordinary opportunity to visit several of the area's finest gardens at the height of the spring season. Details will be announced soon. Event registration, garden descriptions, photographs, and more information can be found at

gardenconservancy.org/opendays

NONPROFIT PARTNER

CHARLESTON HORTICULTURAL SOCIETY

The Charleston Horticultural Society (CHS), founded in 2000, is a nonprofit organization with membership open to all.

The Society offers a wide array of horticultural information and involvement to its more than 1,300 individual and business members through lectures, educational workshops, garden tours, special events, and publications.

📷 Photos permitted   ♿ Partially accessible   **NEW** garden or section   🖋 Nature-friendly

Joe and Sharon Pryse - Knoxville TN
Photo by Finch Photography

Tennesee

TENNESSEE

Knoxville
Saturday, October 1

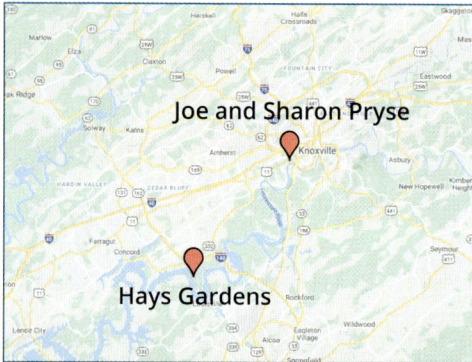

Joe and Sharon Pryse

Hays Gardens

KNOXVILLE
JOE AND SHARON PRYSE
NEW
Hours: 10 a.m. to 4 p.m.

On the banks of the Tennessee River, this steep hillside garden includes meandering paths, a lower lawn, as well as an upper formal rose garden, including more than 120 hybrid tea roses designed by the late Ryan Gainey.

HAYS GARDENS
📷 | ♿ partial
Hours: 10 a.m. to 4 p.m.

The Hays Gardens, constructed and planted by Lane Hays and her late husband Charles Hays about 20 years ago, are located on the shores of Fort Loudon Lake.

There are four distinct gardens: a formal rose garden that includes a large variety of roses, a white moon garden, a fenced cottage garden with a rose arbor and

a variety of perennials, and a quarry woodland garden with a pool and waterfalls over natural marble formations.

The waterfalls were designed and installed in 2014 by Mark Furhman, a local landscape designer. The setting on the lake is beautiful with an expansive lawn separating the various areas.

Hays Garden - Knoxville, Tennesee
Photo by Lane Hays

Gardens of Gordon and Mary Hayward - Putney, VT
Photo by Gordon and Mary Hayward

Vermont

VERMONT

Upper Valley
Saturday, June 25

★ There are two additional gardens open on this date in the nearby Monadnock Region of New Hampshire:
Gardens of Maude & John Odgers, Peterborough, NH
The Gardens at Beechwood Farm, Temple, NH
For garden description and details, *see page 124.*

WESTMINSTER WEST
GORDON & MARY HAYWARD'S GARDEN
📷 | ♿ partial | 🌿
Hours: 10 a.m. to 4 p.m.

Gordon and Mary Hayward's 1.5-acre garden surrounds their 220-year-old farmhouse in southeastern Vermont.

Over the past 38 years they have developed a hybrid of Old England and New England gardens to reflect Gordon's growing up on an orchard in northwestern Connecticut, and Mary's growing up on

a farm outside Chipping Campden in the North Cotswold Hills of England.

The garden, the subject of their book *The Intimate Garden* (WW Norton, 2005), comprises fourteen garden rooms. One area includes a pair of 90-foot perennial borders that terminate in a post-and-beam gazebo framing views of twenty acres of meadows.

More than 40 planted terra-cotta pots and many garden ornaments, several from England, figure into the mood of this garden.

Gordon & Mary Hayward's Garden
Photo by Brian Jones

Anne Spencer Garden - Lynchburg, VA
Photo by Jane White

Virginia

VIRGINIA

Charlottesville
Saturday, April 23

Anne Spencer House and Garden Museum

LYNCHBURG

NON-PROFIT PRESERVATION PARTNER

ANNE SPENCER HOUSE AND GARDEN MUSEUM

📷 | ♿ | **NEW**

Hours: 10 am. to 4 p.m.

The Anne Spencer House and Garden is the only restored garden of an African American in the United States of America.

The Hillside Garden Club began restoration of the Anne Spencer Garden in 1983, and the Garden Club of Virginia won two Commonwealth Awards for their restoration efforts in the historic Spencer Garden, in 1985 and 2009. The Anne Spencer House & Garden Museum is a Virginia Historic Landmark, listed on the National Register of Historic Places.

The Spencer residence reopened its doors as a House Museum in 1977 and is the only intact house museum of an African American in the United States.

Anne spent many hours in the flower garden and cottage. Edward, her husband, handcrafted objects and adorned the garden with a black gothic fence and a fountain head named Prince Ebo, a gift from W.E.B. Dubois.

Harlem luminaries have walked these garden paths. Anne wrote poetry and prose in the garden and planted by sunlight, moonlight, and candlelight. The two worked together to cultivate four garden rooms and took immense pleasure in spending time together traveling to New York parks, national arboretums, and Virginia Byways to acquire rare and native flora.

Anne cultivated a black poppy and narcissus. She ordered roses from flower and seed catalogs and purchased nasturtium packets from the ten-cent store. Farmers driving wagons downtown to the city farmers market shared seeds and plants with Anne when she jumped onto the wayback in order to boycott segregated seating on public transportation.

The Anne Spencer House and Garden Museum, Inc., and Hillside Garden Club have benefited from the guidance and preservation assistance of the Garden Conservancy. The 40-year-long story of the restoration and maintenance of the historic garden is documented in Jane Baber White's book, *Lessons Learned*

📷 Photos permitted   ♿ Partially accessible   **NEW** garden or section   🌿 Nature-friendly

from a Poet's Garden (2011, out of print). The award-winning book, *Half My World* (2003), by Rebecca Frischkorn and Reuben Rainey, explores the history and design of the garden and its influence on her work as a poet.

The Anne Spencer Garden is open to the public year round, sunrise to sunset.

The Anne Spencer House and Garden will also be open for tours on "Garden Day in Virginia," April 26, 2022, from 10 a.m. to 3 p.m. From April 27 through October 31, 2022, tours are by appointment only. Call two weeks in advance to schedule your tour at 434-845-1313.

annespencermuseum.com

Anne Spencer House and Garden, Lynchburg, Virginia
Photo provided by Shaun Spencer Hester

Paulsen Garden, Puyallup, WA
Photo by Camile Paulsen

Washington

WASHINGTON

Pierce County
Saturday, May 21

GRAHAM
OLD GOAT FARM

📷 | ♿ partial
Hours: 10 a.m. to 4 p.m.

Old Goat Farm is a small nursery located in the foothills below Mt. Rainier. The property includes a very small farm with a 118-year-old farmhouse and a large garden featuring both sun and shade beds.

A substantial part of the garden is used for growing vegetables. The nursery specializes in unusual plants, many of which also flourish in the garden.

Another highlight of the farm are the animals: six old goats, nine peacocks, ten ducks, about 60 chickens, and Charley the donkey, all rescue animals.

GARDEN EXTRAS
10 a.m. to 4 p.m. — Plant sale

PUYALLUP
ERNIE & JULIA GRAHAM GARDEN

📷 | 🖊
Hours: 10 a.m. to 4 p.m.

Situated on a sloped acre looking out to Mt. Rainier, this peaceful, award-winning garden focuses on foliage color, texture, and contrast.

Paths lead visitors through several distinct areas: a tranquil woodland featuring Japanese maples and other plantings native to the Pacific Northwest and Asia; a colorful poolside container garden; a contemporary courtyard; Ernie's vegetable garden; and eclectic spaces in between.

Water features, seating areas, and metal and glass garden art are spotted throughout. The garden is a wildlife sanctuary organically maintained solely by its owners. It is a mature garden, although always undergoing redesign here and there.

PAULSEN GARDEN

📷 | ♿ partial | 🖋

Hours: 10 a.m. to 4 p.m.

Located on a ridge above the Orting Valley, the Paulsen Garden encompasses many styles while retaining a quintessentially Pacific Northwest feel.

The front garden features a vine-covered pergola, a waterfall/pond and a wide variety of sun-loving plants. A staircase leads to a large Torii gate, which marks the entrance to a peaceful shade garden with an Asian flair.

Highlights of the back garden include a woodland waterfall/pond, colorful tropical bed, shade pavilion, and greenhouse. An arbor bordered by a fernery leads visitors back to the front entrance.

Flagstone paths and stone terraces connect the various garden rooms, which feature container plantings, dwarf conifers, Japanese maples, and a fun mix of rare and unusual plants. Benches and other seating areas are tucked into many spots around the garden to relax and take in the beautiful views of Mt. Rainier and the Cascades.

— TROWEL TALK—

I love our weeping giant sequoia (*Sequoiadendron giganteum* 'Pendulum') because it's a living sculpture!

My first garden was in Alpharetta, Georgia. Unfortunately, one of our neighbors used the little stream between our yards to dump his lawn clippings, so the mosquitoes outnumbered the plants!

Heucheras limp along in my garden and never grow as fat and fluffy as the ones in the garden magazines.

My favorite garden tool is a pair of Japanese garden scissors for deadheading flowers and cutting stems and small branches. Very sharp and less bulky than a lot of pruners.

— 👍 —

Bainbridge Island

Sunday, June 5

**DRAGON'S LAIR –
THE DEMIANEW GARDENS**

📷 | 🖋

Hours: 10 a.m. to 4 p.m.

We are situated on a hill overlooking beautiful Puget Sound. Our property includes both shady woodland and full sun areas, so we are able to grow a diverse selection of plants.

We have several goals for ourselves as caretakers of our property. One is to have something in bloom from early spring through fall. The other is to use water and our labor resources efficiently. In addition, we love fragrance and color. So we have used many different types of plants throughout our gardens to achieve these goals. We also have many garden accents made of glass that give the garden a playful feeling.

In spring we have a profusion of bulbs and early blooming perennials such as epimediums and terrestrial orchids. As spring gives way to summer, we have blue Himalayan poppies, more orchids, peonies, delphiniums, and finally roses. Midsummer is full of Oriental lilies, roses, and many other perennials. Late summer gives us perennial lobelia, sedum, and many fuchsias. A collection of arisaemas blooms throughout the season in the various beds.

We have fruits, vegetables, and herbs in sunny beds, so we enjoy our own organic produce throughout the season. Grasses add texture as well as low water requirements. We have two mature ponds that give us many hours of pleasure. Waterlilies give us color and habitat for many goldfish and frogs that hatch out and mature each year.

— TROWEL TALK—

We met in a college chemistry class, but made it official as partners collecting specimens for a field botany class!

We have been collecting favorite plants ever since. We have grown many plants over the years, but orchids are still our favorites.

This will be our 28th season here, so some of our terrestrial orchids have grown to large clumps.

— 👍 —

THE COLE GARDEN

📷

Hours: 10 a.m. to 2 p.m.

This garden is small but beautiful. It's a Victorian, shabby chic, perennial garden full of flowers, vignettes, pathways, a rose garden, birdbaths, arbors, and a charming porch for entertaining. Many containers filled with blooming everything, sweet peas, annuals, fuchsias, and hydrangeas. So many beautiful trees, birds galore, and busy squirrels!

There is an amazing collection of garden accoutrements and established bamboo. This garden has a lot of shade for hot afternoons and just the right amount of sun for flowers to bloom vigorously and keep the sweet peas performing from April to September. A wonderfully easy-on-the-eyes garden.

DIGGING DEEPER

In Full Bloom with Teri Cole
Teri Cole
Sunday, June 5, 2 p.m. to 4 p.m.

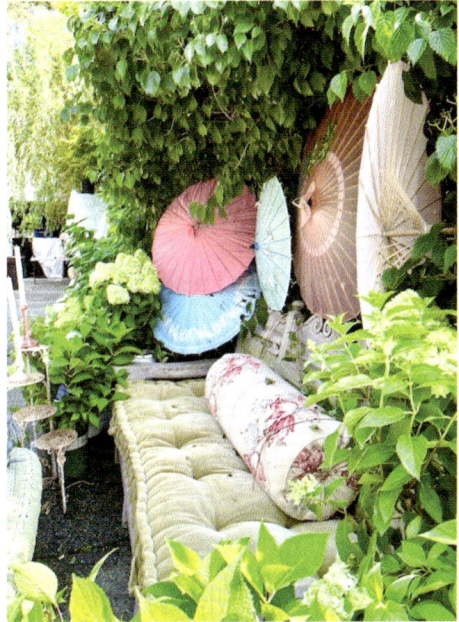

The Cole Garden, Bainbridge Island, WA
$30 Garden Conservancy members;
$40 General

Visit the Cole Garden during the height of rose season for a guided walk with its owner. Small but beautiful, this compact, Victorian, shabby-chic perennial garden offers "blooming everything."

Learn the tricks of the trade to growing great roses and keeping flowers in vigorous bloom from April to September.

WEISSMAN GARDEN

📷 | ♿ partial
Hours: 10 a.m. to 4 p.m.

Barbara and Eric began their stewardship
of this beautifully laid-out garden eleven
years ago, and have enhanced it with many
personal touches. Sunny borders and
shady, fern-lined paths feature Barbara's
extensive plant collection. A complete
renovation of the water feature led to
rethinking the northern half of the garden,
including a seating area next to the pond,
an extended birch grove, and a new
collection of pines.

The latest expansion of the garden, begun
three years ago, opened up a wooded
area south of the house to make room
for an extensive collection of species
rhododendrons and woodland plants.

Clark County
Saturday, June 18

Matsu Kaze (Wind in the Pines)

VANCOUVER

MATSU KAZE (WIND IN THE PINES)

📷 | ♿ partial | 🌿
Hours: 10 a.m. to 4 p.m.

I designed and developed our Asian-
inspired garden twenty years ago when
this 2.5-acre property was a horse pasture.
It is now filled with rare and unusual
plants, including many varieties of conifers,
ginkgos, Japanese maples, and dogwoods,
as well as lilies, peonies, daphnes, clematis,
rhododendrons, and other perennials.

Meandering pathways lead to various
seating areas, a pond with a waterfall, a
covered bridge over a dry creek bed, a fire
pit, an outdoor kitchen, and a guesthouse.
We created this garden to give us
something to do in our retirement. It has
given us that and so much more.

📷 Photos permitted   ♿ Partially accessible   **NEW** garden or section   🌿 Nature-friendly

Notes

The Robbins Garden, River Hills, WI
Photo by Lisa Robbins

Wisconsin

WISCONSIN

Milwaukee Area
Saturday, June 11

Dragonfly Farm

MEQUON

DRAGONFLY FARM

📷 | ✒

DIGGING DEEPER

Creating the Canvas:
The Making of Dragonfly Farm
Cheryl Brickman
Saturday, June 11, 10 a.m. to 12 p.m.

Dragonfly Farm, Mequon, WI
$30 Garden Conservancy members
$40 General

Mark and I bought this 15½-acre property in 1998. It was degraded post agricultural and was used to graze cattle. It had a David Torphy–designed house on it, and that was it. We fell in love with the house first. I am a botanist/horticulturist/garden designer who, after designing gardens for more than 30 years, suddenly had a blank canvas. We called it Dragonfly Farm after witnessing the late August migration of literally thousands of large darners in migration across our property. It was a magical and defining moment.

What happened next was 23 years of restoring, and creating what is now Dragonfly Farm. We have created destinations across our 15½ acres that ecologically and aesthetically complement one another. One of the things I have noticed now that I have three Open Days under my belt is that I am never able to give visitors as much time individually as they have questions. As a professional I also feel a need to share the story, the decisions, and even the mistakes we have made in the creation of this very special place we call home.

I am hoping to give Digging Deeper guests the ultimate tour of the farm and all of its destinations, with the time to tell its story and to answer all the questions they might have. This is a great opportunity for visitors who have been here before and found themselves wanting more.

📷 Photos permitted   ♿ Partially accessible   **NEW** garden or section   ✒ Nature-friendly

The Milwaukee Art Museum Garden Club, founded in 1921, is the oldest and largest garden club in Wisconsin. It supports the museum's projects and promotes education, environmental awareness and community service as well as the enjoyment of gardening, landscape design, horticulture and flower arranging.
www.mamgardenclub.org

The Milwaukee Art Museum has 30,000 works of art dating from antiquity to the present. In 2001, expanding on Eero Saarinen's War Memorial Center and the Kahler Building, Santiago Calatrava designed the Quadracci Pavilion addition, increasing the museum's space to 341,00 square feet. The same year, landscape architect Dan Kiley redesigned the museum's grounds. Time magazine called the Milwaukee Art Museum "one of the country's finest examples of modern architecture put to work for civic purposes."
www.mam.org

Milwaukee Area
Saturday, July 30

BAYSIDE
THE TSAI GARDEN

Hours: 10 a.m. to 4 p.m.

📷 | ♿ | 🌿 | NEW

Color and texture are the touchstones of this garden, more than twenty years in the making. The location is challenging—a low-lying parcel with lots of shade and wet. But Anna Tsai is a determined and optimistic gardener who is constantly trialing new plants, replacing those that don't meet her high expectations for vigor and color, and moving plants to create colorful and unexpected vignettes that capture the eye and spark the creativity of visitors.

While the garden is rich in shade plants, Anna has also carved out areas for a multitude of sun-loving plants to thrive. Visits to Japan expanded the owners' exposure to the color and texture potential of evergreens, which now constitute an important tool in Anna's constant pursuit to create interesting, unexpected, and beautiful plant combinations in every season.

RIVER HILLS
THE ROBBINS GARDEN

Hours: 10 a.m. to 4 p.m.

📷 | ♿ partial | **NEW**

An atmospheric drive leads you deep into this River Hills property, emerging at their 1920s English Tudor granite home. As you walk down this picturesque acreage, to the right is the prairie garden—an ongoing project to convert areas originally overgrown with buckthorn and thistle into a colorful assemblage of Wisconsin prairie plants that bloom from late spring into fall. Beyond the prairie garden lies the apiary, consisting of Flow Hives—a new technology that allows you to harvest honey without removing the frames or disturbing the bees.

Through the hand-pegged walkway is a vintage stucco and beam barn where the art studio of Marion Coffey resides. As you proceed through their bluestone patio you will find their formal perennial gardens. The English Garden is outlined by a custom-made fence, designed by landscape architect Judith Stark, with an arched entryway. The full sun garden's bright yellows, purples, and pinks create a colorful display throughout the summer. Don't miss the hand-painted scuba diver and marine creatures in the bottom of the pool, one of several artist-designed works on the property.

THE VINEYARD AT RIVER HILLS

Hours: 10 a.m. to 4 p.m.

📷 | ♿ partial | 🖋

When the owners purchased their five-acre property 35 years ago, the two outstanding features were an allée of Norway spruces and the rolling terrain. There was no landscaping to speak of around the now 100-year-old house, and thickets of invasive, non-native plants predominated. Influenced by an early book by Rosalind Creasy and by gardens visited on their travels, the owners decided to focus on edible landscaping, while at the same time featuring expansive gardens of shade and sun perennials.

Among the special features are a two-acre vineyard planted with 500 vines of winter-hardy grapes, a large vegetable and cutting garden, and many nut, fruit, and espaliered apple and pear trees. In the last few years, the owners have expanded their gardening focus with a goal of making their property more ecologically sensitive and friendly to birds, small mammals and amphibians, and pollinators and other insects. After removing more than 80 ash trees felled by the emerald ash borer, they have planted diverse varieties of native trees and understory plants, installed a wildlife pond, stopped mowing parts of their lawn, and favored native plants when re-planting areas.

Vignettes from this garden were highlighted monthly from May to November of 2021 in "In My Garden: A Visual Diary," published by the Garden Conservancy. Read more at https://www.gardenconservancy.org/news/in-my-garden-2021/in-my-garden-koenig

---

📷 Photos permitted   ♿ Partially accessible   **NEW** garden or section   🖋 Nature-friendly

Milwaukee Area
Sunday, July 31

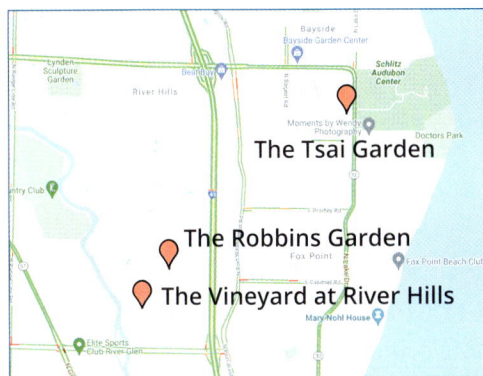

BAYSIDE
THE TSAI GARDEN
Hours: 10 a.m. to 4 p.m.

📷 | ♿ | 🖋 | **NEW**

Color and texture are the touchstones of this garden, more than twenty years in the making. The location is challenging—a low-lying parcel with lots of shade and wet. But Anna Tsai is a determined and optimistic gardener who is constantly trialing new plants, replacing those that don't meet her high expectations for vigor and color, and moving plants to create colorful and unexpected vignettes that capture the eye and spark the creativity of visitors.

While the garden is rich in shade plants, Anna has also carved out areas for a multitude of sun-loving plants to thrive. Visits to Japan expanded the owners' exposure to the color and texture potential of evergreens, which now constitute an important tool in Anna's constant pursuit to create interesting, unexpected, and beautiful plant combinations in every season.

RIVER HILLS
THE ROBBINS GARDEN
Hours: 10 a.m. to 4 p.m.

📷 | ♿ partial | **NEW**

An atmospheric drive leads you deep into this River Hills property, emerging at their 1920s English Tudor granite home. As you walk down this picturesque acreage, to the right is the prairie garden—an ongoing project to convert areas originally overgrown with buckthorn and thistle into a colorful assemblage of Wisconsin prairie plants that bloom from late spring into fall. Beyond the prairie garden lies the apiary, consisting of Flow Hives—a new technology that allows you to harvest honey without removing the frames or disturbing the bees.

Through the hand-pegged walkway is a vintage stucco and beam barn where the art studio of Marion Coffey resides. As you proceed through their bluestone patio you will find their formal perennial gardens. The English Garden is outlined by a custom-made fence, designed by landscape architect Judith Stark, with an arched entryway. The full sun garden's bright yellows, purples, and pinks create a colorful display throughout the summer. Don't miss the hand-painted scuba diver and marine creatures in the bottom of the pool, one of several artist-designed works on the property.

THE VINEYARD AT RIVER HILLS
Hours: 10 a.m. to 4 p.m.

📷 | ♿ partial

When the owners purchased their five-acre property 35 years ago, the two outstanding features were an allée of Norway spruces and the rolling terrain.

📷 Photos permitted   ♿ Partially accessible   **NEW** garden or section   🖋 Nature-friendly

There was no landscaping to speak of around the now 100-year-old house, and thickets of invasive, non-native plants predominated. Influenced by an early book by Rosalind Creasy and by gardens visited on their travels, the owners decided to focus on edible landscaping, while at the same time featuring expansive gardens of shade and sun perennials.

Among the special features are a two-acre vineyard planted with 500 vines of winter-hardy grapes, a large vegetable and cutting garden, and many nut, fruit, and espaliered apple and pear trees. In the last few years, the owners have expanded their gardening focus with a goal of making their property more ecologically sensitive and friendly to birds, small mammals and amphibians, and pollinators and other insects. After removing more than 80 ash trees felled by the emerald ash borer, they have planted diverse varieties of native trees and understory plants, installed a wildlife pond, stopped mowing parts of their lawn, and favored native plants when re-planting areas.

Vignettes from this garden were highlighted monthly from May to November of 2021 in "In My Garden: A Visual Diary," published by the Garden Conservancy. Read more at https://www.gardenconservancy.org/news/in-my-garden-2021/in-my-garden-koenig

Milwaukee Area
Saturday, August 20

The Garden Gone Wild

FOX POINT
THE GARDEN GONE WILD
♿ | ✒ | NEW

DIGGING DEEPER

The Garden Gone Wild
Sally Edgett
Saturday, August 20, 2 p.m.

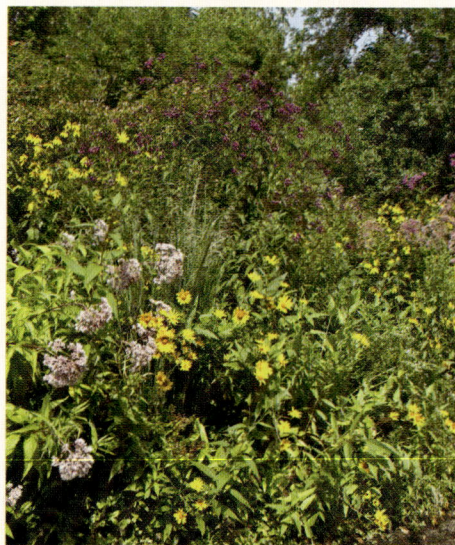

The Garden Gone Wild, Fox Point, WI
$30 Garden Conservancy members
$40 General

📷 Photos permitted   ♿ Partially accessible   **NEW** garden or section   ✒ Nature-friendly

Gardening with native plants has been growing in popularity as gardeners have become educated about the needs and challenges of pollinators and the importance of restoring our ecological web for the healthy future of the planet.

Visit Sally Edgett's Garden Gone Wild and learn how to successfully incorporate native plants into your garden depending on soil type, moisture, space available, light requirements and other key factors. Sally lives in a 150-year-old farmhouse built when Fox Point, its dense forests removed, was farm country. She took continuing education classes with Darrel Morrison, referred to as "the elder stateman of the ecological landscaping movement" by the New York Times, at the University of Wisconsin – Madison in the 1970s, building on a childhood fascination with "wild flowers".

She has put her knowledge to work over the last 40 years by developing a border with wet and mesic prairie plants ranging in height from 2 feet to 11 feet, as well as cultivating other native plants throughout her garden, including a 40-foot-tall Dutchman's Pipe vine which is colonizing a nearby Norway spruce. Join Sally and discover the wealth of native plants that can enrich your garden, provide habitat for butterflies, bees, and other pollinators, and help restore the ecology of your landscape. Sally also has a wealth of non-native plants and will discuss some of her favorites and how to incorporate natives into an established landscape.

Milwaukee Area
Sunday, August 21

Kelton House Farm

The Garden Gone Wild

★ There is a Garden Masters Series event on this date in nearby Fredonia.

FOX POINT
THE GARDEN GONE WILD
♿ | 🌿 | NEW

DIGGING DEEPER

The Garden Gone Wild
Sally Edgett
Sunday, August 21, 10 a.m.

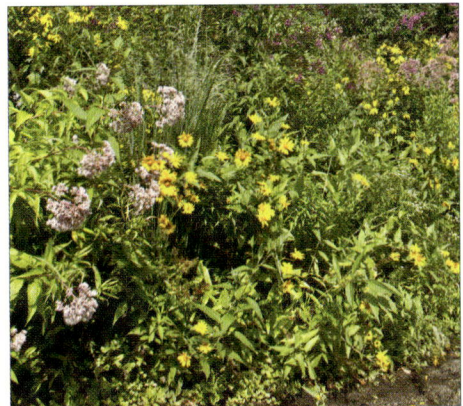

The Garden Gone Wild, Fox Point, WI
$30 Garden Conservancy members
$40 General

📷 Photos permitted   ♿ Partially accessible   NEW garden or section   🌿 Nature-friendly

Gardening with native plants has been growing in popularity as gardeners have become educated about the needs and challenges of pollinators and the importance of restoring our ecological web for the healthy future of the planet.

Visit Sally Edgett's Garden Gone Wild and learn how to successfully incorporate native plants into your garden depending on soil type, moisture, space available, light requirements and other key factors. Sally lives in a 150-year-old farmhouse built when Fox Point, its dense forests removed, was farm country. She took continuing education classes with Darrel Morrison, referred to as "the elder stateman of the ecological landscaping movement" by the New York Times, at the University of Wisconsin – Madison in the 1970s, building on a childhood fascination with "wild flowers".

She has put her knowledge to work over the last 40 years by developing a border with wet and mesic prairie plants ranging in height from 2 feet to 11 feet, as well as cultivating other native plants throughout her garden, including a 40-foot-tall Dutchman's Pipe vine which is colonizing a nearby Norway spruce. Join Sally and discover the wealth of native plants that can enrich your garden, provide habitat for butterflies, bees, and other pollinators, and help restore the ecology of your landscape. Sally also has a wealth of non-native plants and will discuss some of her favorites and how to incorporate natives into an established landscape.

FREDONIA
KELTON HOUSE FARM

Tours by reservation at 1:30 p.m. and 3:30 p.m

GARDEN MASTER'S SERIES

**Kelton House Farm:
Celebrating the American Colonial
Spirit in House and Garden**
Joe Gromacki
Sunday, August 21, 1 p.m. to 5 p.m.

Kelton House Farm, Fredonia, WI
$150 Garden Conservancy members
$175 General

Spend an afternoon at Kelton House Farm, touring with the owner—a noted collector of seventeenth and early eighteenth-century American furniture and decorative arts—exploring the heirloom cutting, perennial, and vegetable gardens, walking the meadows, and enjoying an English tea.

Kelton House Farm is intended to evoke a sense of place that celebrates the colonial period of American history. The early eighteenth-century saltbox house (moved from New England) is set in the context of a rural American farmstead. Gardens of historic design feature pre-1750 heirloom varieties of flowers, herbs, fruits, and vegetables, surrounded by a pastoral landscape. Objects of antique garden ornament from England and New England punctuate the gardens.

Kelton House Farm will be open from 1 p.m. to 5 p.m. for pre-registered guests, who will arrive via horse and carriage. Tickets are for a specific tour with the garden owner, 1:30 p.m. or 3:30 p.m.

At 2:30 p.m., an English tea will be served in the Potting Shed for all to enjoy. The tea will feature jams, jellies, and preserves made with fruits, flowers, and herbs from the garden, as well as honey from the farm's hives. (Please note that the Potting Shed is open-sided and this event will be held rain or shine.)

NOTES

Open Days 2022 Indices

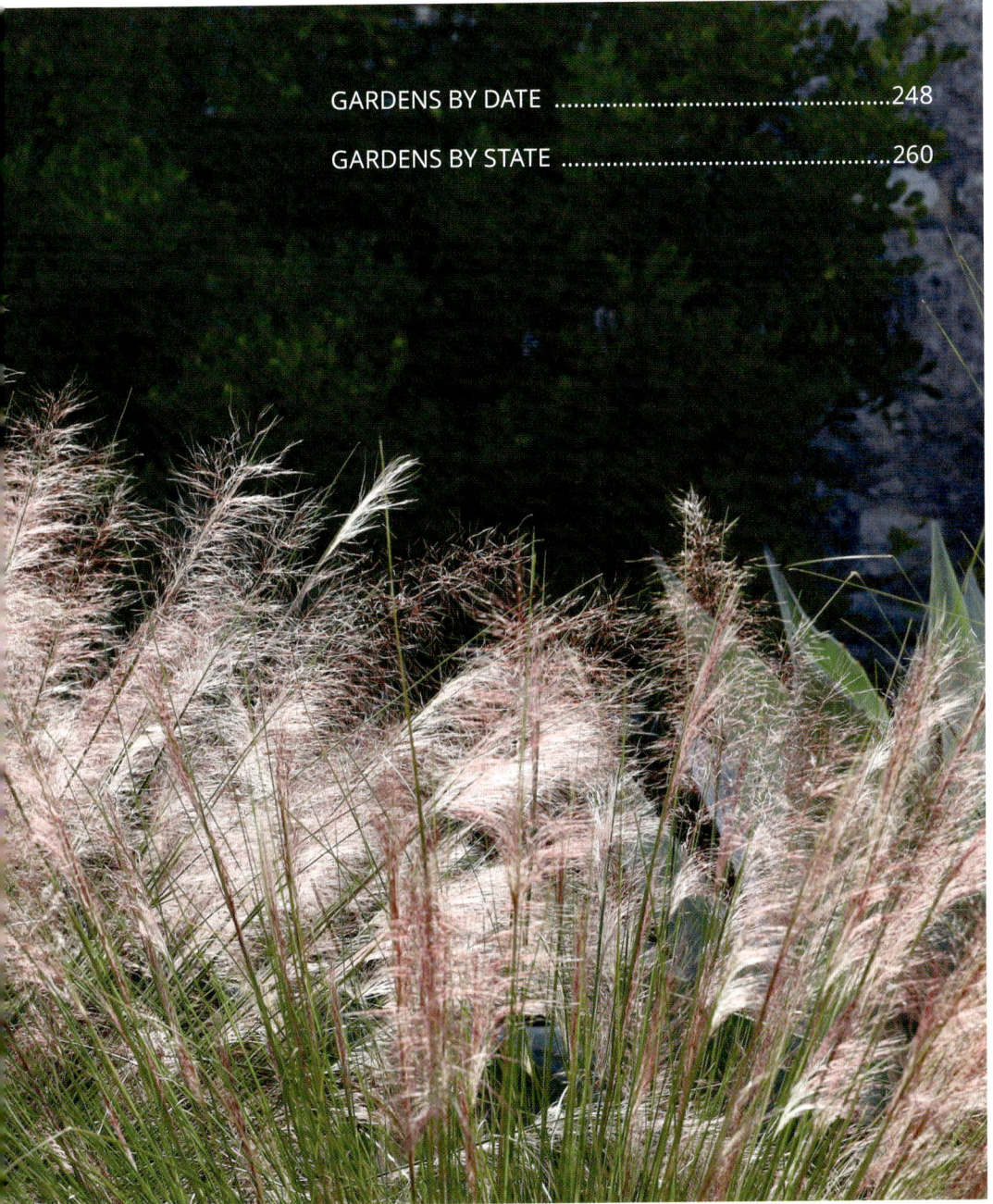

GARDENS BY DATE
MARCH

SATURDAY, MARCH 26
Florida (Jacksonville)
Jacksonville
Cummer Museum of Art & Gardens,
11 a.m. to 4 p.m.
Garden of Ann Hicks, 12 p.m. to 4 p.m.
Lanakila Gardens, 12 p.m. to 4 p.m.

APRIL

SATURDAY, APRIL 16
New Jersey (Essex County)
Nutley
The Mountsier Garden, 10 a.m. to 4 p.m.

SATURDAY, APRIL 9
South Carolina (Spartanburg)
Campobello
Forty Oaks Farm, 10 a.m. to 4 p.m.
Spartanburg
Meeks Garden, 10 a.m. to 4 p.m.

SATURDAY, APRIL 23
Virginia (Charlottesville)
Lynchburg
Anne Spencer House and Garden Museum,
10 a.m. to 4 p.m.

SUNDAY, APRIL 24
California (Pasadena & Environs)

SAVE THE DATE — APRIL 24

Details coming soon!

SUNDAY, APRIL 24
New York (Westchester County)
Lewisboro
The White Garden, 10 a.m. to 3 p.m.

SATURDAY, APRIL 30
Connecticut (Litchfield County)
Falls Village
Garden of Bunny Williams,
    Morning session, 10 a.m. to 1 p.m.
    Afternoon session, 1 p.m. to 4 p.m.

MAY

SUNDAY, MAY 1
California (Los Angeles)

SAVE THE DATE — MAY 1

Details coming soon!
Save the date! Detail.

SATURDAY, MAY 7
California (San Francisco East Bay)
Albany
Keeyla Meadows Gardens & Art,
10 a.m. to 4 p.m.
Berkeley
Aging Gracefully, 10 a.m. to 4 p.m.
Santa Clara Habitat Gardens,
10 a.m. to 4 p.m.

SATURDAY, MAY 7
New York (Dutchess County)
Millbrook
Clove Brook Farm Christopher Spitzmiller
& Anthony Bellomo, 10 a.m. to 4 p.m.
Wappingers Falls
Garden of Anne Spiegel, 10 a.m. to 4 p.m.

SATURDAY, MAY 7
New York (Eastern Long Island)
East Hampton
Garden of Marshall Watson,
10 a.m. to 4 p.m.
Glade Garden—Abby Jane Brody,
10 a.m. to 4 p.m.
The Garden of Dianne B., 10 a.m. to 3 p.m.
Wainscott
Biercuk & Luckey Garden, 10 a.m. to 4 p.m.

SUNDAY, MAY 8
Illinois (Far Western Suburbs)
Elburn
Hummer Haven, 10 a.m. to 4 p.m.

SUNDAY, MAY 8
New Jersey (Hunterdon County)
Pottersville
Anita Shearan Garden, 10 a.m. to 4 p.m.
Bird Haven Farm, 10 a.m. to 4 p.m.
New Jersey (Somerset County)
Far Hills
The Hay, Honey Farm, 10 a.m. to 4 p.m.

SUNDAY, MAY 8
New York (Greene County)
Cornwallville
Greene Bee Greenhouse, 10 a.m. to 4 p.m.

SATURDAY, MAY 14
New Jersey (Passaic County)
Ringwood
Ringwood Water Gardens, 10 a.m. to 4 p.m.
Wanaque
The Sichaks' Garden, 10 a.m. to 4 p.m.

SATURDAY, MAY 14
New York (Westchester County)
Chappaqua
Garden of Shobha Vanchiswar & Murali
Mani, 10 a.m. to 4 p.m.
Cortland Manor
Vivian & Ed Merrin, 10 a.m. to 4 p.m.

Mount Kisco
Rocky Hills, 10 a.m. to 4 p.m.
South Salem
West Lane Farm, 10 a.m. to 5 p.m.

SUNDAY, MAY 15
Massachusetts (Middlesex County)
Groton
Garden of Pepe and John Maynard,
10 a.m. to 4 p.m.
*Gardens are also open this day in nearby
Worcester County.*

SUNDAY, MAY 15
Massachusetts (Worcester)
Petersham
Swift River Farm, 10 a.m. to 4 p.m.
Worcester
Garden of Matt Mattus and Joe Philip,
10 a.m. to 4 p.m.
*A garden is also open this day in nearby
Middlesex County.*

SUNDAY, MAY 15
New Jersey (Essex County)
Montclair
Claire's Meditation Garden,
10 a.m. to 4 p.m.
Nutley
The Mountsier Garden, 10 a.m. to 4 p.m.
*Gardens are also open this day in nearby
Bucks County, PA.*
New Jersey (Morris County)
Chatham
Jack Lagos, 10 a.m. to 4 p.m.

SUNDAY, MAY 15
New York (Dutchess County)
Amenia
Broccoli Hall—Maxine Paetro,
10 a.m. to 4 p.m.

SUNDAY, MAY 15
New York (Ulster County)
Boiceville
Brunel Sculpture Park,
10 a.m. to 4 p.m.

SUNDAY, MAY 15
Pennsylvania (Bucks County)
New Hope
Gardens at Half Moon, 10 a.m. to 4 p.m
Paxson Hill Farm, 10 a.m. to 4 p.m.
*Gardens are also open this day in nearby
Essex County, NJ.*

SATURDAY, MAY 21
California (Mendocino County)
Boonville
Woodshop Grounds, 10 a.m. to 4 p.m.
Navarro
Pepperwood Pottery, 10 a.m. to 4 p.m.
Philo
Wildwood, 10 a.m. to 4 p.m.

SATURDAY, MAY 21
Connecticut (Fairfield County)
Greenwich
Sleepy Cat Farm,
    Morning session, 10 a.m. to 1 p.m.
    Afternoon session, 1 p.m. to 4 p.m.

SATURDAY, MAY 21
Connecticut (New Haven County)
Stony Creek
Uptop—Garden of Fred Bland,
10 a.m. to 4 p.m.

SATURDAY, MAY 21
Washington (South Sound)
Graham
Old Goat Farm, 10 a.m. to 4 p.m.
Puyallup
Ernie & Julia Graham Garden,
10 a.m. to 4 p.m.
Paulsen Garden, 10 a.m. to 4 p.m.

SUNDAY, MAY 22
Massachusetts (Greater Boston)
West Roxbury
Dustman-Ryan Garden - The Artful
Garden, 10 a.m. to 4 p.m.
Milton
Spalding Garden, 10 a.m. to 2 p.m.

SUNDAY, MAY 22
New York (Eastern Long Island)
Old Field
Two Grey Achers, 12 p.m. to 4 p.m.
Wading River
Bill & Veronica Schiavo—Woodland
Garden, 10 a.m. to 4 p.m.

SUNDAY, MAY 29
Connecticut (Fairfield County)
Westport
Blau House & Gardens, 10 a.m. to 4 p.m.

JUNE

SATURDAY, JUNE 4
California (San Jose)
San Jose
Garden of Cevan Forristt, 10 a.m. to 4 p.m.
Ginko Forristt Tea House, 10 a.m. to 1 p.m.

SATURDAY, JUNE 4
Connecticut (Hartford County)
Burlington
Garden of Robin Lensi, 10 a.m. to 4 p.m.
The Salsedo Family Garden,
10 a.m. to 4 p.m.
*Gardens are also open this day in nearby
Litchfield County, CT & Dutchess County, NY.*

SATURDAY, JUNE 4
Connecticut (Litchfield County)
Litchfield
Glenn Hillman, 11 a.m. to 5 p.m.
Roxbury
Japanese Gardens at Cedar Hill,
10 a.m. to 4 p.m.
Warren
Mulla Garden, 10 a.m. to 4 p.m.
Washington
Hollister House Garden, 10 a.m. to 4 p.m.
The Sumacs, 10 a.m. to 4 p.m.
A garden is also open this day in nearby Dutchess County, NY.

SATURDAY, JUNE 4
Missouri (St. Louis)

SAVE THE DATE — JUNE 4

Details coming soon!.

SATURDAY, JUNE 4
New Jersey (Essex County)
Nutley
The Mountsier Garden, 10 a.m. to 4 p.m.

SATURDAY, JUNE 4
New York (Dutchess County)
Millerton
Highgrove Cottage, 10 a.m. to 4 p.m.
Gardens are also open this day in nearby Litchfield County, CT.

SATURDAY, JUNE 4 / SUNDAY, JUNE 5
Rhode Island (Providence County)

SAVE THE DATES — JUNE 4, 5

Details coming soon!

SUNDAY, JUNE 5
New York (Nassau County)
Glen Cove
Kippen Hill, 10 a.m. to 4 p.m.
Locust Valley
Carol & Jim Large's Garden,
10 a.m. to 4 p.m.
Oyster Bay
The Barnyard, 10 a.m. to 4 p.m.
Port Washington
The Gardens at Sands Light,
10 a.m. to 4 p.m.

SUNDAY, JUNE 5
New York (Westchester County)
Pleasantville
Garden of Michael and Suzanne Inglis,
10 a.m. to 4 p.m.

SUNDAY, JUNE 5
Washington (Bainbridge Island)
Bainbridge Island
Dragon's Lair - The Demianew Gardens,
10 a.m. to 4 p.m.
The Cole Garden, 10 a.m. to 2 p.m.
Weissman Garden, 10 a.m. to 4 p.m.

SATURDAY, JUNE 11
Connecticut (New London County)
Stonington
Kentford Farm, 10 a.m. to 4 p.m.

SATURDAY, JUNE 11
Massachusetts (Berkshires)
Sheffield
1391 Barnum Street, 10 a.m. to 4 p.m.
Gardens are also open this day in nearby Columbia & Dutchess Counties, NY.

Saturday, June 11
Massachusetts (Bristol County)
Rehoboth
McIlwain Garden, 10 a.m. to 4 p.m.
Seekonk
Landscape Designer Andrew Grossman's
Display Gardens, 10 a.m. to 4 p.m.
*A garden is also open this day in nearby Kent
County, RI.*

SATURDAY, JUNE 11
New York (Columbia County)
Ancram
Heaven's Gate, 10 a.m. to 4 p.m.
Millerton
Garden of Helen Bodian, 10 a.m. to 4 p.m.
*Gardens are also open this day in nearby
Dutchess County, NY & Sheffield, MA.*

SATURDAY, JUNE 11
New York (Dutchess County)
Millbrook
Katie Ridder & Peter Pennoyer,
10 a.m. to 4 p.m.
Millerton
Hyland/Wente Garden, 10 a.m. to 2 p.m.
*Gardens are also open this day in nearby
Columbia County, NY & Sheffield, MA.*

SATURDAY, JUNE 11
Rhode Island (Kent County)
East Greenwich
Villa Kunterbunt, 10 a.m. to 4 p.m.
*Gardens are also open this day in nearby
Bristol County, MA.*

SUNDAY, JUNE 12
California (San Francisco East Bay)
Berkeley
Camp Shasta, 10 a.m. to 4 p.m.
Orinda
Simpson Garden, 10 a.m. to 4 p.m.
Piedmont
The Shartsis Gardens, 10 a.m. to 4 p.m.

SUNDAY, JUNE 12
Connecticut (Fairfield County)
Fairfield
Inwood Cottage Garden, 10 a.m. to 4 p.m.
Greenwich
Chelmsford, 10 a.m. to 4 p.m.
Garden of Allison Bourke, 10 a.m. to 4 p.m.
Ridgefield
Ken Eisold's Garden, 10 a.m. to 4 p.m.
Westport
Greens Farms Botanical Gardens,
10 a.m. to 4 p.m.

SUNDAY, JUNE 12
New Jersey (Hunterdon County)
Califon
Garden of Dan Ruhland, 10 a.m. to 4 p.m.
Pottersville
Jardin de Buis, 10 a.m. to 4 p.m.
Stockton
The Garden at Federal Twist,
10 a.m. to 4 p.m.

SATURDAY, JUNE 18
California (San Francisco)
San Francisco
Dry Garden on Surrey, 10 a.m. to 4 p.m.
Geary Street Garden, 10 a.m. to 4 p.m.

SATURDAY, JUNE 18
New York (Columbia County)
Claverack
Ketay Garden, 10 a.m. to 4 p.m.
West Taghkanic
Arcadia - Ronald Wagner & Timothy Van
Dam, 10 a.m. to 4 p.m.

SATURDAY, JUNE 18
New York (Saratoga Springs)
Middle Grove
Dalton Garden, 10 a.m. to 4 p.m.
Saratoga Springs
A Place to Nest - Moe's Garden,
10 a.m. to 4 p.m.
Foxglove - Sarah Patterson's Garden,
10 a.m. to 4 p.m.
Winterberry Cottage Garden,
10 a.m. to 4 p.m.
Schuylerville
Susie Kane-Kettlewell's Garden, 10 a.m. to
4 p.m.

SATURDAY, JUNE 18
New York (Westchester County)
Bedford
Brae Willows, 10 a.m. to 4 p.m.
The Great Hill Schoolhouse, 10 a.m. to 4 p.m.
Bedford Hills
Garden of Phillis Warden, 10 a.m. to 4 p.m.
Pound Ridge
James and Ellen Best's Sara Stein Garden,
10 a.m. to 2 p.m.

SUNDAY, JUNE 18
Rhode Island (Newport)
Bristol
Blithewold Mansion, Gardens &
Arboretum, 10 a.m. to 4 p.m.

SUNDAY, JUNE 18
Washington (Clark County)
Vancouver
Matsu Kaze (Wind in the Pines),
10 a.m. to 4 p.m.

SUNDAY, JUNE 19
Connecticut (Hartford County)
Glastonbury
The Murray Gardens, 10 a.m. to 4 p.m.
*Gardens are also open this day in nearby
Tolland and Litchfield Counties.*

SUNDAY, JUNE 19
Connecticut (Litchfield County)
Cornwall Bridge
Debby and Bart Jones' Garden,
10 a.m. to 4 p.m.
Lakeville
Juniper Ledge, 10 a.m. to 4 p.m.
Sharon
Garden of Lee Link, 10 a.m. to 4 p.m.
West Cornwall
Garden of Jane Garmey, 11 a.m. to 4 p.m.
Garden of Michael Trapp, 10 a.m. to 4 p.m.
Roxana Robinson - Treetop,
10 a.m. to 4 p.m.
*Gardens are also open this day in nearby
Tolland and Hartford Counties.*

SUNDAY, JUNE 19
Connecticut (Tolland County)
Tolland
Bear Run, 10 a.m. to 4 p.m.
*Gardens are also open this day in nearby
Hartford and Litchfield Counties.*

SATURDAY, JUNE 25
California (Marin County)
Bolinas
Garden of Sculpture, 10 a.m. to 4 p.m.
Visions of Paradise—Sally Robertson
Garden & Studio, 10 a.m. to 4 p.m.
Stinson Beach
A Panoramic Garden, 10 a.m. to 4 p.m.

SATURDAY, JUNE 25

Connecticut (Litchfield County)
Falls Village
Church House - The Garden of Page Dickey
and Bosco Schell, 10 a.m. to 4 p.m.
Salisbury
Catriona Pike, 10 a.m. to 4 p.m.
Washington
Brush Hill Gardens, 10 a.m. to 4 p.m.
Hollister House Garden, 10 a.m. to 4 p.m.
Washington Depot
Appledore, 10 a.m. to 3 p.m.

SATURDAY, JUNE 25

Maine (York)
York
Braveboat Harbor Farm, 10 a.m. to 4 p.m.

SATURDAY, JUNE 25

New Hampshire (Monadnock Region)
Peterborough
Gardens of Maude & John Odgers,
10 a.m. to 4 p.m.
Temple
The Gardens at Beechwood Farm,
10 a.m. to 4 p.m.
*A garden is also open this day in nearby
Westminster West, VT.*

SATURDAY, JUNE 25

New Jersey (Bergen County)
Mahwah
Sisko Gardens, 10 a.m. to 4 p.m.
Paramus
Sharon Ma's Garden, 10 a.m. to 4 p.m.
Waldwick
Noel Schulz's Garden, 10 a.m. to 4 p.m.

SATURDAY, JUNE 25

Pennsylvania (Chester County)
Phoenixville
Donald Pell Gardens, 10 a.m. to 4 p.m.

SATURDAY, JUNE 25

Vermont (Upper Valley)
Westminster West
Gordon & Mary Hayward's Garden,
10 a.m. to 4 p.m.
*Gardens are also open this day in nearby
Peterborough & Temple, NH.*

SUNDAY, JUNE 26

Maine (York)
York
Braveboat Harbor Farm, 10 a.m. to 4 p.m.

SUNDAY, JUNE 26

New York (Dutchess County)
Dover Plains
Lossing Manor, 10 a.m. to 4 p.m.
Millbrook
Squirrel Hall, 10 a.m. to 4 p.m.
Poughkeepsie
Dappled Berms - The Garden of Scott
VanderHamm, 10 a.m. to 4 p.m.
Stanfordville
Uplands Farm - Zibby & Jim Tozer,
10 a.m. to 2 p.m.

JULY

SATURDAY, JULY 9

New York (Delaware County)
Andes
Cynthia & Charles Bonnes,
10 a.m. to 4 p.m.
Roscoe
Henderson Hollow Farm - Mermer
Blakeslee & Eric Hamerstrom,
10 a.m. to 4 p.m.

SATURDAY, JULY 9
New York (Eastern Long Island)
Bridgehampton
Entwood Garden, 10 a.m. to 4 p.m.
East Hampton
Garden of Arlene Bujese, 10 a.m. to 4 p.m.
Previti/Gumpel Garden, 10 a.m. to 4 p.m.
Mattituck
The Landcraft Garden Foundation,
10 a.m. to 4 p.m.

SATURDAY, JULY 16
New York (Eastern Long Island)
Cutchogue
Conni Cross Garden Designer,
10 a.m. to 2 p.m.
Southold
Mayfield, 10 a.m. to 4 p.m.

SUNDAY, JULY 17
Rhode Island (Little Compton)
Little Compton
Sakonnet, 9 a.m. to 5:30 p.m.

SATURDAY, JULY 23
Connecticut (Litchfield County)
Falls Village
Garden of Bunny Williams,
    Morning session, 10 a.m. to 1 p.m.
    Afternoon session, 1 p.m. to 4 p.m.
Norfolk
Fernwood, 10 a.m. to 4 p.m.

SUNDAY, JULY 24
Massachusetts (Marblehead)
Marblehead
Seaside Farm, 10 a.m. to 4 p.m.
Swampscott
Glass House Gardens, 10 a.m. to 4 p.m.

SUNDAY, JULY 24
New York (Columbia County)
Canaan
Rockland Farm, 10 a.m. to 4 p.m.
Spencertown
Landscape of Linda B. Horn,
10 a.m. to 2 p.m.

SATURDAY, JULY 30
New York (Eastern Long Island)
Shelter Island Heights
Birdhouse Garden, 10 a.m. to 4 p.m.

SATURDAY, JULY 30
Wisconsin (Milwaukee)
Bayside
The Tsai Garden, 10 a.m. to 4 p.m.
River Hills
The Robbins Garden, 10 a.m. to 4 p.m.
The Vineyard at River Hills,
10 a.m. to 4 p.m.

SUNDAY, JULY 31
Connecticut (Litchfield County)
Kent
Sculpturedale, 10 a.m. to 4 p.m.
*Gardens are also open this day in nearby
Dutchess County, NY.*

SUNDAY, JULY 31
New York (Dutchess County)
Millbrook
Garden of Belinda & Stephen Kaye,
10 a.m. to 4 p.m.
Wassaic
Neverest, 10 a.m. to 4 p.m.
*A garden is also open this day in nearby
Litchfield County, CT.*

SUNDAY, JULY 31

Wisconsin (Milwaukee)
Bayside
The Tsai Garden, 10 a.m. to 4 p.m.
River Hills
The Robbins Garden, 10 a.m. to 4 p.m.
The Vineyard at River Hills,
10 a.m. to 4 p.m.

AUGUST

SATURDAY, AUGUST 6

New York (Dutchess County)
Hopewell Junction
Wiccopee Garden - Dedicated to My
Mother Albertina, 10 a.m. to 4 p.m.
*Gardens are also open this day in nearby
Putnam and Westchester Counties.*

SATURDAY, AUGUST 6

New York (Putnam County)
Brewster
Rumford Hall, 10 a.m. to 4 p.m.
*Gardens are also open this day in nearby
Dutchess and Westchester Counties.*

SATURDAY, AUGUST 6

New York (Westchester County)
Bedford Hills
Garden of Phillis Warden,
10 a.m. to 4 p.m.
Croton on Hudson
Rivermere on the Hudson,
10 a.m. to 4 p.m.
Mount Kisco
The Greneker Retreat, 10 a.m. to 4 p.m.
South Salem
Garden of Bernard Marquez & Tim Fish,
10 a.m. to 4 p.m.
*Gardens are also open this day in nearby
Dutchess and Putnam Counties.*

SUNDAY, AUGUST 7

Connecticut (New Haven County)
Meriden
George Trecina, 10 a.m. to 4 p.m.
Northford
Reeds Gap West Residence,
10 a.m. to 4 p.m.

SUNDAY, AUGUST 14

New York (Columbia County)
Claverack
Peter Bevacqua & Stephen King,
10 a.m. to 4 p.m.
Hudson
Versailles on Hudson, 10 a.m. to 4 p.m.
*A garden is also open this day in nearby
Greene County, NY.*

SUNDAY, AUGUST 14

New York (Greene County)
Catskill
Abeel House Prairie, 10 a.m. to 4 p.m.
*Gardens are also open this day in nearby
Columbia County, NY.*

SATURDAY, AUGUST 20

New Jersey (Hunterdon County)
Stockton
Bellsflower Garden, 10 a.m. to 4 p.m.
Pretty Bird Farm, 10 a.m. to 4 p.m.

SATURDAY, AUGUST 27

Connecticut (Fairfield County)
Redding
InSitu, 10 a.m. to 4 p.m.
Ridgefield
Old Barlow's Carriage House and Garden,
10 a.m. to 4 p.m.
*Gardens are also open this day in nearby
Litchfield County, CT & Westchester County,
NY.*

SATURDAY, AUGUST 27
Connecticut (Litchfield County)
Bridgewater
Maywood Gardens, 10 a.m. to 2 p.m.
Gardens are also open this day in nearby Fairfield County, CT & Westchester County, NY.

SATURDAY, AUGUST 27
New York (Westchester County)
North Salem
Perrin Garden, 10 a.m. to 3 p.m.
Gardens are also open this day in nearby Litchfield and Fairfield County, CT.

SEPTEMBER

SATURDAY, SEPTEMBER 10
Connecticut (New Haven County)
Cheshire
Garden of David & Janet Andrews, 10 a.m. to 4 p.m.
Meriden
George Trecina, 10 a.m. to 4 p.m.
Oxford
Garden of Susan & Richard Kaminski, 10 a.m. to 4 p.m

SATURDAY, SEPTEMBER 10
New Jersey (Essex County)
Nutley
The Mountsier Garden, 10 a.m. to 4 p.m.

SUNDAY, SEPTEMBER 11
Connecticut (Litchfield County)
Warren
Mulla Garden, 10 a.m. to 4 p.m.
Washington
Brush Hill Gardens, 10 a.m. to 4 p.m.
Gardens at North House, 10 a.m. to 4 p.m.
Hollister House Garden, 10 a.m. to 4 p.m.
The Sumacs, 10 a.m. to 4 p.m.

SATURDAY, SEPTEMBER 17
Connecticut (Fairfield County)
Greenwich
Sleepy Cat Farm,
    Morning session, 10 a.m. to 1 p.m.
    Afternoon session, 1 p.m. to 4 p.m.
Weston
Garden of Frances Palmer,
12 p.m. to 4 p.m.
Westport
Prospect Gardens Westport,
10 a.m. to 4 p.m.
A garden is also open this day in nearby Westchester County, NY.

SATURDAY, SEPTEMBER 17
Massachusetts (Greater Boston)
Carlisle
Gardens at Clock Barn Home of Maureen & Mike Ruettgers, 10 a.m. to 4 p.m.

SATURDAY, SEPTEMBER 17
New Jersey (Somerset County)
Far Hills
The Hay, Honey Farm, 10 a.m. to 4 p.m.

SATURDAY, SEPTEMBER 17
New York (Eastern Long Island)
East Hampton
Marshouse - Garden of Edwina von Gal, 10 a.m. to 4 p.m.

SATURDAY, SEPTEMBER 17
New York (Westchester County)
South Salem
West Lane Farm, 10 a.m. to 5 p.m.
Gardens are also open this day in nearby Fairfield County, CT.

SUNDAY, SEPTEMBER 18
Connecticut (Fairfield County)
Westport
Blau House & Gardens, 10 a.m. to 4 p.m.

SATURDAY, SEPTEMBER 24
New York (Dutchess County)
Millbrook
Clove Brook Farm Christopher Spitzmiller
& Anthony Bellomo, 10 a.m. to 4 p.m.
Stanfordville
Bear Creek Farm, 10 a.m. to 4 p.m.
Ellen Petersen, 10 a.m. to 4 p.m.

OCTOBER

SATURDAY, OCTOBER 1
Tennessee (Knoxville)
Knoxville
Hays Gardens, 10 a.m. to 4 p.m.
Joe and Sharon Pryse, 10 a.m. to 4 p.m.

SATURDAY, OCTOBER 22
California (Mendocino County)
Gualala
Mendocino Stone Zone, 10 a.m. to 4 p.m.
Point Arena
Frog Song Farm, 10 a.m. to 4 p.m.

SATURDAY, OCTOBER 29
New York (Dutchess County)
Pawling
The Brine Garden—Duncan & Julia Brine,
1 p.m. to 5 p.m.

SUNDAY, OCTOBER 30
New York (Dutchess County)
Pawling
The Brine Garden—Duncan & Julia Brine,
1 p.m. to 5 p.m.

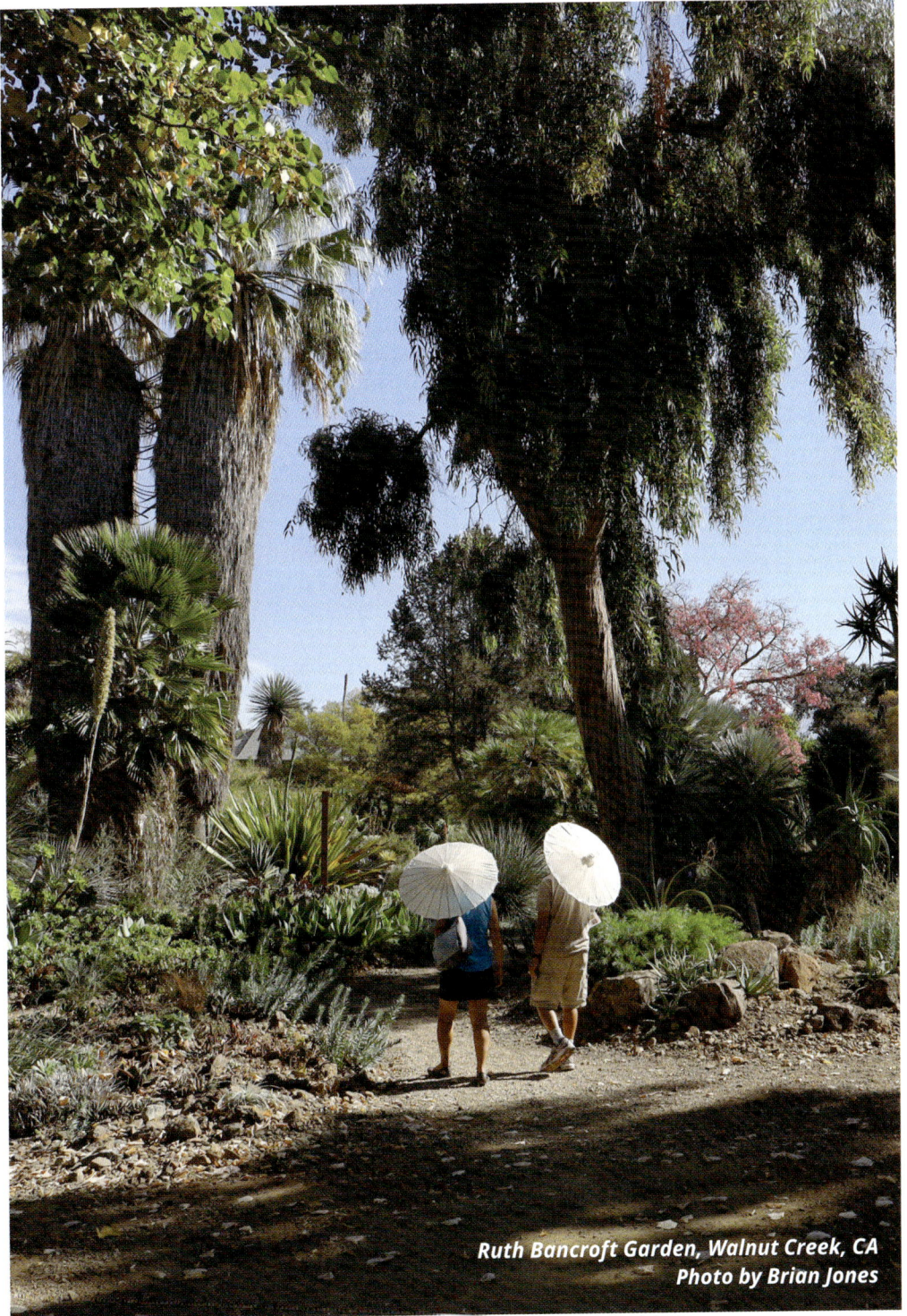

Ruth Bancroft Garden, Walnut Creek, CA
Photo by Brian Jones

GARDENS BY STATE

California

LOS ANGELES

SAVE THE DATE — MAY 1

Details coming soon!

MARIN COUNTY

Bolinas
Garden of Sculpture, Saturday, June 25, 10 a.m. to 4 p.m.
Visions of Paradise—Sally Robertson Garden & Studio, Saturday, June 25, 10 a.m. to 4 p.m.
Stinson Beach
A Panoramic Garden, Saturday, June 25, 10 a.m. to 4 p.m.

MENDOCINO COUNTY

Boonville
Woodshop Grounds, Saturday, May 21, 10 a.m. to 4 p.m.
Gualala
Mendocino Stone Zone, Saturday, October 22, 10 a.m. to 4 p.m.
Navarro
Pepperwood Pottery, Saturday, May 21, 10 a.m. to 4 p.m.
Philo
Wildwood, Saturday, May 21, 10 a.m. to 4 p.m.
Point Arena
Frog Song Farm, Saturday, October 22, 10 a.m. to 4 p.m.

PASADENA & ENVIRONS

SAVE THE DATE — APRIL 24

Details coming soon!

SAN FRANCISCO EAST BAY

Albany
Keeyla Meadows Gardens & Art, Saturday, May 7, 10 a.m. to 4 p.m.
Berkeley
Aging Gracefully, Saturday, May 7, 10 a.m. to 4 p.m.
Camp Shasta, Sunday, June 12, 10 a.m. to 4 p.m.
Santa Clara Habitat Gardens, Saturday, May 7, 10 a.m. to 4 p.m.
Orinda
Simpson Garden, Sunday, June 12, 10 a.m. to 4 p.m.
Piedmont
The Shartsis Gardens, Sunday, June 12, 10 a.m. to 4 p.m
San Francisco
Dry Garden on Surrey, Saturday, June 18, 10 a.m. to 4 p.m.
Geary Street Garden, Saturday, June 18, 10 a.m. to 4 p.m.

SAN JOSE

San Jose
Garden of Cevan Forristt, Satuday, June 4, 10 a.m. to 4 p.m.
Ginko Forristt Tea House, Saturday, June 4, 10 a.m. to 1 p.m.

Connecticut

FAIRFIELD COUNTY

Fairfield
Inwood Cottage Garden, Sunday, June 12, 10 a.m. to 4 p.m.

Greenwich
Chelmsford, Sunday, June 12, 10 a.m. to 4 p.m.
Garden of Allison Bourke, Saturday, June 12, 10 a.m. to 4 p.m.
Sleepy Cat Farm, Saturday, May 21
    Morning session, 10 a.m. to 1 p.m.
    Afternoon session, 1 p.m. to 4 p.m.
Saturday, September 17,
    Morning session, 10 a.m. to 1 p.m.
    Afternoon session, 1 p.m. to 4 p.m.

Redding
InSitu, Saturday, August 27, 10 a.m. to 4 p.m.

Ridgefield
Ken Eisold's Garden, Sunday, June 12, 10 a.m. to 4 p.m.
Old Barlow's Carriage House and Garden, Saturday, August 27, 10 a.m. to 4 p.m.

Weston
Garden of Frances Palmer, Saturday, September 17, 12 p.m. to 4 p.m.

Westport
Greens Farms Botanical Gardens, Sunday, June 12, 10 a.m. to 4 p.m.
Prospect Gardens Westport, Saturday, September 17, 10 a.m. to 4 p.m.
The Blau Gardens, Sunday, May 29, 10 a.m. to 4 p.m.
Sunday, September 18, 10 a.m. to 4 p.m.

HARTFORD COUNTY

Burlington
Garden of Robin Lensi, Saturday, June 4, 10 a.m. to 4 p.m.
The Salsedo Family Garden, Saturday, June 4, 10 a.m. to 4 p.m.

Glastonbury
The Murray Gardens, Sunday, June 19, 10 a.m. to 4 p.m.

LITCHFIELD COUNTY

Bridgewater
Maywood Gardens, Saturday, August 27, 10 a.m. to 2 p.m.

Cornwall Bridge
Debby and Bart Jones' Garden, Sunday, June 19, 10 a.m. to 4 p.m.

Falls Village
Church House - The Garden of Page Dickey and Bosco Schell, Saturday, June 25, 10 a.m. to 4 p.m.
Garden of Bunny Williams, Saturday, April 30,
    Morning session, 10 a.m. to 1 p.m.
    Afternoon session, 1 p.m. to 4 p.m.
Saturday, July 23,
    Morning session, 10 a.m. to 1 p.m.
    Afternoon session, 1 p.m. to 4 p.m.

Kent
Sculpturedale, Sunday, July 31, 10 a.m. to 4 p.m.

Lakeville
Juniper Ledge, Sunday, June 19, 10 a.m. to 4 p.m.

Litchfield
Glenn Hillman, Saturday, June 4, 11 a.m. to 5 p.m.

Norfolk
Fernwood, Saturday, July 23, 10 a.m. to 4 p.m.

Roxbury
Japanese Gardens at Cedar Hill, Saturday, June 4, 10 a.m. to 4 p.m.

Salisbury
Catriona Pike, Saturday, June 25,
10 a.m. to 4 p.m.
Sharon
Garden of Lee Link, Sunday, June 19,
10 a.m. to 4 p.m.
Warren
Mulla Garden, Saturday, June 4,
10 a.m. to 4 p.m.
Sunday, September 11, 10 a.m. to 4 p.m.
Washington
Brush Hill Gardens, Saturday, June 25,
10 a.m. to 4 p.m.
Sunday, September 11, 10 a.m. to 4 p.m.
Hollister House Garden, Saturday, June 4,
10 a.m. to 4 p.m.
    Saturday, June 25, 10 a.m. to 4 p.m.
    Sunday, September 11, 10 a.m. to 4 p.m.
The Sumacs, Saturday, June 4,
10 a.m. to 4 p.m.
Sunday, September 11, 10 a.m. to 4 p.m.
Washington Depot
Appledore, Saturday, June 25,
10 a.m. to 3 p.m.
West Cornwall
Garden of Jane Garmey, Sunday, June 19,
11 a.m. to 4 p.m.
Garden of Michael Trapp, Sunday, June 19,
10 a.m. to 4 p.m.
Roxana Robinson - Treetop, Sunday, June
19, 10 a.m. to 4 p.m

NEW HAVEN COUNTY
Cheshire
Garden of David & Janet Andrews,
Saturday, September 10, 10 a.m. to 4 p.m.
Meriden
George Trecina, Sunday, August 7,
10 a.m. to 4 p.m.
Saturday, September 10, 10 a.m. to 4 p.m.
Northford
Reeds Gap West Residence, Sunday,
August 7, 10 a.m. to 4 p.m.
Oxford
Garden of Susan & Richard Kaminski,
Saturday, September 10, 10 a.m. to 4 p.m
Stony Creek
Uptop—Garden of Fred Bland, Saturday,
May 21, 10 a.m. to 4 p.m.
Stonington
Kentford Farm, Saturday, June 11,
10 a.m. to 4 p.m.

TOLLAND COUNTY
Tolland
Bear Run, Sunday, June 19,
10 a.m. to 4 p.m.

Florida

JACKSONVILLE
Jacksonville
Cummer Museum of Art & Gardens,
Saturday, March 26, 11 a.m. to 4 p.m.
Garden of Ann Hicks, Saturday, March 26,
12 p.m. to 4 p.m.
Lanakila Gardens, Saturday, March 26,
12 p.m. to 4 p.m.

Illinois

FAR WESTERN SUBURBS

Elburn
Hummer Haven, Sunday, May 8,
10 a.m. to 4 p.m.

Maine

YORK

York
Braveboat Harbor Farm, Saturday, June 25,
10 a.m. to 4 p.m.
Sunday, June 26, 10 a.m. to 4 p.m.

Massachusetts

BERKSHIRES

Sheffield
1391 Barnum Street, Saturday, June 11,
10 a.m. to 4 p.m.

BRISTOL COUNTY

Rehoboth
McIlwain Garden, Saturday, June 11,
10 a.m. to 4 p.m.
Seekonk
Landscape Designer Andrew Grossman's
Display Gardens, Saturday, June 11,
10 a.m. to 4 p.m.

GREATER BOSTON

Carlisle
Gardens at Clock Barn Home of Maureen
& Mike Ruettgers, Saturday, September 17,
10 a.m. to 4 p.m.
West Roxbury
Dustman-Ryan Garden - The Artful
Garden, Sunday, May 22, 10 a.m. to 4 p.m.

MARBLEHEAD

Marblehead
Seaside Farm, Sunday, July 24,
10 a.m. to 4 p.m.
Swampscott
Glass House Gardens, Sunday, July 24,
10 a.m. to 4 p.m.

MIDDLESEX COUNTY

Groton
Garden of Pepe and John Maynard,
Sunday, May 15, 10 a.m. to 4 p.m.

NORFOLK COUNTY

Milton
Spalding Garden, Sunday, May 22,
10 a.m. to 2 p.m.

WORCESTER COUNTY

Petersham
Swift River Farm, Sunday, May 15,
10 a.m. to 4 p.m.
Worcester
Garden of Matt Mattus and Joe Philip,
Sunday, May 15, 10 a.m. to 4 p.m.

Missouri

ST. LOUIS

SAVE THE DATE — JUNE 4

Details coming soon!

New Hampshire

MONADNOCK REGION

Peterborough
Gardens of Maude & John Odgers, Saturday, June 25, 10 a.m. to 4 p.m.

Temple
The Gardens at Beechwood Farm, Saturday, June 25, 10 a.m. to 4 p.m.

New Jersey

BERGEN COUNTY

Mahwah
Sisko Gardens, Saturday, June 25, 10 a.m. to 4 p.m.

Paramus
Sharon Ma's Garden, Saturday, June 25, 10 a.m to 4 p.m.

Waldwick
Noel Schulz's Garden, Saturday, June 25, 10 a.m. to 4 p.m.

ESSEX COUNTY

Montclair
Claire's Meditation Garden, Sunday, May 15, 10 a.m. to 4 p.m.

Nutley
The Mountsier Garden, Saturday, April 16, 10 a.m. to 4 p.m.
Sunday, May 15, 10 a.m. to 4 p.m.
Saturday, June 4, 10 a.m. to 4 p.m.
Saturday, September 10, 10 a.m. to 4 p.m.

HUNTERDON COUNTY

Califon
Garden of Dan Ruhland, Sunday, June 12, 10 a.m. to 4 p.m.

Pottersville
Anita Shearan Garden, Sunday, May 8, 10 a.m. to 4 p.m.
Bird Haven Farm, Sunday, May 8, 10 a.m. to 4 p.m.
Jardin de Buis, Sunday, June 12, 10 a.m. to 4 p.m.

Stockton
Bellsflower Garden, Saturday, August 20, 10 a.m. to 4 p.m.
Pretty Bird Farm, Saturday, August 20, 10 a.m. to 4 p.m.
The Garden at Federal Twist, Sunday, June 12, 10 a.m. to 4 p.m.

MORRIS COUNTY

Chatham
Jack Lagos, Sunday, May 15, 10 a.m. to 4 p.m.

PASSAIC COUNTY

Ringwood
Ringwood Water Gardens, Saturday, May 14, 10 a.m. to 4 p.m.

Wanaque
The Sichaks' Garden, Saturday, May 14, 10 a.m. to 4 p.m.

SOMERSET COUNTY

Far Hills
The Hay, Honey Farm, Sunday, May 8,
10 a.m. to 4 p.m.
Saturday, September 17, 10 a.m. to 4 p.m.

New York

COLUMBIA COUNTY

Ancram
Heaven's Gate, Saturday, June 11,
10 a.m. to 4 p.m.
Canaan
Rockland Farm, Sunday, July 24,
10 a.m. to 4 p.m.
Claverack
Ketay Garden, Saturday, June 18,
10 a.m. to 4 p.m.
Peter Bevacqua & Stephen King, Sunday,
August 14, 10 a.m. to 4 p.m.
Hudson
Versailles on Hudson, Sunday, August 14,
10 a.m. to 4 p.m.
Millerton
Garden of Helen Bodian, Saturday, June 11,
10 a.m. to 4 p.m.
Spencertown
Landscape of Linda B. Horn, Sunday, July
24, 10 a.m. to 2 p.m.
West Taghkanic
Arcadia - Ronald Wagner & Timothy Van
Dam, Saturday, June 18, 10 a.m. to 4 p.m.

DELAWARE COUNTY

Andes
Cynthia & Charles Bonnes, Saturday, July 9,
10 a.m. to 4 p.m.
Roscoe
Henderson Hollow Farm - Mermer
Blakeslee & Eric Hamerstrom, Saturday,
July 9, 10 a.m. to 4 p.m.

DUTCHESS COUNTY

Amenia
Broccoli Hall—Maxine Paetro, Sunday, May
15, 10 a.m. to 4 p.m.
Dover Plains
Lossing Manor, Saturday, June 26,
10 a.m. to 4 p.m.
Hopewell Junction
Wiccopee Garden - Dedicated to My
Mother Albertina, Saturday, August 6,
10 a.m. to 4 p.m.
Millbrook
Clove Brook Farm Christopher Spitzmiller
& Anthony Bellomo, Saturday, May 7,
10 a.m. to 4 p.m.
Saturday, September 24, 10 a.m. to 4 p.m.
Garden of Belinda & Stephen Kaye, Sunday,
July 31, 10 a.m. to 4 p.m.
Katie Ridder & Peter Pennoyer, Saturday,
June 11, 10 a.m. to 4 p.m.
Squirrel Hall, Sunday, June 26,
10 a.m. to 4 p.m.
Millerton
Highgrove Cottage, Saturday, June 4,
10 a.m. to 4 p.m.
Hyland/Wente Garden, Saturday, June 11,
10 a.m. to 2 p.m.
Pawling
The Brine Garden—Duncan & Julia Brine,
Saturday & Sunday, October 29 & 30,
1 p.m. to 5 p.m.
Poughkeepsie
Dappled Berms - The Garden of Scott
VanderHamm, Sunday, June 26,
10 a.m. to 4 p.m.

Stanfordville
Bear Creek Farm, Saturday, September 24, 10 a.m. to 4 p.m.
Ellen Petersen, Saturday, September 24, 10 a.m. to 4 p.m.
Uplands Farm - Zibby & Jim Tozer, Sunday, June 26, 10 a.m. to 2 p.m.

Wappingers Falls
Garden of Anne Spiegel, Saturday, May 7, 10 a.m. to 4 p.m.

Wassaic
Neverest, Sunday, July 31, 10 a.m. to 4 p.m.

EASTERN LONG ISLAND

Bridgehampton
Entwood Garden, Saturday, July 9, 10 a.m. to 4 p.m.

Cutchogue
Conni Cross Garden Designer, Saturday, July 16, 10 a.m. to 2 p.m.

East Hampton
Garden of Arlene Bujese, Saturday, July 9, 10 a.m. to 4 p.m.
Garden of Marshall Watson, Saturday, May 7, 10 a.m. to 4 p.m.
Glade Garden - Abby Jane Brody, Saturday, May 7, 10 a.m. to 3 p.m.
Marshouse - Garden of Edwina von Gal, Saturday, September 17, 10 a.m. to 4 p.m.
Previti/Gumpel Garden, Saturday, July 9, 10 a.m. to 4 p.m.
The Garden of Dianne B., Saturday, May 7, 10 a.m. to 3 p.m.

Mattituck
The Landcraft Garden Foundation, Saturday, July 9, 10 a.m. to 4 p.m.

Old Field
Two Grey Achers, Sunday, May 22, 12 p.m. to 4 p.m.

Shelter Island Heights
Birdhouse Garden, Saturday, July 30, 10 a.m. to 4 p.m.

Southold
Mayfield, Saturday, July 16, 10 a.m. to 4 p.m.

Wading River
Bill & Veronica Schiavo—Woodland Garden, Saturday, May 22, 10 a.m. to 4 p.m.

Wainscott
Biercuk & Luckey Garden, Saturday, May 7, 10 a.m. to 4 p.m.

GREENE COUNTY

Catskill
Abeel House Prairie, Sunday, August 14, 10 a.m. to 4 p.m.

Cornwallville
Greene Bee Greenhouse, Sunday, May 8, 10 a.m. to 4 p.m.

NASSAU COUNTY

Glen Cove
Kippen Hill, Sunday, June 5, 10 a.m. to 4 p.m.

Locust Valley
Carol & Jim Large's Garden, Sunday, June 5, 10 a.m. to 4 p.m.

Oyster Bay
The Barnyard, Sunday, June 5, 10 a.m. to 4 p.m.

Port Washington
The Gardens at Sands Light, Sunday, June 5, 10 a.m. to 4 p.m.

PUTNAM COUNTY

Brewster
Rumford Hall, Saturday, August 6, 10 a.m. to 4 p.m.

SARATOGA SPRINGS

Middle Grove
Dalton Garden, Saturday, June 18, 10 a.m. to 4 p.m.

Saratoga Springs
A Place to Nest - Moe's Garden, Saturday, June 18, 10 a.m. to 4 p.m.
Foxglove - Sarah Patterson's Garden, Saturday, June 18, 10 a.m. to 4 p.m.
Winterberry Cottage Garden, Saturday, June 18, 10 a.m. to 4 p.m.

Schuylerville
Susie Kane-Kettlewell's Garden, Saturday, June 18, 10 a.m. to 4 p.m.

ULSTER COUNTY

Boiceville
Brunel Sculpture Park, Sunday, May 15, 10 a.m. to 4 p.m.

WESTCHESTER COUNTY

Bedford
Brae Willows, Saturday, June 18, 10 a.m. to 4 p.m.
The Great Hill Schoolhouse, Saturday, June 18, 10 a.m. to 4 p.m.

Bedford Hills
Garden of Phillis Warden, Saturday, June 18, 10 a.m. to 4 p.m.
Saturday, August 6, 10 a.m. to 4 p.m.

Chappaqua
Garden of Shobha Vanchiswar & Murali Mani, Saturday, May 14, 10 a.m. to 4 p.m.

Cortlandt Manor
Vivian & Ed Merrin, Saturday, May 14, 10 a.m. to 4 p.m.

Croton on Hudson
Rivermere on the Hudson, Saturday, August 6, 10 a.m. to 4 p.m.

Lewisboro
The White Garden, Sunday, April 24, 10 a.m. to 3 p.m.

Mount Kisco
Rocky Hills, Saturday, May 14, 10 a.m. to 4 p.m.
The Greneker Retreat, Saturday, August 6, 10 a.m. to 4 p.m.

North Salem
Perrin Garden, Saturday, August 27, 10 a.m. to 3 p.m.

Pleasantville
Garden of Michael and Suzanne Inglis, Sunday, June 5, 10 a.m. to 4 p.m.

Pound Ridge
James and Ellen Best's Sara Stein Garden, Saturday, June 18, 10 a.m. to 2 p.m.

South Salem
Garden of Bernard Marquez & Tim Fish, Saturday, August 6, 10 a.m. to 4 p.m.
West Lane Farm, Saturday, May 14, 10 a.m. to 5 p.m.
Saturday, September 17, 10 a.m. to 5 p.m.

Pennsylvania

BUCKS COUNTY

New Hope
Gardens at Half Moon, Saturday, May 15, 10 a.m. to 4 p.m.
Paxson Hill Farm, Sunday, May 15, 10 a.m. to 4 p.m.

CHESTER COUNTY

Phoenixville
Donald Pell Gardens, Saturday, June 25, 10 a.m. to 4 p.m.

Rhode Island

KENT COUNTY

East Greenwich

Villa Kunterbunt, Saturday, June 11,
10 a.m. to 4 p.m.

LITTLE COMPTON

Little Compton

Sakonnet, Sunday, July 17,
9 a.m. to 5:30 p.m.

NEWPORT AREA

Bristol

Blithewold Mansion, Gardens &
Arboretum, Saturday, June 18,
10 a.m. to 4 p.m.

PROVIDENCE COUNTY

Providence Area

SAVE THE DATES — JUNE 4, 5

Details coming soon!

South Carolina

CHARLESTON

**SAVE THE DATES
MAY 28 AND JUNE 4**

Details coming soon!

SPARTANBURG AREA

Campobello

Forty Oaks Farm, Saturday, April 9,
10 a.m. to 4 p.m.

Spartanburg

Meeks Garden, Saturday, April 9,
10 a.m. to 4 p.m.

Tennessee

KNOXVILLE AREA

Knoxville

Hays Gardens, Saturday, October 1,
10 a.m. to 4 p.m.
Joe and Sharon Pryse, Saturday, October 1,
10 a.m. to 4 p.m.

Vermont

UPPER VALLEY

Westminster West

Gordon & Mary Hayward's Garden,
Saturday, June 25, 10 a.m. to 4 p.m.

Virginia

CHARLOTTESVILLE AREA

Lynchburg
Anne Spencer House and Garden Museum,
Saturday, April 23, 10 a.m. to 3 p.m.

Washington

BAINBRIDGE ISLAND

Bainbridge Island
Dragon's Lair - The Demianew Gardens,
Sunday, June 5, 10 a.m. to 4 p.m.
The Cole Garden, Sunday, June 5,
10 a.m. to 4 p.m.
Weissman Garden, Sunday, June 5,
10 a.m. to 4 p.m.

CLARK COUNTY

Vancouver
Matsu Kaze (Wind in the Pines), Sunday,
June 18, 10 a.m. to 4 p.m.

SOUTH SOUND

Graham
Old Goat Farm, Saturday, May 21,
10 a.m. to 4 p.m.
Puyallup
Ernie & Julia Graham Garden, Saturday,
May 21, 10 a.m. to 4 p.m.
Paulsen Garden, Saturday, May 21,
10 a.m. to 4 p.m.

Wisconsin

MILWAUKEE AREA

Bayside
The Tsai Garden, Saturday, July 30,
10 a.m. to 4 p.m.
Sunday, July 31, 10 a.m. to 4 p.m.
River Hills
The Robbins Garden, Saturday, July 30,
10 a.m. to 4 p.m.
Sunday, July 31, 10 a.m. to 4 p.m.
The Vineyard at River Hills, Saturday, July
30, 10 a.m. to 4 p.m.
Sunday, July 31, 10 a.m. to 4 p.m.

NOTES